COPS ON CAMPUS

ABOLITION:
EMANCIPATION
FROM THE CARCERAL

Michael Roy Hames-García
and Micol Seigel
Series Editors

Edited by Yalile Suriel, Grace Watkins,
Jude Paul Matias Dizon, and John J. Sloan III

COPS ON CAMPUS

RETHINKING SAFETY AND CONFRONTING POLICE VIOLENCE

University of Washington Press *Seattle*

Copyright © 2024 by the University of Washington Press

Design by Mindy Basinger Hill / Composed in Minion Pro

All rights reserved. No part of this publication may be reproduced or transmitted in any form or by any means, electronic or mechanical, including photocopy, recording, or any information storage or retrieval system, without permission in writing from the publisher.

UNIVERSITY OF WASHINGTON PRESS
uwapress.uw.edu

LIBRARY OF CONGRESS CATALOGING-IN-PUBLICATION DATA

Names: Suriel, Yalile, editor.

Title: Cops on campus : rethinking safety and confronting police violence / edited by Yalile Suriel, Grace Watkins, Jude Paul Matias Dizon, and John J. Sloan III.

Description: Seattle : University of Washington Press, 2023. | Series: Abolition : emancipation from the carceral | Includes bibliographical references and index.

Identifiers: LCCN 2023035974 | ISBN 9780295752204 (hardcover) | ISBN 9780295752211 (paperback) | ISBN 9780295752228 (ebook)

Subjects: LCSH: Campus police—United States. | Police violence—United States. | Campus violence—United States. | College students—Violence against—United States. | Universities and colleges—Security measures—United States. | Universities and colleges—United States—Safety measures. | Mass incarceration—United States.

Classification: LCC HV8291.U6 C664 2023 | DDC 363.28/9—dc23/eng/20230926

LC record available at https://lccn.loc.gov/2023035974

∞ This paper meets the requirements of ANSI/NISO Z39.48-1992 (Permanence of Paper).

CONTENTS

Acknowledgments / vii

Introduction / A Fresh Perspective on Campus Policing in America / *Yalile Suriel, Grace Watkins, Jude Paul Matias Dizon, John J. Sloan III* / ix

PART I *Critical Perspectives on the Organization, Culture, and Tactics of Campus Police*

1 The End of *In Loco Parentis* and Institutionalization of Campus Policing / *John J. Sloan III* / 3

2 A Critical Legal Analysis of Campus Police Authority / *Vanessa Miller* / 17

3 "Just Protecting the University Property" / Campus Policing as Extraterritorial Expansion / *Davarian L. Baldwin* / 33

4 Pushing Back on Campus Police Unions / Histories and Strategies / *Lucien Baskin, Erica R. Meiners, and Grace Watkins* / 41

PART II *Challenging the Narrative of Campus Policing*

5 Locking the Gates / Yale University and the Police Power in the Postindustrial City, 1959–1976 / *Jacob Anbinder* / 57

6 Anti–Sexual Assault Activism and the Legitimacy of Campus Police in Philadelphia / *Matt Johnson* / 77

7 The War on Drugs Meets Campus Police / *Yalile Suriel* / 95

8 "The King of Sting" / A History of the UCLA Police Department / *Andrew Pedro Guerrero* / 108

PART III *Current Issues in Campus Policing*

9 "You're Not Even in the United States. You're in Georgia Tech" / Campus Police, Urban Governance, and the Creation of the Client-Student / *Stephen Averill Sherman* / 127

10 Uncovering the Racial Power of Campus Police / *Jude Paul Matias Dizon* / 144

11 Campus Police and Racialized Barriers to Reporting Sexual Assault for Black Women / *Kamaria B. Porter* / 160

12 Ed Tech Is Surveillance Tech / Pedagogies of Surveillance in Physical and Digital Campuses / *Vineeta Singh* / 178

PART IV *Transforming Campus Safety*

13 Campus Policing and the Experiences of Formerly Incarcerated Students / An Interview with Ryan Flaco Rising / 195

14 How Student Activists Are Working to Defund, Disarm, and Abolish the Campus Police / An Interview with Jael Kerandi / 203

15 Rethinking the Archives on Campus Policing / An Interview with Kacie Lucchini Butcher / 209

16 An Interview with Cops Off Campus Research Collective / Eli Meyerhoff, Nick Mitchell, Brendan Hornbostel, and Zach Schwartz-Weinstein / 223

17 "A Moment of Profound Counterinsurgency" / A Reflection on Faculty Abolitionist Praxis with Dylan Rodríguez / 236

Afterword / *Yalile Suriel, Grace Watkins, Jude Paul Matias Dizon, and John J. Sloan III* / 245

List of Contributors / 251

Index / 259

ACKNOWLEDGMENTS

The coeditors sincerely thank all of the contributors to this volume, whose chapters expanded and reshaped our understanding of this burgeoning and critical field. We also thank the student, staff, and faculty activists who, while tirelessly working on issues of campus policing across the country, nonetheless took time to share their insights with us in the interviews found in part 4 of the book. We are immensely grateful to each of them! Yalile, Grace, and Jude Paul thank John Sloan for his guidance and mentorship. It is an honor to work with and learn from a scholar whose work laid the very foundations for the study of campus policing as it now exists. We greatly appreciate his generosity and willingness to help usher in a new generation of scholarship. Finally, we thank Andrew Berzanskis (our former editor) and Michael Baccam (our current editor) and the staff at the University of Washington Press for their support throughout the process of producing this volume.

Yalile thanks her parents and her mentors from several walks of life for their continued support.

Grace thanks her parents and her friends James and Foo for their love and encouragement.

Jude Paul thanks his family—mom, Justin, Monique, Arieus, and Miles—and partner, Kristine, for their unwavering support. He is eternally grateful to the student leaders at the University of Maryland, College Park, for their activism and courage in the face of police violence. This book is for you!

John thanks Grace, Jude, and Yalile for agreeing to work with him on this project and tolerating his "old school" foibles; his life partner Tavis for supporting another book project; his faithful companion Savannah—*un chien merveilleux*—and Professor Max Bromley for the many hours spent discussing the campus police and the humanity he brought to campus policing practice. This one's for Dad . . .

Lastly, we thank you, the reader, for picking up this volume. Whether you are a student, a researcher, a faculty or staff member, or unaffiliated with a university, we hope you find it useful for better understanding the complexities of higher education and its impact on the world around us.

INTRODUCTION

A Fresh Perspective on Campus Policing in America

YALILE SURIEL, GRACE WATKINS,
JUDE PAUL MATIAS DIZON, AND JOHN J. SLOAN III

For years the police departments that are nearly ubiquitous on university and college campuses attracted little scholarly or public attention due to their reputation as "rent-a-cop" operations. However, the last five years witnessed an explosion of interest in these departments and officers. Headline after headline has thrust campus police departments from relative obscurity into the national spotlight and raised questions about their powers and impact:[1]

- In 2017, a nonbinary student named Scout Schultz was shot and killed by Georgia Tech police while experiencing a mental health crisis.[2] In the past decade, multiple other students have been injured or killed by campus police while experiencing severe mental distress.
- In 2018, brothers Thomas Kanewakeron Gray and Lloyd Skanahwati Gray, members of the Mohawk nation, were pulled from a campus tour by University of Colorado police officers for "looking like they didn't belong."[3] Just a few days later, a Black student named Lolade Siyonbola was questioned by Yale police for sleeping in a common room for graduate students.[4] These incidents prompted others across the nation to recount, on social media and to reporters, their experiences with racial profiling by campus police officers.
- In 2019, a Yale University police officer and a local city police officer opened fire into a car containing a Black couple named Stephanie Washington and Paul Witherspoon, resulting in serious injuries to Washington.[5] The incident drew parallels to past instances where campus police

killed Black people on and off campus, such as the 2015 murder of Sam Dubose by a University of Cincinnati officer during a traffic stop.[6] The shooting also raised questions about the frequent and often dangerous collaborations between campus and municipal police.
- In 2020, it was discovered that campus police at the University of California, Santa Cruz, used military-grade technology to surveil a graduate student strike, which raised concerns about the technology available to campus police and their connections to the US Department of Defense and federal intelligence agencies.[7]

In the aftermath of George Floyd's 2020 murder by City of Minneapolis police officer Derek Chauvin, increased attention on police violence turned into a national movement. Black, Indigenous, Latinx, Asian American, and other students of color brought the demands of Black Lives Matter and the summer of 2020 uprisings against police violence to the setting they knew best: colleges and universities. As a result, a new generation of undergraduate student activists—along with their supporters—called for their institutions to disarm,[8] defund,[9] or abolish[10] campus police departments. In their demands, students cited evidence of the abusive practices of campus police, such as pervasive racial profiling;[11] targeted surveillance of LGBTQ people;[12] and the routine dismissal of women's reports of sexual violence, with some victims even experiencing sexual harassment from campus officers themselves.[13]

Over two-thirds of universities and colleges in the United States enrolling 2,500 or more students have sworn and armed campus police departments with jurisdiction beyond school grounds.[14] These departments' organizational and jurisdictional characteristics mirror those of traditional law enforcement agencies: paramilitary-oriented bureaucracies featuring a rank structure, specialization, and multifunctionality. They recruit and hire new officers using tactics and processes similar to those used by state, county, and municipal police departments across the nation. Newly hired campus police officers then undergo basic training at more than 350 police academies across the county that also train new hires from state, county, and municipal police departments. At the academy, new campus officers receive an average of twenty weeks of training across multiple areas including firearms and nonlethal weapons (e.g., batons), defensive and arrest/control tactics, constitutional and criminal law, self-improvement (e.g., stress management) and operations (e.g., patrol procedures, emergency vehicle driving; report writing; interviewing and interrogation). Successful completion of basic training is followed by a variable period of field training (typically 90 to 120 days) supervised by a Field Training Officer (FTO) who evaluates the new officers' performances. On successful completion of field training, the new officers begin their law enforcement and order maintenance duties as full-fledged campus police officers.

With the Cops Off Campus Movement as its backdrop, this volume examines the history, operations, and impact of the campus police and its role in the symbiotic relationship between higher education and the carceral state.[15] The volume's chapters span a range of fields (e.g., history, American studies, ethnic studies, criminology, higher education, and sociology), critical perspectives, and methodologies (e.g., case studies, surveys, archival research, ethnographies, and oral histories) to explore different facets of campus policing. Contributors possess a variety of backgrounds both within and outside the academy and use their different perspectives to excavate narratives about campus police abuses.

Collectively, the volume explores new directions in the burgeoning field of critical campus police studies, which challenges the hegemonic conception of colleges and universities as "safe havens" detached from "real-world" issues like racial profiling, illegal surveillance, and police violence. It also challenges the assumption that universities exist to "serve the public good."[16] The contemporary American university has been cast as a center for expanding access, especially following the years of the Student Protest Movement, which contributed to significant postsecondary educational attainment among Black, Latinx, and Asian American students.[17] Yet, at the same time that universities moved away from being exclusive spaces for elites, higher education leaders and state lawmakers constructed a new kind of police that has caused significant harm to marginalized communities.[18]

In this introduction, we first present a brief history of the evolution of campus policing in the United States. Next, we provide an overview of existing and emerging scholarship on campus police. We then conclude with a summary of the chapters that follow.

THE HISTORY AND EVOLUTION OF CAMPUS POLICING

The first known occurrence of armed, sworn police officers patrolling a college campus in the United States was in 1894, when Yale University hired two officers from the New Haven Police Department to create a "campus police department."[19]

Over the next 130 years, campus security slowly became institutionalized in higher education, culminating with the presence of sworn, uniformed, and armed campus police officers or nonsworn security guards at nearly every American postsecondary institution in the United States.[20] This evolution occurred throughout multiple eras, each influenced by factors both internal and external to postsecondary institutions that resulted in a particular "model" of campus security becoming preeminent.

ERAS OF CAMPUS SECURITY IN AMERICAN POSTSECONDARY INSTITUTIONS

Era	Timing	Influence(s)	Key features of the era
Faculty	17th–19th centuries	In loco parentis	Faculty and administrators responsible for physical plant maintenance and identifying rule-breakers
Watchman	late 19th–early 20th centuries	Rapidly expanding access to higher education via creation of public land grant colleges	Patrol and control access to campus; identify rule-breakers; raise alarms for fires or other threats
Security guard	mid-20th century	Post–World War II GI Bill and continuing expansion of access to higher education	Traffic control and parking oversight; routine patrol of campus and access control to it
Policing	late 20th century–present	End of in loco parentis; campus protests of 1960s; end of segregation and continuing expansion of access to higher education for members of previously excluded groups	Sworn, uniformed, armed; random, routine patrol; rapid response to calls for service; police academy trained; ongoing "professionalization"

THE FACULTY ERA AND *IN LOCO PARENTIS*

As shown in the table, the evolution of campus policing requires an understanding of how contextual influences helped shape campus police as they exist today. Spanning nearly three centuries of American history, the *in loco parentis* era in higher education saw no need for formalized campus security like what is seen at today's colleges and universities. Largely due to the fact that postsecondary institutions were uncommon, relatively small—both in size and complexity of their physical plants—and had few enrollees, professors and institutional administrators tended to campus maintenance and "security" needs.[21] When students were caught violating codes of conduct, they were summarily expelled. In cases of larger-scale disorders occurring on campus, local police were summoned to address the situation. When threats to the physical plant arose from fire or flood, institutions sought help from the surrounding community. Not until the latter part of the nineteenth century and the creation of land-grant colleges and universities in the United States did institutional security needs change enough to warrant formalizing security operations. It was then that colleges and universities began using watchmen and janitors to address campus security.

THE WATCHMAN/JANITOR ERA

Seymour Gelber posits campus watchmen as being the direct lineal predecessor of the contemporary campus police or security officer.[22] Gelber also suggests the likely origins of the watchman system in US higher education was with the bedels at the University of Oxford during the fifteenth century. As described by Gelber, bedels were "servants appointed to execute the orders of the university Chancellor and the proctors" and performed such functions as collecting fines, escorting people to prison, and administering punishment to offending students.[23] In the United States, college or university watchmen carried out tasks such as responding to burglaries and fires. They also worked to prevent incursions onto campus by livestock, stoked stoves during winter, and tended the campus gate(s).

Along with watchmen, also important to the evolving system of campus security were janitors (now known as custodians).[24] At Colby College, for example, janitors served as unofficial policemen and advisors to students and faculty alike,[25] while at Lehigh University janitors were considered "officers of the university" and placed in charge of buildings and grounds. They were also empowered to direct student-involved disorders to cease and were responsible for reporting damages and breaches of order to the university president.[26]

THE SECURITY GUARD ERA

With the arrival of the twentieth century came further changes to campus security as the number of postsecondary institutions in the United States grew and many of the original land-grant colleges became full-fledged universities featuring increasingly large physical plants and enrollments. Gelber points to the invention of the mass-produced automobile and its arrival on college and university campuses as marking the emergence of what most experts would consider "modern" campus security operations.[27] As more cars appeared on campus, university administrators increasingly needed a way to control traffic, address parking issues, and ensure that "students act[ed] within proper moral constraints," particularly women riding around campus (and beyond) in cars.

These changes led to the creation of security personnel who were equipped to patrol the campus and its immediate environs, as well as address growing traffic problems, including issues surrounding parking on campus. The years following the end of World War II "saw a divestment of the watchman-janitor image and the formation of a formal organizational police structure in the form of campus security departments."[28] For example, the 1950s witnessed the creation of a national-level professional association to represent campus security interests and professionalize their work.[29] In November 1958, eight campus security officers representing colleges and universities from a geographic cross-section of the country met in Tempe, Arizona, to create the International Association of College and University Security Directors (IACUSD), which is now known as the International Association of Campus Law Enforcement Administrators (IACLEA).[30] The first formal meeting of the organization occurred just over a year later in Houston, Texas, with representatives from twenty-eight colleges and universities attending. Prior to the creation of IACUSD, campus security personnel associated themselves with several other national groups including the Association of Physical Plant Directors, the Higher Education Section of the Campus Safety Association, and the Association of College Business Officers. Regional campus security groups were also organized such as the Northeast College and University Security Association, which included the Ivy League institutions. In multiple states, campus security officials also gathered informally to share ideas and identify emerging security issues on campus.[31]

Until the 1960s and 1970s, the legal authority of campus security officials to stop, question, detain, or arrest was uncertain. Almost no state legislation had been passed specifically addressing campus security officers, their duties, and their legal authority. Most officers functioned under derivative authority through deputization by the local sheriff or municipal chief of police. Some departments relied upon state statutes that appeared to provide the color of legal authority to them but had not been formally tested in court.[32]

THE CAMPUS POLICE ERA

The Student Protest and Black Campus Movements sparked mass demonstrations over civil rights, the Vietnam War, and free speech. University administrators often responded by calling state and municipal police to campus to quell the unrest. The result was a series of near-fatal and fatal encounters between students and police that swept the nation. For example, in 1967 officers from the City of Houston Police Department fired thousands of rounds of ammunition at Black protestors at Texas Southern University.[33] In 1970, members of the Ohio National Guard opened fire on protesters gathered at Kent State University, killing four students and injuring nine others.[34] Just two weeks later, state and municipal police fired on a women's dormitory at the historically Black institution Jackson State College in Jackson, Mississippi, killing two students and injuring twelve others.[35]

In the aftermath of these violent and deadly encounters, higher education officials faced mounting pressure from state governors and other officials to crack down on the increasing number of student-led protests.[36] College and university administrators—with assistance from state legislatures and attorneys general—then took the steps necessary to create their own campus police forces. States passed enabling legislation (or attorneys general issued formal opinions) that officially authorized colleges and universities to create their own campus *police* departments whose personnel would include sworn officers, which addressed the previous uncertainty surrounding the legal authority of these departments. This step would not only have serious consequences for the future of policing of race, gender, and sexuality within university spaces but would also change town-gown relations as campus police increasingly focused their attention on keeping out members of the larger community in the name of "campus security."

Over the following decades, as more campus police departments were created, colleges and universities chose two different paths for campus security operations. One path, taken mostly by smaller private postsecondary institutions, resulted in the continued use of nonsworn security guards (either hired directly or contracted through third-party vendors) to patrol campus and provide other security services. The other path, chosen mainly by larger public institutions of higher learning, involved creating campus police departments staffed by sworn officers.[37]

Colleges and universities choosing the campus police path first hired senior-level officers away from municipal and state law enforcement agencies to establish state-sanctioned campus police departments. This fact helps explain why campus police departments possess many of the same organizational and tactical characteristics of municipal police departments including a rank structure, task specialization, top-down communication, use of routine patrol and rapid response to calls for service, and sanctioned use of both lethal and nonlethal weapons.[38] Like their municipal counterparts, sworn campus police officers now complete basic training at police academies and a period of on-the-job field training. They also have to complete some number of hours of department-established annual in-service training.

In summary, modern campus police—replete with all of the regalia commonly associated with municipal police such as uniforms with insignia, sidearms, batons, handcuffs, and communication devices—were the end result of an evolutionary process that began with professors, administrators, and janitors handling "campus security" and ended with academy-trained, sworn, "professional" law enforcement personnel within agencies whose organizational and tactical features resemble modern municipal police. With this brief review of the origins and evolution of the campus police in mind, attention now turns to an overview of what scholars have written about campus policing.

CAMPUS POLICING SCHOLARSHIP:
THE STATE OF THE FIELD

Diane Bordner and David Petersen commented in 1983 that "much of the existing literature on campus police may be generally characterized as highly descriptive and particularistic, concerned with specific issues and statements of opinion, and lacking in substantive research evidence."[39] Although important scholarly contributions have since been made, Bordner and Petersen's point that campus police departments remain an understudied topic is still valid, especially in light of their significant impact not only in shaping university life for students, faculty, and staff but also in gentrifying surrounding neighborhoods.

The lack of scholarship on campus policing partly stems from the popular misconception of campus police as not "real" police, resulting from their association with security guards and night watchmen.[40] Campus police also do not neatly fit within existing areas of study because of their unusual hybrid status and powers. For example, they have largely been excluded from histories of American municipal police and private police forces in the United States, both of which have received significant attention in recent years.[41]

Further hindering campus policing scholarship is the ability of many departments, especially those at private universities, to avoid public access to their records.[42] Only campus police at public universities are subject to Freedom of Information Act requests.[43] There is also evidence of campus forces regularly destroying their records.[44] Additional hindrances arise when university archives are able to deaccess or otherwise restrict access to materials that do exist. Finally, comprehensive aggregate data on the budgets, powers, and size of campus police departments across the United States is limited to occasional surveys conducted by the US Department of Justice's Bureau of Justice Statistics.[45] As a result of these obstacles, the majority of scholarship on campus police departments has tended to focus on one or a few institutions at a time and is generally restricted to departments or institutions willing to release relevant records.

The majority of what might be considered "traditional" scholarship on campus police originated in the fields of criminology and criminal justice.[46] These scholars have examined such topics as campus police departmental organizational structures and tactical practices;[47] campus police officer discretion;[48] and campus crime reduction effectiveness.[49]

Members of campus police leadership have also published on this topic through trade publications such as *Campus Law Enforcement Quarterly*, *Police Chief Magazine*, and the FBI *Law Enforcement Bulletin*. The majority of this scholarship is descriptive and highlights issues and innovations in the field. Much of this scholarship assumes the necessity of campus policing in design and tactics.[50] Such assumptions thus shape the focus and intent of the research, often geared toward formulating research- or evidence-based improvements. For example, research on legitimacy issues in campus policing have mostly focused on how to improve relations between campus police officers and students.[51]

Turning from practitioner-oriented scholarship, John Sloan has been a central figure in efforts to bring scholarly attention to the topic of campus policing.[52] Beginning with his comprehensive account of the origins and growth of campus police forces nationally, to charting the political and cultural histories of campus securitization efforts, his scholarship has promoted the study of campus police as its own distinct field, rooted in discussions of evolving perceptions of and responses to "campus crime."[53] Sloan's analyses demonstrate how campus policing has traditionally been framed as both a legitimate *and* primary solution to lawbreaking, violence, and disorder at colleges and universities.[54] Accordingly, his work also shows how campus police promoted themselves as a "safeguard" against all manner of "threats" to institutions of higher education.[55]

In recent years, a range of scholars outside of criminology and the social sciences have built on Sloan's work to make important contributions to the study of campus police as well. These scholars have brought new methodologies, archival sources, and a critical framework that questions the necessity and legitimacy of campus policing. Their scholarship presents campus policing as a multifaceted story with many actors and turning points involving higher education, the US Congress, state-level political actors, and municipal law enforcement agencies—all of which continue to seek more effective and efficient ways to surveil and control university space.

Following the infamous "pepper-spray incident" at the University of California, Davis, in 2011—during which a campus police officer pepper-sprayed student protesters sitting on the ground during an Occupy demonstration—several important publications laid much of the groundwork for a critical reinterpretation of campus police duties. Principally, essays by Dylan Rodríguez, Sunaina Maira, and Julie Sze in a 2012 issue of *American Quarterly*, as well as the 2013 anthology *Policing the Campus: Academic Repression, Surveillance, and the Occupy Movement*, connected campus policing to global struggles against police violence and the suppression of activist movements.[56]

The growing field of carceral studies has also produced new ways of conceptualizing and analyzing the impact of campus police and their participation in the US government's War on Crime initiative. In 2017, Roderick Ferguson published *We Demand: The University and Student Protests*, which demonstrates how "police violence, administrative violence, and ideological violence have come together in an institution that is at once a bureaucracy, a school, and a police station."[57] Davarian L. Baldwin's book *In the Shadow of the Ivory Tower: How Universities Are Plundering Our Cities* extended this analysis to demonstrate the impact campus police have on communities surrounding colleges and universities. Teona Williams's recent article "For 'Peace, Quiet, and Respect': Race, Policing, and Land Grabbing on Chicago's South Side" uses literature on environmental justice to demonstrate how "green initiatives shape the intersections of gentrification and racial profiling" through campus police. Contributions from critical university studies and abolitionist university studies—especially the works of S. A. Smythe, Nick Mitchell, Abigail Boggs, Eli Meyerhoff, and Andy Hines—center abolitionist thought and connect the growth of campus police departments to broader ongoing campaigns of austerity and militarization in higher education.[58] In a similar vein, David Allen's recent analysis of how public, postsecondary institutions engage in self-protection via the use of campus police suggest there is much to be uncovered from closer analysis of available campus police budgetary information.[59]

In the field of higher education research, attention to campus police is growing as a factor shaping the experiences of students of color. William Smith and colleagues identified a consistent pattern of Black undergraduate men being targeted by campus police for "fitting the description" of suspects.[60] Campus police officers are frequent contributors to the racially hostile interactions Black undergraduates encounter at historically white institutions, reinforcing marginalization and exclusion.[61] Amalia Dache-Gerbino and Julie White's research demonstrates that geographic location and racial composition of different colleges and universities inform the different styles and tactics of policing that campus departments deploy. For example, their observational study of a suburban community college and its urban branch campus suggested that the latter campus functioned to criminalize the majority student of color population by maintaining a much more visible police force.[62] These emerging contributions from higher education scholars demonstrate the range of adverse impacts that campus police have on student life, thus troubling the assumption that police promote a safe learning environment.

In summary, the scholarship of campus policing that began as a trickle in the 1990s has increased as previously ignored and marginalized perspectives come to the fore. Slowly, campus policing scholarship—originating in criminal justice and criminology—is now being expanded to include many other disciplines. These works go beyond discussions of how campus police might be reformed to question their very existence and examine their impact on marginalized people. It is in this emerging critical line of inquiry that this volume is situated.

BOOK OVERVIEW

The contributors of this volume critically analyze campus police in the context of the institutional arrangements that justify state-sanctioned violence, increased surveillance, racial injustice, economic inequality, nativism, and gender-based oppression. The book is divided into four parts. In part 1, researchers uncover the structure, organization, and culture of campus policing. In chapter 1, John J. Sloan III discusses the implications of the end of *in loco parentis* and the subsequent institutionalization of campus policing. Chapter 2, by Vanessa Miller, establishes the legal history around campus police authority. Chapter 3, by Davarian L. Baldwin, explores how urban colleges and universities deploy the blunt force of campus police as an act of "extraterritorial expansion." In chapter 4, Lucien Baskin, Erica R. Meiners, and Grace Watkins examine the role of police unions in organizing campus police and helping to shield violent officers from disciplinary sanctions.

Part 2 excavates histories of campus police at a wide array of higher education institutions and challenges previously held narratives of the trajectory of these forces. In chapter 5, Jacob Anbinder examines the development of the Yale University Police Department—a national leader in campus law enforcement—as an important case study of the interactions between school integration, coeducation, and shifts in municipal politics during the years of the Student Protest Movement and its aftermath. In chapter 6, Matt Johnson examines the relationship between campus activism against sexual assault activism at the University of Pennsylvania in the 1970s and 1980s and the parallel expansion of the Penn police, which has since become one of the largest private police forces in the world. In chapter 7, Yalile Suriel explores how the US government's War on Drugs initiative shaped the development of campus policing. In chapter 8, Andrew Pedro Guerrero chronicles how the UCLA Police Department's (UCLA PD) efforts to guard campus property grew into extensive undercover sting operations that criminalized not only UCLA affiliates but also thousands of Los Angeles residents. Together, this section brings to light the long-overlooked histories that shaped the evolution of American campus policing and frames the use of campus police as a means for postsecondary administrators to better maintain control of students, especially students of color, in the unique campus context.[63]

The chapters in part 3 address current issues in campus policing such as racial profiling and the surveillance of marginalized communities on and off campus. In chapter 9, Stephen Averill Sherman uses fieldwork conducted at the Georgia Institute of Technology and Georgia State University to illustrate that campus police are important agents of urban governance, thereby complicating scholarly understandings of urban citizenship. In chapter 10, Jude Paul Matias Dizon examines the power of campus police to shape racial dynamics within a university community. Chapter 11, by Kamaria B. Porter, focuses on the specific experiences of Black women and nonbinary sexual assault survivors in reporting sexual violence to campus police. In chapter 12, Vineeta Singh argues that education technology (ed tech) has become a legal battleground not just for college students' privacy rights but also for conversations about campus policing. Together, this section challenges our understanding of "safety" and the bounds of campus policing.

Part 4 consists of interviews with students, staff, and faculty who are working to transform campus safety and "disrupt what must be dismantled or transformed to reduce harm and build supportive, sustainable communities, and to join in making connections between struggles across various thresholds."[64] There has been a tidal wave of organizing within the national Cops Off Campus Movement since 2020, and it is essential that these efforts be recorded. Therefore, part 4 is intended to preserve the reflections and observations of activists for the future. The interviewees each work in a variety of positions within and outside of the university to document campus police abuses, interrogate existing structures within higher education, and explore new ways of providing safety and support services. Chapter 13 is an interview with Jael Karendi, the former president of the University of Minnesota's Student Government, who led a successful campaign for UMN to sever ties with the City of Minneapolis Police Department (MPD) during the 2020 uprising. In chapter 14, Ryan Flaco Rising—a member of the Underground Scholars Initiative, which helps formerly incarcerated students navigate the University of California system—discusses the unique challenges related to campus policing faced by system-impaired and formerly incarcerated students. Chapter 15 features an interview with the University of Wisconsin–Madison Public History Project director Kacie Lucchini Butcher on the challenges of researching the history of campus police, as well as her efforts to make archival discoveries accessible to the public. In chapter 16, members of the Cops Off Campus Research Collective discuss their efforts to work with students across the country to gather quantitative data on campus police departments and their ongoing educational projects related to campus policing. Part 4 concludes with chapter 17, which features an interview with Professor Dylan Rodríguez at the University of California, Riverside, on the Cops Off Campus Movement, its intersections with other radical and abolitionist organizing, and the specific role that faculty activists can play within these efforts. Together, these interviews showcase the vast array of efforts to redefine and reimagine campus safety by challenging the legitimacy of campus police and exploring alternatives for the future.

NOTES

1. Kate Mabus and Noah Tesfaye, "What the Cops Off Campus Movement Looks Like across the Country," *Nation*, April 12, 2021.

2. Avi Selk, T. Rees Shapiro, and Wesley Lowery, "Call about Suspicious Man Was Made by Georgia Tech Student Killed by Police, Investigators Say," *Washington Post*, September 18, 2017.

3. Austin Fisher, "Wrongfully Detained Brothers Get ACLU Help," *Rio Grande Sun*, May 18, 2018.

4. Britton O'Daly, "Yale Responds after Black Student Reported for Napping in Common Room," *Yale Daily News*, May 10, 2018, https://yaledailynews.com/blog/2018/05/10/yale-responds-after-black-student-reported-for-napping-in-common-room.

5. Sharon Otterman, "Police Shoot at a Black Couple Near Yale, Prompting a Week of Protests," *New York Times*, April 24, 2019.

6. Simon McCormack, "Cop Shoots, Kills Unarmed Black Man after Routine Traffic Stop," *Marshall Project*, July 22, 2015, www.huffpost.com/entry/cop-shoots-kills-unarmed-black-man_n_55af9a7de4b0a9b948530a26.

7. Lauren Kaori Gurley, "California Police Used Military Surveillance Tech at Grad Student Strike," *VICE News*, May 15, 2020, www.vice.com/en/article/7kppna/california-police-used-military-surveillance-tech-at-grad-student-strike.

8. KGW Staff, "Portland State University to Have Fully Disarmed Police Officers by September," *KGW8*, June 12, 2021, www.kgw.com/article/news/local/portland-state-university-disarming-police-officers-by-september/283-d00711af-a8d6-409e-844b-c4f5dc222fc3.

9. Lee Gaines, "A Debate over Defunding the Campus Police Takes Root at the University of Illinois," *Illinois NewsRoom*, January 25, 2021, https://illinoisnewsroom.org/a-debate-over-defunding-the-campus-police-takes-root-at-the-university-of-illinois/.

10. Davarian Baldwin, "Why We Should Abolish the Campus Police," *Chronicle of Higher Education*, May 19, 2021, www.chronicle.com/article/why-we-should-abolish-campus-police.

11. Ellen Burstein and Michelle Kurilla, "Students and Alumni Rally outside University President's House to Call for the Abolition of Campus Police," *Harvard Crimson* (Cambridge, MA), July 30, 2020, www.thecrimson.com/article/2020/7/30/abolish-hupd-elmwood-protest/.

12. Patrick Dilley, *Gay Liberation to Campus Assimilation: Early Non-Heterosexual Student Organizing at Midwestern Universities* (Cham, Switzerland: Palgrave Macmillan, 2019).

13. Grace Watkins, "The Crimes of Campus Police," *Chronicle of Higher Education*, October 20, 2020.

14. Brian Reaves, *Campus Law Enforcement, 2011–12*, Office of Justice Programs, Bureau of Justice Statistics, January 15, 2015, www.ojp.gov/library/publications/campus-law-enforcement-2011-12.

15. Royel M. Johnson and Jude Paul Matias Dizon, "Toward a Conceptualization of the College-Prison Nexus," *Peabody Journal of Education* 96, no. 5 (2021): 508–26.

16. Barnard Longden and Charles Belanger, "Universities: Public Good or Private Profit," *Journal of Higher Education Policy and Management* 35, no. 5 (August 2013): 501–22, DOI/abs/10.1080/1360080X.2013.825417; Susan Wright and Davydd J. Greenwood, "Recreating Universities for the Public Good: Pathways to a Better World," *Learning and Teaching* 10, no. 1 (Spring 2017): 1–4, DOI:10.3167/latiss.2017.100101.

17. Bill Hussar, Jijun Zhang, Sarah Hein, Ke Wang, Ashley Roberts, Jiashan Cui, Mary Smith, Farah Bullock Mann, Amy Barmer, and Rita Dilig, *The Condition of Education 2020*, National Center for Education Statistic publication no. 2020–144, US Department of Education, Washington, DC: National Center for Education Statistics, May 2020, https://nces.ed.gov/pubsearch/pubsinfo.asp?pubid=2020144; US Census Bureau, *Statistical Abstract of the United States: 1999*, December, 9, 1999; www.census.gov/library/publications/1999/compendia/statab/119ed.html.

18. National Research Council, *The Growth of Incarceration in the United States: Exploring Causes and Consequences* (Washington, DC, 2014), https://www.nap.edu/download/18613.

19. Seymour Gelber, *The Role of Campus Security in a College Setting* (Washington, DC: US Government Printing Office, 1972).

20. Reaves, *Campus Law Enforcement, 2011–12*.

21. Gelber, *The Role of Campus Security*.

22. Gelber, *The Role of Campus Security*.

23. Gelber, *The Role of Campus Security*, 16–17.

24. Gelber, *The Role of Campus Security*; Sharon Walker, "A Profile of Campus Police and Security Departments at Four-Year Institutions of Higher Education in Illinois, Indiana, Michigan, and Ohio" (PhD diss., Department of Higher Education, Ohio State University, 1976).

25. Ernest Mariner, *The History of Colby College*, Colby College Press (1953), https://digitalcommons.colby.edu/colbiana_books/5?utm_source=digitalcommons.colby.edu%2Fcolbiana_books%2F5&utm_medium=PDF&utm_campaign=PDFCoverPages; Earl Smith, *Mayflower Hill: A History of Colby College*, Colby Books (1963), https://digitalcommons.colby.edu/colbiana_books/7?utm_source=digitalcommons.colby.edu%2Fcolbiana_books%2F7&utm_medium=PDF&utm_campaign=PDFCoverPages.

26. Catherine Bowen, *A History of Lehigh University*. Lehigh Alumni Bulletin (1924).

27. Gelber, *The Role of Campus Security*, 19–20.

28. Gelber, *The Role of Campus Security*, 28.

29. Grace Watkins, "Cops Are Cops: American Campus Police and the Global Carceral Apparatus," *Comparative American Studies: An International Journal*, 17, no. 3–4 (2020): 242–56.

30. James Ferguson, *Campus Law Enforcement: An Historical Perspective* (Huntsville: Texas Law Enforcement Management Institute, 1990).

31. International Association of Campus Law Enforcement Administrators, "About Us" (2021). www.iaclea.org/about.

32. Gelber, *The Role of Campus Security*, 34.

33. Ayodale Braimah, "Houston (TSU) Riot (1967)," *Black Past*, December 4, 2017, www.blackpast.org/african-american-history/houston-tsu-riot-1967/.

34. Jerry M. Lewis and Terry R. Hensley, "The May 4 Shootings at Kent State University: The Search for Historical Accuracy," Kent State University *M4Y*, https://www.kent.edu/may-4-historical-accuracy.

35. Whitney Blair Wycoff, "Jackson State: A Tragedy Widely Forgotten," *National Public Radio* (Washington, DC), May 3, 2010, www.npr.org/templates/story/story.php?storyId=126426361.

36. Lyle Denniston, "The Campus and the Vietnam War: Protest and Tragedy," *Constitution Daily Blog* (Washington, DC), National Constitutional Center (2017), https://constitutioncenter.org/blog/the-campus-and-the-vietnam-war-protest-and-tragedy.

37. Reaves, *Campus Law Enforcement*, 2011–12.

38. Eugene Paoline and John Sloan, "Variability in the Organizational Structure of Contemporary Campus Law Enforcement Agencies: A National Level Analysis," *Policing: An International Journal* 26, no. 4 (2003): 612–39.

39. Diance C. Bordner and David M. Petersen, *Campus Policing: The Nature of University Police Work* (Lanham, MD: University Press of America, 1983), 2–3.

40. Andrea Allen, "Are Campus Police 'Real' Police? Students' Perceptions of Campus Versus Municipal Police," *Police Journal* 94, no. 2 (2021): 102–21; Shannon K. Jacobsen, "Policing the Ivory Tower: Students' Perceptions of the Legitimacy of Campus Police Officers," *Deviant Behavior* 36, no. 4 (2015): 310–29.

41. Elizabeth Kai Hinton, *America on Fire: The Untold History of Police Violence and Black Rebellion since the 1960s* (New York: Liveright, 2021); Simon Balto, *Occupied Territory: Policing Black Chicago from Red Summer to Black Power* (Chapel Hill: University of North Carolina Press, 2019); Max Felker-Kantor, *Policing Los Angeles: Race, Resistance, and the Rise of the LAPD* (Chapel Hill: University of North Carolina Press, 2018). Stuart Schrader, *Badges without Borders: How Global Counterinsurgency Transformed American Policing* (Berkeley: University of California Press, 2019); Christopher Agee,

The Streets of San Francisco: Policing and the Creation of a Cosmopolitan Liberal Politics, 1950–1972 (Chicago: University of Chicago Press, 2014).

42. Diane Krauthamer, "Journalists' Requests for Campus Crime Records Often Denied by Schools," Student Press Law Center (2005), https://splc.org/2005/03/splc-journalists-requests-for-campus-crime-records-often-denied-by-schools/.

43. Jonah Newman, "Private Colleges Keep Police Policies and Procedures Under Wraps," *Chicago Reporter,* August 25, 2015, www.chicagoreporter.com/private-colleges-keep-campus-police-policies-and-procedures-under-wraps/.

44. Dan Papscun, "How Access to Public Records Is Being Threatened by Police Union Contracts," Reporters Committee for Freedom of the Press, March 4, 2020, www.rcfp.org/police-unions-records-access/; University of Baltimore, "Records Retention Schedule," Police Policies, n.d., www.ubalt.edu/about-ub/offices-and-services/university-police/police-policies-community-service-complaints/records-retention-schedule.cfm; Julie O'Donoghue, "21 Ways LSU Hid or Suppressed Information about Sexual Misconduct," *Louisiana Illuminator,* March 10, 2021, https://lailluminator.com/2021/03/10/21-times-lsu-hid-or-suppressed-information-about-sexual-misconduct/; Jon Parton, "BYU Files Suit in Fight over University Police Public Records," Courthouse News Service, October 23, 2019, www.courthousenews.com/byu-files-suit-in-fight-over-university-police-public-records/.

45. Bureau of Justice Statistics, "Survey of Campus Law Enforcement Agencies," US Department of Justice, Office of Justice Programs, 2009, https://bjs.ojp.gov/data-collection/survey-campus-law-enforcement-agencies.

46. John J. Sloan III, "The Modern Campus Police: An Analysis of Their Evolution, Structure, and Function," *American Journal of Police* 11, no. 1 (1992): 85–104; Paoline and Sloan, Variability in the Organizational Structure"; Max Bromley and Brian Reaves, "Comparing Campus Police and Municipal Police: The Human Resource Dimension," *Policing: An International Journal* 21, no. 3 (1998): 534–46; John Sloan, Mark Lanier, and Deborah Beer, "Policing the Contemporary University Campus: Challenging Traditional Organizational Models," *Journal of Security Administration* 23, no. 1 (2000): 1–21; Kenneth Peak, Emmanuel Barthe, and Adam Garcia, "Campus Policing in America: A 20-Year Perspective," *Police Quarterly,* 11, no. 2 (2008): 239–60; Eugene Paoline and John Sloan, "Community-Oriented Policing (COP) on College Campuses: New Directions?," in *Campus Crime: Legal, Social and Policy Perspectives,* 3rd ed., ed. Bonnie Fisher and John Sloan (Springfield, IL: Charles C. Thomas, 2013), 325–52; Katy Hancock, "Community Policing within Campus Law Enforcement Agencies," *Police Practice and Research* 17, no. 5 (2016): 463–76.

47. Max L. Bromley, "Comparing Campus and Municipal Police Community Policing Practices," *Journal of Security Administration* 26, no. 2 (2003): 37–75; Katherine Hancock, "Community Policing within Campus Law Enforcement Agencies," *Police*

Practice and Research 17, no. 5 (2016): 463–76; Paoline and Sloan, "Variability in the Organizational Structure."

48. Andrea N. Allen, "Campus Police-Citizen Encounters: Influences on Sanctioning Outcomes." *American Journal of Criminal Justice* 40, no. 4 (2015): 722–36; Andrea N. Allen, "Campus Officers' Explanations of Traffic Stop Sanctions," *Police Quarterly* 17, no. 3 (2014): 276–301; Andrea N. Allen, "Campus Officers' Sanctioning of Alcohol-Involved Crime: Influences on Discretionary Decision-Making," *Police Practice and Research* 17, no. 3 (2016): 249–62.

49. Paul Heaton, Priscilla Hunt, John MacDonald, and Jessica Saunders, "The Short- and Long-Run Effects of Private Law Enforcement: Evidence from University Police," *Journal of Law and Economics* 59, no. 4 (2016): 889–912; John MacDonald, Jonathan Klick, and Ben Grunwald, "The Effect of Privately Provided Police Services on Crime," U of Penn, Institute for Law and Economics, Research Paper No. 12-36 (2012), 1–25.

50. Bordner and Petersen, *Campus Policing*; Robert Files Etheridge, "A Study of Campus Protective and Enforcement Agencies in Selected Universities" (PhD diss., Michigan State University, 1958); David N. Falcone and Keith A. Gehrand, "Policing Academia in Illinois: The Evolution of an American Policing Model," *Journal of Crime and Justice* 26, no. 1 (2003): 55–70; Gelber, The Role of Campus Security"; Eric Scott, "College and University Police Agencies," Workshop in Political Theory and Public Policy Analysis, Indiana University, Bloomington, August 12, 1976; Nicholas Michael Perez and Max Bromley, "Comparing Campus and City Police Human Resource and Select Community Outreach Policies and Practices: An Update." *Policing: An International Journal of Police Strategies and Management* 38, no. 4 (2015): 664–74.

51. Michael F. Aiello, "Legitimacy Invariance and Campus Crime: The Impact of Campus Police Legitimacy in Different Reporting Contexts," *Police Practice and Research* 21, no. 3 (2019): 1–16; Ryan Patten, Lucas Alward, Matthew Thomas, and James Wada, "The Continued Marginalization of Campus Police," *Policing: An International Journal of Police Strategies & Management* 39, no. 3 (2016): 566–83; James C. Wada, Ryan Patten, and Kimberlee Candela, "Betwixt and Between: The Perceived Legitimacy of Campus Police," *Policing: An International Journal of Police Strategies & Management* 33, no. 1 (2010): 114–31.

52. Sloan, "The Modern Campus Police"; Paoline and Sloan, "Variability in the Organizational Structure"; Sloan, Lanier, and Beer, "Policing the Contemporary University Campus"; John Sloan, "A Seminal Moment for America's Campus Police?," *British Society of Criminology Blog*, October 7, 2020; John Sloan and Eugene Paoline, "A National Comparison of Police Academies Operated by Academic Institutions and by Law Enforcement Agencies: Different Strokes for Different Folks?," *Journal of Criminal Justice Education*, https://doi.org/10.1080/10511253.2021.1986085; Bonnie Fisher, Mi-

chelle A. Protas, Logan M. Lanson, and John J. Sloan III, "The Evolution of College and University Campus Security in the United States: Congressional Legislation, Administrative Directives, and Policing," in *Handbook of Security*, 3rd ed., ed. Martin Gill (New York: Palgrave Macmillan, 2022), 399–423, https://doi.org/10.1007/978-3-030-91735-7_19.

53. Bonnie Fisher, John Sloan, Francis Cullen, and Chungmeng Liu, "Crime in the Ivory Tower: The Level and Sources of Student Victimization," *Criminology* 36, no. 3 (1998): 671–710; Bonnie Fisher and John Sloan, eds., *Campus Crime: Legal, Social and Policy Perspectives*, 4th ed. (Springfield, IL: Charles C. Thomas, 2023); John Sloan and Bonnie Fisher, *The Dark Side of the Ivory Tower* (New York: Cambridge University Press, 2010).

54. Kelly J. Asmussen and John W. Creswell, "Campus Response to a Student Gunman," *Journal of Higher Education* 66, no. 5 (1995): 575–91; James Alan Fox and Jenna Savage, "Mass Murder Goes to College: An Examination of Changes on College Campuses Following Virginia Tech," *American Behavioral Scientist* 52, no. 10 (2009): 1465–85; Joseph A. Schafer, Eric Heiple, Matthew J. Giblin, and George W. Burruss, "Critical Incident Preparedness and Response on Post-Secondary Campuses," *Journal of Criminal Justice* 38, no. 3 (2010): 311–17; Michael L. Sulkowski and Philip J. Lazarus, "Contemporary Responses to Violent Attacks on College Campuses," *Journal of School Violence* 10, no. 4 (201): 338–54.

55. Andrea N. Allen, "Do Campus Police Ruin College Students' Fun?," *Deviant Behavior* 38, no. 3 (2017): 334–44; Andrea N. Allen, "Stop and Question Campus Policing," *Policing: An International Journal of Police Strategies and Management* 39, no. 3 (2016): 507–20; James D. Griffith, Harry Hueston, Eddie Wilson, Casey Moyers, and Christian L. Hart. "Satisfaction with Campus Police Services," *College Student Journal* 38, no 1. (2004): 150–56; Robert P. Johnson, and Max Bromley, "Surveying a University Population: Establishing the Foundation for a Community Policing Initiative," *Journal of Contemporary Criminal Justice* 15, no. 2 (1999): 133–43.

56. Dylan Rodríguez, "Beyond 'Police Brutality': Racist State Violence and the University of California," *American Quarterly* 64, no. 2 (2012): 301–13; Sunaina Maira and Julie Sze, "Dispatches from Pepper Spray University: Privatization, Repression, and Revolts," *American Quarterly* 64, no. 2 (2012): 315–30; Anthony Nocella and David Gabbard, eds., *Policing the Campus: Academic Repression, Surveillance, and the Occupy Movement* (New York: Peter Lang, 2013).

57. Roderick Ferguson, *We Demand: The University and Student Protests* (Berkeley: University of California Press, 2017), 27.

58. See Paola Bacchetta et al., "Queer of Color Space-Making in and beyond the Academic Industrial Complex," *Critical Ethnic Studies* 4, no. 1 (2018): 44–63; Abigail

Boggs and Nick Mitchell, "Critical University Studies and the Crisis Consensus," *Feminist Studies* 44, no. 2 (2018): 432–63; Andy Hines, "The University Fix and John Edgar Wideman's *Philadelphia Fire*," *American Quarterly* 72, no. 1 (2020): 129–53.

59. David Allen, "Crime, Universities, and Campus Police," *Applied Economics* 53, no. 37 (2021):4276–91.

60. William A. Smith, Allen R. Walter, and Lynette L. Danley, "'Assume the Position . . . You Fit the Description': Psychosocial Experiences and Racial Battle Fatigue among African American Male College Students," *American Behavioral Scientist* 51, no. 4 (December 2007): 551–78.

61. Jude Paul Matias Dizon, "Protecting the University, Policing Race: A Case Study of Campus Policing," *Journal of Diversity in Higher Education*, October 7, 2021; DeMarcus A. Jenkins, Antar A. Tichavakunda, and Justin A. Coles, "The Second ID: Critical Race Counterstories of Campus Police Interactions with Black Men at Historically White Institutions," *Race Ethnicity and Education* 24, no. 2 (March 4, 2021): 149–66; Kristen J. Mills, "'It's Systemic': Environmental Racial Microaggressions Experienced by Black Undergraduates at a Predominantly White Institution," *Journal of Diversity in Higher Education* 13, no. 1 (March 2020): 44–55.

62. Amalia Dache-Gerbino and Julie A. White, "College Students or Criminals? A Postcolonial Geographic Analysis of the Social Field of Whiteness at an Urban Community College Branch Campus and Suburban Main Campus," *Community College Review* 44, no. 1 (January 2016): 49–69.

63. Ross Wolf, Charlie Mesloh, and Mark Henych, "Fighting Campus Crime: Perceptions of Police Canines at a Metropolitan University," *Critical Issues in Justice and Politics* 3, no. 1 (2010): 1–18.

64. Chrissy Anderson-Zavala, Patricia Krueger-Henney, Erica Meiners, and Farima Pour-Khorshid, "Fierce Urgency of Now: Building Movements to End the Prison Industrial Complex in Our Schools," *Multicultural Perspectives* 19, no. 3 (2017): 151–54.

PART I
CRITICAL PERSPECTIVES ON THE ORGANIZATION, CULTURE, AND TACTICS OF CAMPUS POLICE

1

THE END OF *IN LOCO PARENTIS* AND INSTITUTIONALIZATION OF CAMPUS POLICING

JOHN J. SLOAN III

Formal creation of campus police departments at American postsecondary institutions (PSIs) began in the late 1960s and early 1970s, during which *in loco parentis* (in place of the parents)—a cornerstone of higher education law from the colonial era through the height of the civil rights era that defined the legal relationship between PSI and student—was ending.[1] Under it, PSIs were responsible for not only meeting students' physical needs for food and housing but also for developing their moral character through hard work and discipline. Importantly, during much of the *in loco parentis* era, "campus security"—everything from protecting the campus physical plant from fire, flood, or vandalism to addressing student violations of codes of conduct—was overseen by faculty members and administrators. As the number of PSIs increased and they became ever larger in size and more complex in their scope of operation, security responsibilities were passed on first to "watchmen," later to janitors and watchmen, then to nonsworn security guards affiliated with campus buildings and grounds departments, and finally sworn police officers employed by the PSIs and affiliated with their campus security departments or campus police departments.[2] This chapter explores how, with the demise of *in loco parentis*, higher education administrators, with the help of state legislatures and attorneys general, used the police power of the state to create a more invasive, controlling, technology-based version of *in loco parentis*: the campus police.

IN LOCO PARENTIS: A BRIEF HISTORY

In its earliest interpretations under English common law, *in loco parentis* established the legal relationship between the head of a household and young (ages thirteen or fourteen) apprentices or household servants taking up residence there to learn a trade.[3] In exchange for the child's labor, the natural parents expected that the master—serving "in their place"—would provide for the physical and moral well-being of their child(ren). As the doctrine became more widely accepted by the British courts, *in loco parentis* became applicable not only to nongovernmental entities like families, but governmental entities including public and private schools.[4] The doctrine eventually became the cornerstone legal principle used by common law courts for defining a legal relationship among two or more parties in which a temporary guardian or caretaker assumed some or all parental duties of a minor child (i.e., one under the age of majority) in their care.[5]

In Loco Parentis *in American Higher Education*

The importance of *in loco parentis* for American higher education is found in Craig Forest's observation that "without an understanding of *in loco parentis* it is impossible to understand the relationship between students and college administrators prior to the 1970s."[6] Further, the regime was both paternalistic and patriarchal, both hallmarks of the English common law in which it developed and best illustrated by the common law doctrine *parens patriae*, which literally refers to the monarch as the "parent of the fatherland."[7] PSIs serving in the place of the parents [read: *father*] was accomplished via (1) creating strict rules of student conduct (e.g., curfews, limiting time away from campus) and other restrictions on their freedom; (2) instilling in students the discipline needed to complete a difficult academic program of study that copied the so-called British model of higher education in which students were immersed in the ancient languages (i.e., Latin and Greek) and ideas of Western civilization, and recitation was used to measure students' progress; and (3) punishment for rules violations, including expulsion, without due process.[8]

In loco parentis was not designed to foster an egalitarian relationship between student and PSI. Rather, the regime fostered *unilateral control* of students by PSI faculty members and administrators backed by court rulings saying that PSIs had the legal right to impose contemporary moral standards on students and discipline them for violations. Even after the age of college students increased from as young as thirteen years old to the more typical eighteen-to twenty-two-year-old range, with isolated exceptions such as in the immediate aftermath of World War II and the return of GIs who entered college in droves, the guiding assumption of *in loco parentis* was that college students were immature, likely to fall prey to their base instincts, and incapable of making [morally] right choices without PSI oversight. Craig Forest has observed that across multiple historical eras, even though the rules and/or disciplinary procedures changed—including when they were established *by* students *for* students—*in loco parentis* continued to define the relationship between PSIs and students, periodically reinforced by the courts as challenges came before them.[9]

Changing Times

Important to understanding *in loco parentis* is its informal decline and ultimate formal demise. Craig Forest points to several watershed moments occurring late in the history of *in loco parentis* that influenced its decline. The first of these began in the early 1950s, when the last of the World War II–era, GI Bill–funded former soldiers passed through college. Following a period of relaxing the rules and enforcement of them during the late 1940s, PSI administrators reasserted *in loco parentis* oversight on the following generation of students entering college.[10] This turn was largely in response to Americans' concern over a perceived epidemic of "juvenile delinquency" occurring at the time and a view increasingly held by adults that teenagers—including their own—were potential threats to the existing social order.[11]

College administrators reacted to these signals by cracking down on nascent "radical" political views that were developing among students and expressed in student-led or produced publications, such as campus humor magazines, for content that was deemed subversive or obscene but that raised few eyebrows before World War II. Later, during the Cold War, behaviors once considered harmless became feared as threatening to the US government. Campus administrators also systematically used *in loco parentis* to stifle student participation of *any* sort in political battles arising from the Civil Rights, Antiwar, and Free Speech Movements of the early to mid-1960s.

During the remainder of the 1960s, college students pushed back against *in loco parentis* precisely because it had become the legal justification for censoring the spread of students' political ideas, silencing their protests, and stifling their participation in the political battles of the day. Pushback came in the form of lawsuits filed in state and federal courts seeking to "get out from under *in loco parentis* control and political censorship" and "abolish *in loco parentis* once and for all."[12] As it turned out, the courts were quite sympathetic and ruled in students' favor in a series of state and federal court decisions throughout the 1960s. Then, in 1971, with passage of the Twenty-Sixth Amendment and awarding of the voting franchise to eighteen-year-olds, college students were proclaimed adults and were thus entitled to protections of their civil rights, especially those relating to freedom of speech and assembly and due process protections during disciplinary hearings.

The erosion and eventual demise of *in loco parentis* occurred during a period of rapid social change in the United States that not only saw the end of legally sanctioned segregation but also witnessed significant changes in American higher education. During this period, according to the National Center for Education Statistics,[13] PSI enrollments increased by 120 percent over the previous decade. By 1969, PSI national enrollments were as large as 35 percent of the eighteen- to twenty-four-year-old population, and some 41 percent of all college students were women. Public institutions accounted for 74 percent of higher education enrollments, while about 25 percent of all students were enrolled at two-year colleges. In 1960, the average enrollment at a college or university was 1,816 at 2,004 PSIs; by 1970, the figures had increased by 75 percent and 26 percent, respectively, to an average of 3,170 students at 2,525 PSIs. The period also witnessed overall annual higher education revenues increase to $5.785 billion in 1970 from $2.374 billion in 1960, while the overall value of American PSIs' physical plant assets grew by 105 percent from $2.601 billion in 1960 to $5.322 billion in 1970 (figures are in constant 1992 dollars).

In short, the end of *in loco parentis* was largely due to dramatic enhancements in the scale, scope, and complexity in operation of PSIs as ever more students enrolled at ever more PSIs, whose revenues and physical plant values soared. By the mid-1970s, many PSIs—especially large, public, research-oriented land-grant universities—resembled small cities replete with the usual problems of parking, space constraints, traffic congestion, and importantly, dramatic increases in *perceived* levels of crime and violence occurring on their campuses. PSI administrators also had to deal with the turbulence occurring on their campuses. As Richard Brownell has observed: "With the birth of the Free Speech Movement at . . . Berkeley in 1964, college students demonstrated their political and social awareness. Students for a Democratic Society, an influential nationwide network of college students dedicated to leftist political ideals, created a united front to protest [not only] the Vietnam War [but] the racism, imperialism, and economic inequality of the time."[14]

Student uprisings were becoming commonplace at not only elite PSIs like Columbia and Harvard and major public research universities like the University of California, Berkeley, and the University of Wisconsin but also smaller PSIs like Kenyon College and the College of Wooster. Black college students actively organized antisegregation protests in the South and elsewhere, some of which were met with significant backlash such as the Orangeburg Massacre that occurred at South Carolina State University in 1968 and left three dead and thirty others wounded after police and members of the South Carolina National Guard opened fire on unarmed student demonstrators.[15] College women of the day were also involved in these movements.[16] The disturbances culminated with the shooting of unarmed student protesters at Kent State University by members of the Ohio National Guard on May 4, 1970, and ten days later at Jackson State University by Mississippi state troopers and local police. Combined, the two incidents left six people dead and scores wounded or injured while trying to escape the barrage of bullets.[17]

PSI administrators thus found themselves in a quandary. Using local and state police to quell the unrest had gone horribly wrong and resulted in the shooting deaths of students, their sympathizers, and innocent bystanders, and the injuring of scores of others during these conflicts. Campuses were locked down for days on end. Parents were in shock, while politicians, especially state governors, pressured college and university presidents to "do something . . . *or else.*"

University administrators, cognizant of the fact that *in loco parentis* was on its way out, also realized that *outsiders*—local and state police, members of state National Guard units—were the problem: they had no ties to the campus community and were thus both feared and despised by students and many faculty. Administrators then thought, "What if colleges and universities could create their *own* police departments with their own officers who would then be responsible for order maintenance?" Unlike local and state police, *campus* police officers could be assimilated into and become part of the campus community. As a result, the campus police could respond to the unrest and violence that was occurring as internal guardians of the campus community rather than invaders seeking its destruction.

PSI administrators also knew they possessed neither the political power nor the legal authority to do so—only the state could make it happen. The logical next step was to seek the help of sympathetic state legislators and attorneys general to create necessary enabling legislation or issue binding legal opinions that would allow them to create their own police departments. Legislatures and attorneys general could then point to the *police power* of the state as the political and legal justification for allowing PSIs to create their own police departments.

By the late 1960s, campus police departments began appearing at major public land-grant research universities and later at smaller public colleges and universities and even some private PSIs. Former senior-level local police officers or state troopers were then hired by PSIs to organize and manage these new police departments staffed with sworn officers typically "cherry-picked" from local police and county sheriff's departments. These efforts resulted in the successful development of a new form of *in loco parentis* that was backed by the police power of the state and embodied in the person of the sworn, uniformed, and armed *campus* police officer.

In summary, the English common law–based legal regime of *in loco parentis* was a more than three-hundred-year-old cornerstone of higher education law that was paternalistic, patriarchal, and quasi-authoritarian. It allowed PSIs to foster rules and exercise discipline over college students largely without consequence. As PSI numbers and enrollments grew in the post–World War II era, *in loco parentis* slowly began eroding. That process was quickened as a result of federal and state court rulings beginning in 1961 and continuing to the passage of the Twenty-Sixth Amendment in 1971. During that roughly ten-year period, student-led groups demonstrated against perceived injustices of the day including civil rights, women's rights, and the Vietnam War via organized on-campus protests. Sometimes the protests turned violent and were met with the nightsticks of, and bullets from, local and state law enforcement as well as National Guard units. Faced with having to "do something" about the unrest, PSI administrators convinced state legislatures and attorneys general to allow them to create their own campus police departments. The end result of these efforts was the creation of a new form of *in loco parentis* that has ultimately proven harsher than the regime it replaced because it directly brought the vast police powers of the state onto the campuses of institutions of higher learning.[18]

CAMPUS POLICE: ORIGINS AND EVOLUTION

To understand the development of campus police departments, one must first understand that in American law, one of the foremost constitutional principles revolves around the police power of the states.[19] Santiago Legarre presents a useful review of the historical background and development of this key constitutional principle that dates to ancient Greece and the ideas of Plato and Aristotle.[20] In his discussion, Legarre makes the point that "police power," as a constitutive principle in American federalism, is the name the Founders chose to designate to the states—via the Tenth Amendment—a range of legislative powers not specifically delegated to the federal government.[21] Legarre also presents historical evidence that the word *police* actually refers to "the regulation, discipline, and control of a community" or "civil administration and public order" rather than state-sanctioned individuals with arrest powers. From this notion of *police* emerged the legal concept of police *power*, which Legarre then links to the common law principle of *parens patriae*. This principle articulates that the prerogative of the king extends to the care of certain "classes" of people who lack parental care (e.g., abused or neglected children). Thus, the notion that a state has police power is effectively analogous to the patriarchal power that a king would exercise over his subjects or a father over his family. Legarre shows that the constitutional framers—through documents like the Articles of Confederation, early states' Declarations of Rights, and during debate at the Constitutional Convention—envisioned each of the new states fulfilling its *parens patriae* role via the Tenth Amendment's language about powers not specifically delegated to the Congress being reserved to the states.[22]

By allowing PSIs to create their own campus police departments, the states were effectively combining *parens patriae* and *in loco parentis* into the newly minted persona of the uniformed, sworn, and armed campus police officer. Doing this significantly expanded the ability of PSIs to surveil and ultimately control—not to mention discipline via arrest and formal processing by the criminal justice system—both members of the campus community and campus visitors. Further, the reach of *local* police departments via jurisdictional expansion of campus police was accomplished through mutual assistance agreements (MAAs) or memoranda of understanding (MOUs) between PSIs and nearby municipalities.

THE CONTEMPORARY CRISIS OF CAMPUS POLICING

Over the past decade, campus police have illegally pepper-sprayed seated student protesters at the University of California, Davis; shot and killed an eighteen-year-old University of South Alabama undergraduate student who was seeking their help while confused and disoriented from a drug overdose; engaged in illegal off-campus detentions; shot and killed a Black motorist they pulled over well off the University of Cincinnati campus; pulled their guns on a Black Yale graduate student in the student commons; pulled a gun on a University of Oregon student of color after mistaking him for a white suspect; shot and killed a Black man on the campus of Portland State University; and shot a Black University of Chicago student experiencing a mental health crisis.[23] Elsewhere, I have written about issues arising from—but not exclusive to—incidents like those mentioned that have led to a seminal moment in the history of campus policing that involves reimagining their role in American higher education. The issues contributing to this moment include campus police legitimacy, their militarization, lack of accountability, opacity in operations, increasing mission creep, and basic training that emphasizes creating "warriors" rather than "guardians."[24]

Issues That Must Be Resolved

In the present context, *legitimacy* refers to the justification for, or the logical existence of, the campus police and turns at least partly on the belief that police generally respect the bounds of their authority.[25] As Aziz Huq and his colleagues observe: "Individuals do not cede unlimited power to legal authorities. They demarcate their lives into domains, some of which are off-limits to the intrusion of formal authority. The notion of bounded authority goes beyond the relational nature of procedural justice because it captures processes that represent the *misuse of power* [emphasis added]."[26]

If this view is correct, one could then make an argument that the legitimacy of campus police would rest with the fact they exist to safeguard the campus physical plant and members of its community from various threats, while operating within a set of agreed-upon community-established constraints, from an *insider* position—campus police are also members of the campus community. They serve as *guardians* for it—not armed warriors engaging in conflict with it. Their raison d'être is explicitly *not* to wage war on members of the communities being policed. Doing so would represent a serious violation of their bounded authority that is worthy of significant sanction.

Almost from their creation, such an ideal failed to gain traction. First, as the number of campus police departments grew and sworn police patrolling college campuses became common, other police officers expressed skepticism about whether campus officers were "real cops." For many in campus policing, their apparent marginalization by the field more broadly superseded issues of legitimacy. To address that perception and under the guise of "professionalization," campus police departments (and by extension their officers) became ever more like their municipal police counterparts—who themselves currently face a reckoning arising partly from their racist origins in southern slave patrols, as well as a long-standing history of violence perpetrated against Black Americans, along with their involvement in creating the carceral state.[27]

Second, in the post-9/11 era, campus police departments and officers have dutifully followed their policing colleagues in taking on an increasingly "warrior" persona that includes not only donning (or having access to) regalia resembling that worn by soldiers but also taking advantage of the US Department of Defense's 1033 Program, which has brought military-grade weapons and technology to college campuses.[28] That program, created as part of 1997's National Defense Authorization Act, allows the Department of Defense to legally dispose of surplus equipment and weapons by giving them to local authorities, including police departments like those at PSIs. According to the Law Enforcement Support Office (LESO), which coordinates and oversees the equipment procurement process for police agencies, over $7.4 billion of property has been transferred to more than eight thousand enrolled law enforcement agencies, including dozens of campus police departments, since the program's inception.[29] All that militarization has accomplished is harming citizen perceptions of, and trust in, the police, including campus officers, as militarization disproportionately is directed at Black citizens and communities.[30]

Third, according to the AAUP Campus Police Working Group, unlike their municipal counterparts who are accountable to elected officials like mayors and city councils and therefore to voters, campus police departments are ultimately accountable only to an unelected college or university president and gubernatorially appointed members of PSI governing boards.[31] The safety of the campus community thus becomes the responsibility of individuals who are not accountable to the people comprising that community (i.e., faculty members, staff, and students). The problem is exacerbated by the mission creep (see below) occurring in campus policing that has resulted in their jurisdictional authority extending to areas miles away from the college or university.

Fourth, campus policing is rife with opacity, especially in departments operating at private PSIs. Imon Jackson and Frank LoMonte found that departments at private PSIs are even beyond the reach of Freedom of Information Act laws as they apply only to records kept by public entities, thus increasing these departments' opacity. As a result, when a campus police department is operated by a private university, it is far from certain members of the campus community or the larger public will have access to the kind of department records necessary for even nominal oversight.[32] Consistent with these informational gaps, Nathalie Baptiste described campus police departments at private PSIs as "one more case of privatization producing more confusion and less accountability."³³ Even in states that do afford the public a measure of transparency in private PSIS' police department records, wholesale access is generally circumscribed by statute. For instance, Baptiste found that, in North Carolina, Texas, and Virginia, state statutes mandated that police departments operated by private universities disclose the first page of each "incident report" written by officers responding to the scene of a crime, but nothing else. Also relating to transparency are agency processes and procedures for addressing complaints filed against officers. Again, such information is difficult to come by, which makes it hard to track outcomes in these cases.

Fifth, particularly in recent years, jurisdictional limits on the power of campus police officers to patrol, make arrests, or otherwise intervene in areas outside or beyond the legally established physical boundaries of the campus have greatly expanded and continue to do so. I suggest this situation is akin to *mission creep*, a term used by the military to refer to the incremental expansion of an intervention, project, or mission beyond its original scope, focus, or goals. In campus policing, *mission creep* refers to instances where the jurisdictional boundaries of a particular campus police department have expanded well into surrounding areas. Such expansion is made possible through Mutual Aid Agreements (MAAs) or Memoranda of Understanding (MOUs), in which campus police are given the authority by local municipalities to patrol off-campus locations and render assistance to local police as needed. MAAs and MOUs may also accord campus police the authority to respond to calls for service arising from locations near the campus. Thus, it is becoming increasingly common for campus police to patrol areas well outside of their originally established physical and legal boundaries of the campus into communities whose members may neither know who they are or why they are present.

Finally, before any new police officer can begin their duties, they must first complete basic law enforcement training (BLET) that involves about twenty weeks of forty-hour-per-week training at one of more than six hundred police academies nationwide offering this training.³⁴ BLET involves achieving competence in six core areas of a nationally accepted curriculum: operations; weapons/defensive tactics; self-improvement; "special topics" (such as gangs, elder crime, or advanced nonlethal weapons); law (constitutional and criminal); and community-oriented policing (COP). Trainees are also likely to receive additional training beyond the core hours in areas such as weapons, physical control/defensive tactics, patrol tactics, and terrorism.

When one considers the *proportion* of hours devoted to these core areas, however, training in so-called traditional (i.e., "warrior") areas of policing such as operations and weapons/defensive tactics can encompass more than 60 percent of the total training hours, whereas training in COP, for example, typically constitutes only about 10 percent of total hours. In short, much of the BLET experienced by new campus officers stresses the "warrior" aspects of policing while downplaying training in ethics, cultural diversity, problem solving, and deescalation. Unless change occurs with the warrior emphasis in BLET, it is doubtful change will occur in the larger field of policing, which includes *campus* policing.

Like American policing more broadly, campus policing faces multiple crises involving their legitimacy, militarization via ties to the Department of Defense, accountability and transparency relating to the governance of PSIs, expanding legal jurisdiction via mission creep, and officers' early occupational socialization as "warriors" through basic law enforcement training at police academies around the country. Importantly, all of these issues are now infused into the "new" *in loco parentis* in higher education that centers on campus policing.

CAMPUS POLICE DEPARTMENTS employing uniformed, sworn and armed officers are a relatively new thread that has been added to the fabric of American higher education. Personifying a more sophisticated and technology-laden version of *in loco parentis* and grounded in the patriarchy of *parens patriae*, campus police are symbols of the police power of the state as enumerated in the Tenth Amendment to the U.S. Constitution. Because they mimic municipal police departments as quasi-military bureaucracies replete with specialization whose officers are trained as "warriors," they face many of the same crises as their municipal counterparts including issues involving legitimacy, militarization, accountability and transparency, mission creep, and training. Like their municipal counterparts, they are pieces of a criminal justice system that helps maintain the machinery of the American carceral state. At minimum, the current reckoning they face calls for a complete reimagining of their role and function in higher education and could well result in disbanding them entirely.

NOTES

1. Craig A. Forest, "A History of *In Loco Parentis* in American Higher Education" (PhD diss., University of Missouri, 2020); John J. Sloan III, "Holding Postsecondary

Institutions Liable for Civil Wrongs: Surveying the Legal Landscape," in *Campus Crime: Legal, Social and Policy Perspectives*, 4th ed., ed. Bonnie S. Fisher and Sloan (Springfield, IL: Charles C. Thomas, 2022), 115–42; John S. Tieman, "*In Loco Sacerdotis*: Toward a Reimagining of *In Loco Parentis*" (PhD diss., St. Louis University, 1996).

2. See John J. Sloan III, "The Modern Campus Police: An Analysis of Their Evolution, Structure and Function," *American Journal of Police* 11, no. 2 (1992): 85–104.

3. John C. Hogan and Mortimer D. Schwartz, "*In Loco Parentis* in the United States: 1765–1985," *Journal of Legal History* 8, no. 3 (1987): 260–74, www.tandfonline.com/doi/pdf/10.1080/01440368708530908.

4. Philip Lee, "The Curious Life of *In Loco Parentis* in American Universities," *Higher Education Review* 8, no. 1 (2011): 65–90.

5. Hogan and Schwartz, "*In Loco Parentis* in the United States: 1765–1985."

6. Forest, "A History of *In Loco Parentis* in American Higher Education," 7.

7. John S. Tieman, "*In Loco Sacerdotis*: Toward a Reimagining of *In Loco Parentis*" (PhD diss., St. Louis University, 1996).

8. Sarah Packard, *Higher Education in the UK and the US: Converging University Models in a Global Academic World?* (Leiden, The Netherlands: Brill, 2014), https://brill.com/view/title/24845.

9. Forest, "A History of *In Loco Parentis* in American Higher Education."

10. Forest, "A History of *In Loco Parentis* in American Higher Education," 116–19.

11. Isabelle Trueblood, "The Evolution of Fear of Juvenile Delinquency," *ARC GIS Blog*, May 10, 2021, https://storymaps.arcgis.com/stories/ 4be46641c29d4410babfcf0 48d453c19/.

12. Forest, "A History of *In Loco Parentis* in American Higher Education," 17.

13. National Center for Education Statistics, *120 Years of American Education: A Statistical Portrait* (Washington, DC: US Department of Education, 1993), table 23, https://nces.ed.gov/pubsearch/pubsinfo.asp?pubid=93442.

14. Richard Brownell, "From Campus Protest to Armed Insurrection." *Medium*, April 25, 2019, https://medium.com/@rickbrownell/from-campus-protest-to-armed-insurrection-22c0233025b9.

15. Lorraine Boissoneault, "In 1968, Three Students Were Killed by Police: Today, Few Remember the Orangeburg Massacre," *Smithsonian Magazine*, February 7, 2018.

16. Abigail J. Stewart, Isis H. Settles, and Nicolas J. G. Winter, "Women and the Social Movements of the 1960s: Activists, Engaged Observers, and Nonparticipants," *Political Psychology* 19, no. 1(1998): 63–94.

17. Cynthia Harrigan, Isabel Irizarry, Elizabeth Yates, and Jessica Kerley, "The Students They Are A-Changin," *America in the '60s* (2000), www2.kenyon.edu/Khistory/60s/welcome.htm.

18. Recent analyses by observers of higher education, such as Peter Lake, suggest

that PSIs have begun adopting the role of "facilitator" with their students, guiding them to help make better choices relating to their physical, psychological, and moral development and successfully helping shepherd them through the four years of college (see, for example, Vimal Patel, "The 'New' *In Loco Parentis*," *Chronicle of Higher Education*, February 22, 2019). Although the "facilitator university" may be the newest iteration of *in loco parentis*, commensurate with its rise has been militarization of the campus police, expansion of their jurisdictional boundaries into areas well away from campus, and closer ties with local law enforcement through mutual assistance agreements (MAAs) or memoranda of understanding (MOUs).

19. For example, see Noah R. Feldman and Kathleen M. Sullivan, eds., *Constitutional Law*, 20th ed. (St. Paul, MN: West Academic Publishing, 2019).

20. Santiago Legarre, "The Historical Background of the Police Power," *Journal of Constitutional Law* 9, no. 3 (2006): 745–96, https://scholarship.law.upenn.edu/jcl/vol9/iss3/3/.

21. Legarre, "The Historical Background of the Police Power," 747.

22. Rajan Bal, "The Perils of *Parens Patriae*." *Georgetown Journal on Poverty Law & Policy*, November 21, 2017, www.law.georgetown.edu/poverty-journal/blog/the-perils-of-parens-patriae.

23. American Association of University Professors (AAUP) Campus Police Working Group, *On Campus Police Forces* (Washington, DC: American Association of University Professors, 2021), www.aaup.org/report/campus-police-forces.

24. John J. Sloan III, "Five Issues That Will Determine the Future of Campus Policing in America." *Academia Letters*, Article 1813 (2021), https://doi.org/10.20935/AL1813.

25. Peter Fabienne, "Political Legitimacy," in *The Stanford Encyclopedia of Philosophy*, summer 2017 ed., ed. Edward N. Zalta, https://plato.stanford.edu/archives/sum2017/entries/legitimacy/.

26. Aziz Z. Huq, Jonathan Jackson, and Richard Trinkner, "Legitimating Practices: Revisiting the Predicates of Police Legitimacy," *British Journal of Criminology* 57, no. 5 (2016): 1101–122, https://doi.org/10.1093/bjc/azw037.

27. Connie Hasset-Walker, "How You Start Is How You Finish? The Slave Patrol and Jim Crow Origins of Policing," *Human Rights* 46, no. 2 (2021), www.americanbar.org/groups/crsj/publications/human_rights_magazine_home/civil-rights-reimagining-policing/how-you-start-is-how-you-finish/; Kelly Lytle Hernandez, Khalil Gibran Muhammad, and Heather Ann Thompson, "Introduction: Constructing the Carceral State," *Journal of American History* 102, no. 1 (2015): 18–24, https://doi.org/10.1093/jahist/jav259.

28. Brian Barrett, "The Pentagon's Hand-Me-Downs Helped Militarize Police: Here's How," *Wired*, June 2, 2020.

29. Barrett, "The Pentagon's Hand-Me-Downs."

30. Jonathan Mummolo, "Militarization Fails to Enhance Police Safety or Reduce Crime but May Harm Police Reputation," *PNAS* 115, no. 37 (2018): 9181–86.

31. AAUP Campus Police Working Group, *On Campus Police Forces.*

32. Iman J. Jackson and Frank LoMonte, "Policing Transparency," *Human Rights* 44, no. 4 (2020), www.americanbar.org/groups/crsj/publications/human_rights_magazine_home/black-to-the-future-part-ii/policing-transparency/.

33. Nathalie Baptiste, "Campus Cops: Authority without Accountability," *American Prospect*, November 2, 2015, 1, https://prospect.org/civil-rights/campus-cops-authority-without-accountability/.

34. John J. Sloan III and Eugene A. Paoline III, "'They Need More Training!' A National-Level Analysis of Police Academy Basic Training Priorities," *Police Quarterly* 24, no. 4 (2021): 486–518, https://doi.org/10.1177%2F10986111211013311.

2

A CRITICAL LEGAL ANALYSIS OF CAMPUS POLICE AUTHORITY

VANESSA MILLER

Campus police officers enjoy broad authority that is anchored in legal protections. These legal protections constitute multidimensional shields for the creation, function, and accountability of the campus police. For example, most states create and give officers police powers via statutory authority. In fact, nearly every state has enacted a law that codifies the duties and functions of campus police officers. While states have ordinarily delineated the powers of municipal police officers, the use of statutory law to expressly authorize colleges and universities to employ campus police officers is actually rooted in racialized concepts of safety that characterized the 1970s. During the 1960s and 1970s, most statutory laws dedicated to campus policing emerged as a response to the various protests taking place on college campuses across the country. By passing these statutes, states secured the legal authority of campus police officers as sworn "peace officers" of the state.

As law enforcement officers of the state, campus police officers generally have the same rights, protections, and immunities afforded to any other law enforcement officer. Most notably, campus police officers at public postsecondary institutions may be protected from civil lawsuits arising from their professional interactions with citizens and the discretionary authority the officers exercise during them under the doctrine of qualified immunity. The defense allows officers to claim immunity for performing discretionary functions. Also, campus police departments lack community oversight despite patterns of racialized interactions with campus community members. Unlike many of their municipal counterparts, campus police departments or their parent institution (i.e., the university/college) frequently do not have a formal process to submit or review complaints of alleged misconduct against officers. In an effort to hold police departments accountable, multiple current and former campus police officers at the University of Washington (UW) filed a lawsuit against the UW Police Department (UWPD) alleging their work environment was racially hostile.

This chapter presents a critical legal analysis of state-level statutory protections afforded to campus police officers that ultimately make it more difficult for victims of violent and discriminatory police interactions—who are disproportionately racially marginalized members of the campus community—to hold campus police officers accountable. Specifically, it outlines a multilayered model of state-sanctioned protections that ultimately permit campus police to engage in discriminatory conduct with minimal legal intervention or oversight that includes statutes granting police authority to campus officers, the legal doctrine of qualified immunity, and institutional opacity regarding the submitting and receiving of complaints regarding alleged campus police misconduct. The analysis shows the broad legal authority and protection afforded campus police is deeply connected to the surveillance and control of racially marginalized students and community members which should be a cause for concern for university leadership and prompt a reexamination of their reliance on the campus police for order maintenance and law enforcement both on and off campus.

OVERVIEW AND HISTORY OF CAMPUS POLICE STATUTORY AUTHORITY

Colleges and universities have significant policing power partly because of campus police statutes.[1] Campus police statutes grant university leaders and governing boards the lawful authority to create and maintain a campus police department. These statutes authorize campus police officers to serve as sworn law enforcement officers of the state with the power to carry weapons, execute arrests, execute search warrants, serve subpoenas, conduct criminal investigations, collaborate with state or federal law enforcement agencies, and provide relevant law enforcement services on campus. Nearly every state authorizes campus police officers to exist at public institutions and hold full law enforcement authority; many states also authorize campus police officers at private institutions to have law enforcement, private security, or public safety authority. Though many modern campus police departments developed from campus security departments, it is noteworthy that campus police statutes did not develop from general concerns about on-campus safety. Rather, they developed from a deeply rooted history of policing race on campus.[2]

The first state law relating to campus policing dates to 1905 in Rhode Island.[3] The law stated, "The Sheriff of the County of Providence with as many of his deputies as he may deem necessary shall attend the celebration of the annual commencements of Brown University and Providence College and shall preserve peace and good order and decorum during [the] same."[4] In the first half of the twentieth century, very few states enacted laws relating to campus policing or campus security; by 1950, just four more states passed laws that expressly authorized government officials or university leaders to appoint campus police officers, and five states passed laws that authorized government officials to appoint "special officers" for public functions. In theory, the "special officer" laws provided the opportunity for state officials, under the color of legal authority, to appoint officers to a college or university campus. For example, in 1946, a Kentucky statute permitted the governor to appoint "special local police officers to serve as special officers on campus to preserve the peace and protect the property of the institution."[5] The number of campus police statutes remained relatively low for the next several years. By 1960, only ten additional states had passed laws that expressly authorized government officials or university leaders to appoint campus police officers.[6] Between 1960 and 1969, twenty-eight additional states passed campus police statutes.[7] State-level campus police statutes, an anomaly during the prior six decades, nearly tripled in number during a single decade and were inextricably tied to the profound social and political changes concerning racial justice and antiviolence sentiments present during the 1960s.

During the 1960s and into the 1970s, mass student protests and demonstrations concerning segregation, police violence against Black communities, women's rights, freedom of speech, and the Vietnam War flooded American college campuses. The protests significantly increased tensions with government officials and interactions with local police.[8] Some of the mass student protests of the 1960s developed from student opposition to urban renewal plans and university expansion into the majority-Black neighborhoods surrounding them.[9] Students at many urban-based elite higher educational institutions protested the universities' acquisition and commodification of Black neighborhoods by publicly occupying university spaces.

Some of the most prominent examples were the protests at Columbia University in 1968. Student protests and sit-ins resulted in the students involved being violently removed from campus by officers of the New York Police Department (NYPD). Black students who opposed the construction of a segregated campus gymnasium in Harlem, which they labeled "Gym Crow,"[10] called on the university to stop the acquisition of predominantly Black and Hispanic neighborhoods surrounding the campus. White students who opposed the United States' involvement in the Vietnam War demanded the university sever its ties to military-related research. Both groups of student protesters occupied separate university buildings. After several days, university administrators called the NYPD to quash the demonstrations. The Black students relinquished their occupation as soon as the officers arrived, but the white students met police with forceful resistance. The NYPD arrested over seven hundred students that day.[11]

A few years later, Governor James Rhodes of Ohio exclaimed he was ready to forcefully move against campus unrest or uproar and would do so irrespective of the desires of campus administrators.[12] He was willing to quell student activism and expression concerning antiwar sentiments by calling the Ohio National Guard to restore order on campus.[13] Following student expression opposing the expansion of the Vietnam War, student riots broke out and the Reserve Officers' Training Corps (ROTC) building was lit on fire. During a protest held on May 4, 1970, members of the Ohio National Guard fired into a crowd of Kent State University students with live ammunition, killing four and injuring nine.[14] The incident triggered nationwide student strikes at colleges and universities that forced them to close. Only ten days after the Kent State shooting, city and state police officers opened fire on student protesters at Jackson State University, a historically Black university in Jackson, Mississippi, killing two students and injuring twelve.[15] Earlier that year, riot police were sent to the University of Puerto Rico at Río Piedras to prevent students from protesting the presence of ROTC on the campus. Antonia Martínez Lagares shouted "asesinos" (assassins) as she watched police officers beat students. A police officer looked up and shot her in the head.[16]

Universities were faced with unprecedented challenges to their campus authority. Mass anti-establishment student protests consumed many campuses, and higher education law relating to student conduct and discipline radically shifted during the 1960s and 1970s.[17] Student movements simultaneously demanded university policy reform that recognized their right to engage in political activity and assemble on campus and that local police be removed from campus.[18] University leaders lobbied their state representatives to establish and outfit their own police force to respond to increased safety concerns on campus. Senior administrators requested attorney general opinions to determine the scope of university police, including jurisdictional limitations, arrest powers, and the ability to patrol in unmarked vehicles.[19] By establishing their own on-campus police force, universities would not have to delay responding to crises on campus by waiting for municipal police or other law enforcement agencies to arrive. Instead, they would be able to maintain an internal, dedicated police force to meet the needs of the university.[20]

Despite framing "safety" as the rationale for creating campus police departments, universities used the tools of the carceral state to provide legal status for their own police force as a means of social control. By 1970, approximately forty-one states had legally authorized university administrators or governing bodies to appoint campus police officers.[21] The legislative measures established not only the state-sanctioned law enforcement authority of campus police officers but also the legal legitimacy of the presence of the carceral state on campus. Although many of the student protests were peaceful, university leaders supplied their campus police departments with the fiscal resources needed to mirror their municipal police counterparts. Universities resourced their campus police departments with vehicles, uniforms, and professional training to "respond" to the civil unrest of the antiviolence and pro-speech student movements.

By 2020, nearly every state had enacted formal university police statutes or had otherwise codified the legal authority of campus police officers. Although these statutes differ in purpose, scope of authority, delegation of authority, and appointment procedures, they fundamentally authorize universities to maintain and operate a law enforcement agency whose roots can be traced to the slave patrols of the antebellum South and contemporaneously express themselves in racialized conflicts with student activists and members of surrounding Black neighborhoods. For example, in Alabama, there are various state statutes that articulate what power and authority colleges and universities can delegate to their sworn campus police officers.[22] Florida law directs—not just empowers—universities to provide police officers for the university and establishes minimum training requirements.[23] Oregon law gives authority to university presidents to establish a process to receive and respond to complaints about the policies of the police department and conduct of police officers.[24] Kansas law permits university police officers to exercise their law enforcement authority in any area outside of their jurisdiction if assistance is requested from law enforcement officers in the area.[25]

From repressing student activism to patrolling the surrounding communities, race plays a role in how American universities are policed. Campus police statutes were created as a by-product of the carceral state to surveil and control student activism on campus. The student sit-ins, demonstrations, and dissent in response to segregation and violence led institutional leaders to accelerate the legitimizing of campus police departments. The continued expansion of campus police resources and authority during nationwide student activism revealed a need for institutions to maintain an unadulterated image of being safe havens of speech, scholarship, and inquiry despite campus police violence and student dissent arising from it. Increased interactions with the police led to overpolicing and hypervigilant surveillance of racially marginalized students and community members.

QUALIFIED IMMUNITY

In July 2019, a police officer in Georgia shot a ten-year-old child in the leg when he tried to shoot a family's dog.[26] The officer was pursuing a criminal suspect when the suspect went into a local resident's yard. At the time, one adult and six children were in the yard. The officer demanded everyone get on the ground. The family's dog, who posed no immediate threat, walked into the yard. The officer fired his weapon at the dog twice. The second bullet ripped through the child's knee as he lay on the ground. The child's parent filed a civil lawsuit against the officer under 42 U.S.C. § 1983 ("Section 1983") for deprivation of the right to be free from excessive force as guaranteed under the Fourteenth Amendment to the US Constitution. The US Eleventh Circuit Court of Appeals dismissed the civil rights lawsuit against the officer because it found the officer was entitled to *qualified immunity*.[27] This case is a harrowing example of the legal protections that excuse police violence and limit redress for victims.

Qualified immunity shields government officials performing discretionary functions from civil lawsuits. It is a form of *sovereign immunity* first introduced by the US Supreme Court in 1967. In *Pierson v. Ray*, the Court held that police officers should be entitled to a "good faith" and "probable cause" defense to Section 1983 claims.[28] The Court's extension of a good faith defense to Section 1983 claims is important for civil liability suits. Section 1983 claims provide a civil action for a person deprived of "any rights, privileges, or immunities secured by the Constitution and laws" by a state actor.[29] It is one way for victims of police violence or discrimination to recover damages for the violation of their constitutional rights.

In 1982, the Supreme Court fundamentally changed the basis of the qualified immunity doctrine. In the landmark case *Harlow v. Fitzgerald*, the Supreme Court held that government officials would be entitled to qualified immunity so long as their conduct "does not violate clearly established statutory or constitutional rights of which a reasonable person would have known."[30] Critics argue the Supreme Court effectively cloaked government officials in absolute protection from legal accountability. In her dissent in *Kisela v. Hughes*, Justice Sonia Sotomayor, joined by Justice Ruth Bader Ginsburg, wrote: "Such a one-sided approach to qualified immunity transforms the doctrine into an absolute shield for law enforcement officers, gutting the deterrent effect of the Fourth Amendment. The majority . . . sends an alarming signal to law enforcement officers and the public. It tells officers that they can shoot first and think later, and it tells the public that palpably unreasonable conduct will go unpunished."[31] Further, in 1989, the Supreme Court held in *Graham v. Connor* the "reasonable test" for examining police officer's actions in excessive force claims would take into account how officers are "often forced to make split-second judgements."[32] Specifically, the reasonable use of force must be examined from the perspective of a "reasonable officer on the scene" and not from "20/20 hindsight."[33]

In an unprecedented analysis of appellate court records, journalists from *Reuters Investigates* found that courts increasingly grant police officers qualified immunity in use of excessive force cases.[34] For example, between 2005 and 2007, courts favored police in 44 percent of excessive force cases, but between 2017 and 2019, courts favored police in 57 percent of excessive force cases. Qualified immunity continues to protect police officers from accountability by treating police brutality as unfortunate collateral damage in the legal process.

Campus police officers, as statutorily authorized state law enforcement personnel, are also entitled to qualified immunity. The same legal concerns regarding qualified immunity protections of municipal police officers apply to campus police. Qualified immunity can be seen as a fail-safe tool that excuses discriminatory conduct as part of the job. It is a likely explanation for the infrequency of judicial intervention in lawsuits involving campus police. Despite heightened media attention to incidents of racial profiling and harassment by campus police, successful legal challenges against the conduct of campus police officers are infrequent.

Courts have found campus police officers at public universities are entitled to qualified immunity protections *because* they operate as state law enforcement officers, ultimately shielding their discretionary functions from liability for civil damages. Some states, like New Jersey, have extended qualified immunity protections to campus police officers employed at private postsecondary institutions. In *McClendon v. Lewis*, a Pennsylvania District Court held that a defendant's claims against a campus police officer for a stop and arrest were barred because the officer's actions were protected under qualified immunity.[35] In *Giles v. Davis*, the US Third Circuit Court of Appeals found that campus police officers were entitled to qualified immunity because they had probable cause for arrest and any reasonable officer would conclude the plaintiff's actions were an unjustifiable risk of public disturbance.[36] Qualified immunity limits lawsuits against campus police officers employed at public universities. The limitation ultimately makes it difficult for victims of police misconduct—who are disproportionately racially marginalized communities—to seek relief in court and further minimizes the ability for campus police officers to be held accountable for unlawful or discriminatory misconduct.

Even when campus officers are not entitled to qualified immunity, the option for protection can prime officers to believe it will be afforded. In *Collick v. William Paterson University*, William Paterson University (WPU) police officers arrested two Black male students accused of engaging in nonconsensual sex with a classmate.[37] The officers arrested the men while they were off campus during the Thanksgiving break. They were placed in handcuffs, brought to the WPU campus for questioning, and were not told the reason for their arrest. Prior to their arrest, the plaintiffs were not interviewed, notified of the accusation, or offered an opportunity to deny the allegations. The plaintiffs alleged, among other complaints, racial discrimination, false arrest, and false imprisonment.[38] The court held the plaintiffs failed to establish a racial discrimination claim because identifying race as a stand-alone factor is not sufficient to establish bias. The officers contended the plaintiffs failed to establish a claim for false arrest or imprisonment because they had probable cause for the arrest. The officers further contended that even if they lacked probable cause, their conduct was protected under qualified immunity. The court, however, denied the motion to dismiss on the ground of qualified immunity because it did not find the officers' conduct reasonable. Qualified immunity shields government officials from civil liability so long as their conduct does not violate clearly established rights of which a reasonable person would have known.[39] Here, the officers failed to take basic investigatory steps that reasonable officers would have taken and ultimately jumped to the conclusion they had probable cause.

The doctrine of qualified immunity is a critical issue in contemporary police reform and must be a priority for university leaders, especially those responsible for campus security measures. Qualified immunity shields police officers from being held responsible for malfeasance, denying victims of police misconduct their constitutional rights. Qualified immunity creates difficult challenges for victims of police violence to move forward in an already difficult legal process. It requires a plaintiff to demonstrate the officer's conduct was unlawful and the officer should have known they were violating a "clearly established" statutory or constitutional right, limiting the plaintiff from holding officers accountable for their conduct.

INSTITUTIONAL INFRASTRUCTURE FOR CAMPUS POLICE ACCOUNTABILITY

There currently is a lack of institutional infrastructure either to provide community oversight of campus police or to receive and review complaints of alleged campus police misconduct. There is no institutional infrastructure in place to collect or provide to the public information about abuse of campus police authority, results of internal investigations, or justification for policing strategies or tactics. In fact, only a handful of *municipal* police departments, including the New York Police Department (NYPD), operate public databases that release similar information.[40] The NYPD database not only includes complaints received for alleged officer misconduct but also records disciplinary actions taken and relevant results of internal investigations. Government watchdogs and public interest nonprofit organizations, like the Citizens Police Data Project in Chicago, also provide the public with information on allegations of police misconduct that holds officers accountable when recognized patterns of racial discrimination and abuse are otherwise ignored by police departments.[41]

The lack of accountability for campus police misconduct is critical because campus police officers play a role in the way that racial conflict becomes legitimized or delegitimized on campus. They have the discretion to pursue—or not pursue—action against persons who instigate racially hostile environments. When campus police decide to end an investigation into bananas and nooses found hanging around campus after the first Black woman is elected as student body president or arrest a Black student for third-degree assault after a white student attempted to hit her with her car in the campus parking lot, campus police are signaling to the rest of the campus community that racism and oppressive ideologies are tolerated.[42]

Legal Analysis of Campus Police Authority

In an effort to hold campus police departments accountable for their patterns of racially discriminatory conduct, racially marginalized campus police officers have filed legal complaints that challenge the culture of campus policing. The officers have documented their lived experiences with racial discrimination in their work environment and racial hostility within their own departments.[43] Campus police departments are overwhelmingly white and male, and structural racism within policing is well documented.[44] Black, Latino, and other racialized minority campus police officers across the nation are attempting to challenge the culture of entrenched racism that plagues their departments. Their complaints allege their respective departments are spaces of hostile, discriminatory, and retaliatory conduct where Black officers are met with intimidation and disciplinary actions for conduct their white peers also engage in but which is unsanctioned. National demands to reckon with histories of state-sanctioned racial violence by the police as well as the public health crisis created by COVID-19 helped expose the often-muted racial climates within campus police departments. A selection of legal challenges to the campus police culture are listed below:

- Officer Nikki Hendrix, a Black campus police officer at Syracuse University, became the second Black officer within a year to sue the department. In her complaint, Officer Hendrix says the Syracuse University Police Department (SUPD) systematically discriminates against Black officers by unfairly judging them during the hiring and promotional process and incentivizes Black officers to infringe on citizens' rights to advance in the department.[45] Officer Hendrix also says she has been denied for every promotion despite being employed by the department for more than a decade and being a Syracuse resident. She contends white men with less qualifications who reside outside of Syracuse are offered the promotions over her.
- Two Black campus police officers at the University of Florida filed a discrimination complaint with the Equal Employment Opportunity Commission and the Florida Commission on Human Relations.[46] In their complaint, Officer Andrielle Boone and Brian Ausgood allege they experienced racial and gender discrimination and retaliation from members of the university's police department (UFPD). Both officers described incidents of racial discrimination by members of the UFPD command staff. Furthermore, Officer Boone contends she was put on the "Brady" list as retaliation for reporting a coworker. She describes being subject to

rumors, workplace drama, and discrimination from white officers following her promotion to Sergeant in 2017.
- A Black campus police officer at the University of Delaware filed a complaint against the department for racial discrimination after he voiced concerns over management of COVID-19.[47] Officer Raushan Rich was with the department for eight years before being terminated for insubordination. Officer Rich expressed concerns over a university policy that required campus police officers to escort COVID-19–positive students to quarantine. He felt it was an unnecessary risk for non–law enforcement purposes. However, he was instructed to comply "regardless of the risks" and was forced to pick up an officer who was also hesitant to comply with the policy. Officer Rich states that he was disciplined for conduct for which his white colleagues were not.[48]
- Officer Brandon Hanks, a well-known Black officer in the Syracuse community, filed a discrimination complaint against SUPD alleging the department systemically discriminates and retaliates against Black officers, creating what he described as a "Jim Crow culture."[49] In his complaint, he states SUPD maintained a hostile work environment that included racial harassment, racial stereotypes, and the treatment of Black officers as inferior.
- Multiple Black police officers at the University of Washington came forward to share their experiences of racism from their white peers and superiors.[50] Five Black campus officers filed a lawsuit against the university's police department, describing "a culture of entrenched racism that has included racial slurs, vicious comments about Black people and open hostility directed at them and at members of the public."[51] In the complaint, the officers described heinous acts of racial violence and disparagement while at work. For example, Officer Karinn Young said she found bananas in front of her locker, one time with a note referring to her as a "monkey." Officer Hamini said a white supervisor struck him with a stick-like object and remarked, "You people should be used to being hit with these."[52]

The accounts of Black campus police officers experiencing racially hostile and discriminatory workplaces further demonstrates the continued othering of Black persons on campus. Their experiences contribute to a culture of campus policing that is entrenched in racism and hostile to Black community members.

These legal challenges are important because they document resistance from campus police departments to foster a more racially just work environment despite nationwide efforts to defund police departments over racist policing.

Over the last fifty years, institutions of postsecondary education have become quasi-municipalities with social, economic, and political authority over the community. Their status has permitted them to operate their own police force without much community oversight or regulation. The disconnect between the function of campus police and actual public safety needs can help reframe how resources are distributed to meet community needs. Additionally, because of their unique position in society, and available resources, institutions are perfect case studies to rethink policing as it relates to community safety more broadly.

CALLS TO DEMILITARIZE AND DIVEST from campus police departments are calls to recognize the deeply rooted histories of surveilling and controlling students on campus, and to unravel the racial power dynamics between white police forces and the surrounding often Black and Latino neighborhoods. University leaders must listen to community activists who have repeatedly communicated their concerns about using state violence on campus, in particular as they have been weaponized against Black and marginalized populations. Campus police statutes are permissive. They simply authorize university leaders and governing boards to appoint and employ campus police. With few exceptions, there are no directives from campus police officers. Instead, universities should invest their allotted million-dollar budgets and resources into mental health services, food and housing security, community programs and relations, and academic programs.

University leaders should reexamine their reliance on campus police officers because the legal status of campus police is deeply entrenched in the control of racially marginalized campus community members. Campus police officers receive legal protections in connection with their functions and duties that ultimately make it more difficult for victims of police violence or discriminatory conduct to hold campus police officers or their institutions liable for civil rights violations. Under state law, campus police officers are law enforcement of the state and therefore enjoy the rights, protections, and immunities generally reserved for government officials with discretionary functions. Though campus police statutes appear to serve the interests of the campus community because they provide protection to the campus from crime, the statutes are embedded in oppressive systems to surveil and control racially marginalized students and community members. In the courts, qualifying campus police officers are entitled to the defense of qualified immunity, which shields officers from personal liability.

Here, the law serves as a double-edged sword. On the one hand, the law provides campus police officers with the ability to exercise broad authority on campus. On the other, it shields them from exposure to civil liability. Even if campus police officers are not ultimately granted qualified immunity, the option for legal protection for their conduct creates an "act-now, analyze-later" environment. Lastly, a lack of institutional infrastructure to provide community oversight or receive and review complaints of police misconduct contributes to the unbridled exercise of authority by campus police. However, a recent wave of legal challenges to the culture of campus policing by current or former Black and Latino campus police officers seeks to challenge the status quo—from racialized hiring and promotion practices to culture dynamics.

NOTES

1. Also referred to as "university police statutes."
2. See Jude Paul Matias Dizon, "Protecting the University, Policing Race: A Case Study of Campus Policing," *Journal of Diversity in Higher Education*, 2021, advance online publication, https://doi.org/ 10.1037/dhe0000350.
3. In 1896, Rhode Island law permitted the town council to elect "one or more special constables" to attend "any school or meeting for the purpose of preventing any interruption or disturbance therein, with the power of arrest" (Gen. Laws Rhode Island Ch. 16 § 45-16-8 (1896)). However, the legislative history is unclear whether "schools" includes colleges and universities.
4. See Seymour Gelber, *The Role of Campus Security in the College Setting* (Washington, DC: US Government Printing Office, 1972), 25.
5. Ky. Rev. Stat. 61.360 (1946).
6. See Gelber, *The Role of Campus Security in the College Setting*, 171–90.
7. Gelber, *The Role of Campus Security in the College Setting*.
8. See Muhammad Ahmad, "On the Black Student Movement—1960-70," *Black Scholar* 9, no. 8–9 (1978): 2–11, https://doi.org/10.1080/00064246.1978.11414012.
9. See Richard Rothstein, *The Color of Law: A Forgotten History of How Our Government Segregated America* (New York: Liveright, 2018); and Davarian L. Baldwin, *In the Shadow of the Ivory Tower: How Universities Are Plundering Our Cities* (New York: Bold Type Books, 2021).
10. Siobhan Ryan, "Columbia University's 'Gym Crow': What the Contest over a Public Park Reveals about the Link between Race and Space," *Australasian Journal of*

American Studies 39, no. 1 (2020): 101–22, www.jstor.org/stable/26973002.

11. Paul Starr, "How the '68 Uprising Looks Today," *Columbia College Today*, Spring 2018, www.college.columbia.edu/cct/issue/spring18/article/how-68-uprising-looks-today.

12. See Joe Eszterhas and Michael D. Roberts, *Thirteen Seconds: Confrontation at Kent State* (New York: College Notes & Texts, 1970), 162–63.

13. See Eszterhas and Roberts, *Thirteen Seconds*, 162–63.

14. See Jerry M. Lewis and Thomas R. Hensley. "The May 4 Shootings at Kent State University: The Search for Historical Accuracy," Kent State University, www.kent.edu/may-4-historical-accuracy.

15. See Tim Spofford, *Lynch Street: The May 1970 Slayings at Jackson State College* (Kent, OH: Kent State University Press, 1989).

16. Alexandra Acosta-Vilanova, "La historia eterna de Antonia Martinez Lagares," *PULSO Estidiantil*, March 4, 2021, https://pulsoestudiantil.com/la-historia-eterna-de-antonia-martinez-lagares/.

17. See chapter 1 of this volume; Dixon v. Ala. State Bd. Of Educ. (5th Cir. 1961); Robert D. Bickel, and Judith A Brechner, "The Role of College or University Legal Counsel," in *College Administrator and the Courts* (Asheville, NC: College Administration Publications, 1978).

18. Kellie C. Soerey and Dannis Gregory, "Protests in the Sixties," *College Student Affairs Journal* 28, no. 2 (2010): 184–206, https://digitalcommons.odu.edu/efl_fac_pubs/42/.

19. See Gelber, *The Role of Campus Security in the College Setting*, 171–90.

20. Libby Nelson, "Why Nearly All Colleges Have an Armed Police Force," *Vox*, July 29, 2015.

21. See Gelber, *The Role of Campus Security in the College Setting*, 171–90.

22. Ala. Code § 16-52-12.1 grants Jacksonville State University police officers as peace officers with authority "any place in the state." Ala. Code § 16-56-12 delegates authority to the chancellor of Troy University to appoint and employ police officers on campus to eject trespassers and execute arrests on campus. Ala. Code § 16-48-12 authorizes the president of Auburn University to appoint and employ university police officers with the duties and invested powers of police officers. For additional examples, see Ala. Code Title 16: Education.

23. Fla. Stat. § 1012.97.

24. Or. Rev. Stat. § 352.121.

25. Kan. Stat. Ann. § 22-2401(a)(6).

26. Nick Sibilla, "Cop Who Accidentally Shot 10-Year-Old When Aiming for Family Dog Can't Be Sued, Federal Court Rules," *Forbes*, July 18, 2019.

27. Amy Corbitt, Individually and as Parent and Natural Guardian of SDC, a Minor

v. Michael Vickers, No. 17–15566, D.C. Docket No. 5:16-cv-00051-LGW-RSB, U.S. Eleventh Circuit (July 10, 2019), https://media.ca11.uscourts.gov/opinions/pub/files/201715566.pdf.

28. Pierson v. Ray, 386 U.S. 547 (1967).

29. 42 U.S.C. § 1983.

30. Harlow v. Fitzgerald (1982) 457 U.S. 800 at 818.

31. Kisela v. Hughes, 138 S. Ct. 1148, 1162 (2018).

32. Graham v. Connor, 490 U.S. 386, 397 (1989).

33. Graham v. Connor, 490 U.S. 386, 397 (1989).

34. Andrew Chung, Lawrence Hurley, Jackie Botts, and Andrea Januta, "Shielded," Thomson Reuters, May 8, 2020, www.reuters.com/investigates/specialreport/usa-police-immunity-scotus/.

35. McClendon v. Lewis, No. 02-CV7433, 2005 U.S. Dist. LEXIS 1204 (E.D. Pa. Jan. 27, 2005).

36. Giles v. Davis, 427 F.3d 197 (3d. Cir. 2005).

37. Collick v. William Paterson Univ., No. 16–471 (KM) (JBC), 2016 U.S. Dist. LEXIS 160359 (D.N.J. Nov. 17, 2016).

38. Collick v. William Paterson Univ. (D.N.J. Nov. 17, 2016).

39. McGreevy v. Stroup, 413 F.3d 359, 364 (3d Cir. 2005) (quoting Harlow v. Fitzgerald, 457 U.S. 800, 818, 102 S.Ct. 2727, 73 L.Ed.2d 396 (1982)).

40. The City of New York Civil Complaint Review Board, n.d. "NYPD Member of Service Histories," www1.nyc.gov/site/ccrb/policy/MOS-records.page.

41. Citizens Police Data Project, n.d., "CPDP," https://cpdp.co.

42. Gina Cook, "American University Ends Hate Crime Investigation a Year Later," NBC4 Washington, April 29, 2018, www.nbcwashington.com/news/local/american-university-ends-hate-crime-investigation-a-year-later/53518/; Keely Brewer and Isabel Hope, "'It Is Blatant Racism': UA Student Shares Story of Arrest on Instagram," March 3, 2022, https://thecrimsonwhite.com/96173/news/it-is-blatant-racism-ua-student-shares-story-of-arrest-on-instagram.

43. Mike Baker, "Black Campus Police Officers Say They Suffered 'Unbearable' Racism," *New York Times*, June 22, 2021; Radley Balko, "There's Overwhelming Evidence That the Criminal Justice System Is Racist: Here's the Proof," *Washington Post*, June 10, 2020.

44. Brian A. Reaves, *Campus Law Enforcement, 2011–2012*, NCJ 248028 (Washington, DC: Bureau of Justice Statistics, 2016).

45. Chris Libonati, "2nd Black Syracuse Officer Set to Sue Department, Alleges Discrimination on the Job," syracuse.com, May 4, 2022.

46. Gershon Harrell, "University of Florida Police Department under Fire after Racial Discrimination Complaint," *Gainesville Sun*, April 13, 2022, www.gainesville.com

/story/news/2022/04/13/uf-police-department-under-fire-after-racial-discrimination-complaint/7229038001/.

47. Noah A. McGee, "Black Officer Accuses the University of Delaware of Racial Discrimination over Covid Protocols in New Lawsuit," The Root, February 22, 2022, www.theroot.com/black-officer-accuses-the-university-of-delaware-of-rac-1848577985.

48. Yusra Asif, "Lawsuit Accuses UD and Its Police Department of Racial Discrimination over Covid Practices," *Delaware News Journal*, February 14, 2022, www.delawareonline.com/story/news/2022/02/14/university-delaware-sued-police-officer-over-covid-19-protocols-his-dismissal/6708190001/.

49. Chris Libonati, Chris Baker, and Douglass Dowty, "Syracuse's Best-Known Police Officer Attacks Department's 'Jim Crow Culture' in Racial Bias Claim," June 25, 2021, https://www.syracuse.com/news/2021/06/syracuses-best-known-police-officer-attacks-departments-jim-crow-culture-in-racial-bias-claim.html.

50. Olafimihan Oshin, "Black Campus Officers Allege They Suffered 'Unbearable' Racism at University of Washington," *The Hill*, June 23, 2021, https://thehill.com/homenews/state-watch/559892-black-campus-officers-allege-they-suffered-unbearable-racism-at/.

51. Baker, "Black Campus Police Officers Say They Suffered 'Unbearable' Racism."

52. Vanessa Miller and Katheryn Russell-Brown, "Policing the College Campus: History, Race, and Law," *Washington and Lee Journal of Civil Rights and Social Justice* 29, no. 3 (2023): 59–128.

3

"JUST PROTECTING THE UNIVERSITY PROPERTY"

Campus Policing as Extraterritorial Expansion

DAVARIAN L. BALDWIN

Brandy Parker grew up in Woodlawn, just a few blocks south of the University of Chicago's (UChicago) Hyde Park campus. But his neighborhood felt like a world away from the university's bucolic campus oasis in the city, filled with ivy-covered gothic buildings and sleek, glassy research facilities powered by some of the wealthiest families in the world. By contrast, Woodlawn was and perhaps still is a neighborhood ravaged by urban violence and poverty. Parker moved to Sixty-First Street as a preteen and remembers that his mother wouldn't even let him venture away from the block until he was fifteen or sixteen. In fact, he didn't even know a place like Hyde Park could exist so close to where he lived. So as soon as he could, Parker joined his teenage friends to explore the campus. Hyde Park was so different from Woodlawn, "we would walk around just to get away from my environment, from the violence and stuff you know."

While Parker looked at UChicago as a refuge, elements of the university tagged him as a threat. Even at twenty-one, he thought back on those days with a mixture of irritation and fear; "every time I used to step my foot on university campus, [the campus police] always used to follow us." Parker would hear his physical description on a nearby walkie-talkie ("Black male with a mohawk"). Or campus police just flat out declared, "You don't belong over here, what are you doing over here?" While students did not outright question his presence, he noticed how they "crunched their backpacks." He would think, "You could be one of those college students that finna go shoot up a school. . . . I should be crunching my damn book bag!" Parker felt he had every right to enjoy the tranquil green spaces and different environment just blocks away from home. But the harassment wore him down. He devised elaborate, if inconvenient, routes to walk around the main areas of the campus. But UChicago police were "everywhere, I can't escape from them."

It was hardly an exaggeration to say that Parker could not "escape" the University of Chicago Police Department (UCPD). In 2011, the city's Commission on Public Safety passed a municipal ordinance that expanded UCPD's jurisdiction about four miles beyond the main campus, going north to Thirty-Seventh and as far south as Sixty-Fourth.[1] In short, UCPD, an armed private police force that answered only to the private university, was given the public authority to make arrests on city blocks. And their jurisdiction spread all the way from the historic Black neighborhood of Bronzeville right down to the heart of Parker's Woodlawn. Parker explained to me, "It's just like if you hire your own police force, you make your own police force." And the consequences of this expanded jurisdiction were real.

Many residents were happy to have the additional police presence amid the city's violence. Parker, however, was getting stopped by UCPD three or four times a week. He had committed no crimes and could not be found in any criminal database. Yet Parker relayed how cops sometimes jumped out on him before their car even stopped, screaming the now routine mantra, "Where the guns at, where the drugs at?" Parker began to wonder, "What they really protecting[?] . . . [I]s they really protecting the people or is they protecting the soil, the land?"

Parker pointed out that he met some really good police officers who encouraged him to go to school and even welcomed him on campus. But with the UCPD expansion, the campus already spilled over into his neighborhood. He now felt just as unwelcome on his own block as he had in Hyde Park. And it became clear to him UCPD was "just protecting the university property" as the campus expanded across the city's South Side.

BRUTE STRENGTH/SOFT POWER

When I went to Chicago, I wasn't even looking for Brandy Parker. I didn't expect to hear his story. I had come to study UChicago as a critical example of higher education's growing control over economic development and urban governance in working-class neighborhoods and communities of color, or what I call the rise of UniverCities. I was fascinated that an elite institution of higher education had become one of the biggest landholders and low-wage employers in the city.

Campus policing was not really on my radar. But when I talked to the amazing activists at the Invisible Institute about this work on UniverCities, they said, "You have to speak with Brandy."

It didn't take long, while speaking to Brandy, for me to quickly realize how central campus policing was to the larger celebration of higher education as an economic growth engine for cities. His observation that campus policing primarily serves to protect "university property" was more than a casual quip. The City of Chicago's 2011 municipal ordinance applied UCPD jurisdiction to any neighborhood targeted for university development. The details of this policing ordinance are instructive because higher education's growing prosperity has been centrally tied to the conversion of the campus into a lucrative urban planning model for managing real estate development, labor relations, and healthcare services for whole cities.

Brandy's experiences with UCPD, far away from the main campus, reveal how the 2011 ordinance helped convert campus police into an agent of what I call extraterritorial expansion. As schools across the country look to fill neighborhood blocks with prosperous housing, laboratories, retail operations, and other amenities, campus policing functions to regulate behavior, clear ground, and eventually protect the assets of one of the largest forces in today's political economy: higher education. Colleges and universities are increasingly turning to the brute strength of campus policing, alongside the soft power of campus building, to enact a violent confiscation and control of local communities.

UChicago serves as a titanic case of the growing encroachment of university police on our daily lives. It has one of the largest private security forces in the world, outside of the Vatican, with jurisdiction over fifty thousand nonstudent residents.[2] And the campus police hold this kind of public power in the same area where the university is one of the largest employers, landholders, and major economic engines. But UCPD's role in extraterritorial expansion is not singular. It has become a model for campus policing across the country.

A VATICAN CITY WITHIN BALTIMORE

Universities justifiably argue that the increased jurisdiction of sworn and armed campus police serves the interests of students and faculty coming into sometimes dangerous urban environments. This added police presence is also showcased as an act of public service to help overextended municipal officers and the residents they are tasked with protecting. But as Brandy's story reveals, soon after UChicago extended its jurisdiction, Black students and Black residents worried about racial profiling or at least the undue surveillance of nonwhite citizens by a police force with the primary task of serving the interests of a largely white institution.

Community organizations like the Invisible Institute and Southside Together Organizing for Power (STOP) could rattle off to me countless stories where Chicago's South Side residents had been directly harassed, thrown up against a squad car, or constantly followed by UCPD. In 2016, African Americans made up 59 percent of the population under UCPD jurisdiction, but according to a report from the Illinois Department of Transportation, they accounted for 100 percent of UCPD's investigation stops conducted on foot.[3] By early 2018, Black drivers made up nearly three-quarters of all the drivers stopped by the university police. And lest one argue that these numbers simply verify how Black people commit more crimes, this data did not include interactions with the majority-white student body. Former UCPD chief Fountain Walker confirmed that incidents with students are typically referred to the university. Campus activists charged that the glaring difference in treatment has created an unjust "two-tiered system of policing."[4] A student and community member can be accused of the same infraction, but the former meets with the dean and the latter is shuttled through the criminal justice system.

Despite the clear racial disparities of a two-tiered system, schools all across the country looked to UChicago for answers. After a 2017 spike in robberies and assaults, senior administrators at Johns Hopkins University even made a trip to the South Side.[5] And in March 2018, university president Ronald Daniels and Hopkins Hospital CEO Paul Rothman sent a surprise email to the campus community announcing their intent to establish a private police department in Baltimore. Hopkins officials insisted that a new hope rested in ramping up campus security, frequently citing a 2015 study lauding UCPD's ability to reduce crime by 45–60 percent.[6] And students and Baltimore residents also looked at UChicago as a model for campus policing. But what they saw was horror. Apprehensive critics highlighted the 2018 UCPD shooting of a mixed-race student in the midst of a mental health crisis.[7] While no one could deny the need for solutions to Baltimore's violence, strong local voices denounced the idea of a private campus police force as the remedy.

"It's akin to establishing a Vatican City within Baltimore," is how state senator Mary Washington described Hopkins's policing plan to me.[8] Her district includes the main campus, and Washington grew livid just thinking about the idea of this private, elite, majority-white school seeking to establish a security force in one of the country's most impoverished cities. She pointed out the racial and class disparity but also decried the idea of a private police force with the public authority of law enforcement powers in local neighborhoods.

Maryland had little history of private campus police holding public authority in its cities. And yet the Johns Hopkins campaign for this police force would establish the school as a quasi-municipality, "with its own army, its own laws," Washington explained. Normally, public officials held what she called the "power of the purse" to change police budgets or incentivize desired behavior. But here, the officers would answer to no one but the school's board of trustees and its donors. Hopkins already held considerable weight in Baltimore. Still, little compared to these efforts to push through a private police force with no public oversight.

Despite a cross-section of political operatives lining up to support the Hopkins police plan, students, faculty, and residents never wavered in their staunch opposition. Protesters demonstrated at the Garland Hall administration building for the entire month of April 2019. Detractors never used the language of extraterritorial expansion, but they explicitly warned that Hopkins would use campus police to gentrify neighborhoods while remaining silent about the largely white campus's crimes of substance abuse violations and sexual assault.[9] Senator Washington backed the protest and pointed out that many of the community "sweeteners" included in the police bill to appease skeptics would actually come from the taxpayers, not the university. Critics made a strong case for rejecting the plan. But Maryland legislators followed the national trend and gave Johns Hopkins the power to establish its own private police force in the middle of Baltimore.[10] But the fight still continues in Baltimore and across the country.

THE RACIAL RECKONING OF 2020 AND CAMPUS POLICING

A long simmering frustration with the racial injustice of urban policing came to a boil in the summer of 2020. The COVID-19 pandemic forced the world to confront a series of killings that included George Floyd, Breonna Taylor, Tony McDade, and Rayshard Brooks on a digital feedback loop. The terror and trauma were unrelenting. Yet these deaths galvanized years of grassroots organizing into global mobilization. In words that were unthinkable just months earlier, people were able to bring to the mainstream calls to abolish the current policing apparatus, clearly identifying it as a state-sanctioned expression of white supremacy. And as the call for police abolition rang out, a growing number of folks also realized that the biggest carceral force in their daily lives was not the municipal police but, in fact, the campus police. This time policing, for many, became a window into a broader analysis of higher education's growing dominance over the political economy of US cities and towns. My thinking around extraterritorial expansion was no longer theoretical. It confirmed people's daily lives, in the midst of struggle.

Despite the boogeyman of the campus rapist, a specter that has kept campus police armed to the teeth and stalking streets, sexual violence and substance abuse among students remain prevalent. And after the summer of 2020, more residents wanted answers. The failure of policing was not a matter of capacity. Police were everywhere. A growing chorus of skeptics began to look at the actual function of campus police as a reason for the incongruence between more policing and the failure to reduce student crime. It became clear that actual *campus* policing would bring greater attention to white-on-white student crime and devalue the institutional brand in today's lucrative knowledge economy. By contrast, images of highly armed campus security forces storming city blocks reassure parents, researchers, and investors that schools are open for business. In the end, the current practice of campus policing helps higher education prosper while both students and residents are sacrificed at the altar of the UniverCity.

For decades, city schools responded to white flight and economic divestment by demolishing whole blocks and building institutional walls to help protect their campuses from the so-called urban crisis of an increased population of Black and Latinx residents in their surroundings. But as residents and industry flooded back into cities, higher education's urban renewal could no longer mean hunkering down behind the walls of campus buildings. Universities had to maximize profits from the knowledge economy by remaking cities in their own image. And to secure the urban planning strategy of the "innovation district" or the "knowledge community," schools have embraced a "velvet hammer" approach to expansion. Here retail, laboratories, and high-end housing follow behind a militarized version of the campus police, who secure various sections of host communities for university development. What holds constant is the scant concern for most students or the needs and interests of longtime residents fighting for a right to remain. Public safety has become the language of displacement and wealth capture.

NOTES

A portion of this chapter was first published in Davarian L. Baldwin, *In the Shadow of the Ivory Tower: How Universities Are Plundering Our Cities* (New York: Bold Type Books, 2021).

1. The ordinance gives the University of Chicago Police Department jurisdiction in any area targeted for university development (Alia Shahzad, "The Bill That Would Have Subjected UCPD to FOIA," *Chicago Maroon*, May 28, 2018).

2. Jonah Newman, "More Than Half of Chicago Area Universities Have Armed Police Departments," *Chicago Reporter*, July 30, 2015; Nathalie Baptiste, "Campus Cops: Authority without Accountability," *American Prospect*, November 2, 2015.

3. Jonah Newman, "New Data Supports Old Accusations of Racial Profiling by University of Chicago Police Department," *Chicago Reporter*, April 5, 2016.

4. Ashvini Katrik-Narayan, "The Fight over Chicago's Largest Private Police Force," *South Side Weekly*, July 16, 2018; Jonah Newman, "U. of C. Police Shooting Came at Time of Increased Stops, Continued Disparities," *Chicago Reporter*, April 6, 2018. See also Aaron Gettinger, "UCPD Pedestrian, Traffic Stops Involve Disproportionate Number of Blacks, Minorities," *Hyde Park Herald*, July 3, 2018.

5. Luke Broadwater, "Despite Intensive Lobbying Effort, Johns Hopkins Private Police Legislation Faces Uncertain Future," *Baltimore Sun*, February 8, 2019; Rollin Hu, "The Winding and Contested Path to a Johns Hopkins Police Force," *Baltimore Beat*, March 21, 2019.

6. Brandon Soderberg, "What a Private Police Force Would Mean for Johns Hopkins University and Baltimore," *Real News Network*, March 13, 2018; "Opposition Grows to Hopkins Armed, Private Police Force Proposal," *Real News Network*, February 21, 2019.

7. Newman, "U. of C. Police Shooting Came at Time of Increased Stops, Continued Disparities"; University Faculty and Staff, "Open Letter Regarding the UCPD Shooting," April 5, 2018.

8. Bruce DePuyt, "Senator on Hopkins Bill: 'It's Akin to Establishing a Vatican City within Baltimore,'" *Maryland Matters*, February 21, 2019.

9. Fern Shen, "Citing School Officials' Contribution to Pugh, Hopkins Students Protest Private Police Plan," *Baltimore Brew*, April 9, 2019; Larry Smith, "Johns Hopkins University's Private Police Force Would Bring More Cops to an Overpoliced Baltimore," *Appeal*, May 16, 2019; Abdallah Fayyad, "The Criminalization of Gentrifying Neighborhoods," *Atlantic*, December 20, 2017; Brandon Soderberg, "How to Protest Campus Cops and Save Lives," *The Outline*, May 15, 2019, https://theoutline.com/post/7431/johns-hopkins-university-campus-occupation-arrests-private-police-ice.

10. It should be noted that organizing pressure did force Maryland lawmakers to alter the original proposal. The approved law includes requirements for activated body cameras; Baltimore residency for at least 25 percent of the officers; and a ban on using surplus military equipment. Unlike campus police departments in other states, the Hopkins police force will be subject to Maryland's Public Information Act. But still, Hopkins appoints thirteen of the fifteen members of an Accountability Board that has no power to discipline officers (see Laura Pugh, "Johns Hopkins Police Bill Signed into Law, Despite Student and Community Objections," *Biomedical Odyssey*, April 28, 2019).

4

PUSHING BACK ON CAMPUS POLICE UNIONS

Histories and Strategies

LUCIEN BASKIN, ERICA R. MEINERS, AND GRACE WATKINS

In 2019, on the precipice of the COVID-19 pandemic, graduate student workers at the University of California, Santa Cruz, represented by the United Auto Workers (Local 2865), were sick and tired. After a hard bargaining year, all that was on the table was a paltry contract that did not address crucial community needs. Spending up to 70 percent of their meager wages on housing, graduate student workers rebelled by refusing to submit grades or teach. The ensuing wildcat strike lasted for months. Their demands for living wages resonated with other graduate student workers and soon spread to UC campuses in Santa Barbara, Berkeley, and San Diego.

University of California police—often in full riot gear—were deployed to manage the uprising. In February 2020, the University of California Police Department (UCPD) arrested seventeen graduate student workers (eighty-two students were also fired for participating in the strike). Images of armed police—outfitted in face shields and carrying batons—hit the headlines of local and national newspapers.[1] After the strike concluded, documents obtained through the California Public Records Act revealed that the UCPD was also using FBI and military-grade surveillance technology to gather intelligence on students participating in the work stoppage.[2]

At the same time that the UCPD was violently cracking down on labor organizing, its officers were also the proud members of their own union. The Federated University Police Officers' Association (FUPOA) has more than three hundred members across the ten University of California campuses, making it the largest campus police union in the United States. FUPOA exists to "[protect] and [enhance] the rights and benefits of its members" with respect to "employee and employer relations."[3] Through its partnership with the Peace Officers Research Association of California (PORAC), FUPOA also lobbies the state legislature against "the mistreatment and unfair laws piling up against law enforcement."[4] Union president Wade Stern stated that FUPOA has "[sent] a clear message as to why we shouldn't be abolished or defunded."[5]

There is not much public information about campus police unions due to the ability of many of these forces to keep private records. However, investigating these organizations is key to understanding the power, operations, and objectives of campus police forces. Unions and professional associations have been instrumental in helping campus police to obtain the status of full-service police departments and firmly entrench their place within higher education. For years they have engaged in collective bargaining for member officers, threatened and organized strikes, and waged public relations campaigns. This chapter first investigates the histories and roles of these labor organizations on postsecondary educational campuses. The following two sections explore the analytic and organizing issues that situate campus police unions within a wider abolitionist landscape. We conclude with strategic action steps for building anticarceral campaigns on campus and through the structures of labor unions.

THE HISTORY AND STRUCTURE OF CAMPUS POLICE UNIONS

In the 1960s, campus police across the United States underwent a period of rapid growth and transformation from their origins as security guards in groundskeeping departments. Black power, antiwar, and other mobilizations unfolded on campuses, and, in response, campus police engaged in racist profiling and violence in an attempt to manage uprisings, including forcing local residents off of school grounds.[6] During this period, campus police departments doubled or even tripled in size and funding, and state legislatures began to codify their powers. Campus officers largely welcomed these changes as an opportunity to assert their professional status as "real" police and expand their resources to include new weapons and off-campus jurisdiction.

Campus forces were not content with these expansions to their powers, however, and began to turn to police unions in the 1970s as a means to lobby for more weapons, funding, and benefits. For example, University Police Association documents from 1972 state that the primary objective of (an early version of) FUPOA was "to enhance the stature of this Police Department."[7] Of particular importance was compensation and, specifically, being paid as much as the local city police.[8] Wage parity with municipal police was meant to signal that campus police were "legitimate" equals to their city counterparts.

In the early years of campus police unionization, many joined local Fraternal Order of Police (FOP) chapters or formed their own campus police unions modeled after the FOP. In some cases, these unions joined together to form university system–wide unions like FUPOA or statewide systems like the Louisiana University Police Association (LUPA). Through these unions, campus officers formed new working partnerships and joined an expanding network of carceral unions for police officers, prison guards, and parole officers. For example, the Stony Brook University Police are associated with both the New York State Correctional Officers & Police Benevolent Association and the New York State Troopers Police Benevolent Association.[9]

Campus police departments across the United States were building their own unions at the same time that they were surveilling and suppressing the organizing efforts of other university employees. Zach Schwartz-Weinstein details how the Yale Police Department, represented by the Yale Police Benevolent Association, used violence, undercover officers, surveillance, and intimidation tactics to suppress labor organizing efforts.[10] Another example was recorded by an independent newsletter in Lawrence, Kansas, called the *Kansas Free Press*. In 1965, "the [Central Missouri State College] janitors met to form a union. A campus cop was outside the meeting—taking down license plate numbers. Of those attending the meeting, some were merely threatened with losing their jobs and others were summarily dismissed."[11]

One of the chief tactics at the disposal of campus police unions was going on strike when contract negotiations broke down. Campus officers knew that the threat of a strike was a powerful bargaining chip to leverage against administrators. Department-wide strikes presented the risk of seriously disrupting campus operations and attracting negative media attention to the university. While municipal police associations were often limited in their ability to strike (due to agreements with city and state officials preventing "essential" workers from engaging in work stoppages), campus police unions had far fewer restrictions due to their university affiliation.[12] Throughout the 1980s and 1990s (and continuing to the present), campus officers staged protests, strikes, and "blue flus" during union conflicts—in some cases lasting for weeks or months—at schools such as the University of Chicago, Southern Illinois University, the University of Pittsburgh, Yale University, and the University of Pennsylvania.[13]

Another tactic that campus police unions wielded was taking their complaints to the press, knowing that administrators were concerned about negative media coverage, especially with respect to campus safety. Representatives from campus police unions pushed for changes by publicly attacking administrators in student newspaper op-eds and interviews with local newspapers.[14] In one such case, the president of the FOP lodge representing the Brookdale Community College police in New Jersey complained to a local newspaper in 1977 that the "emasculating" policy restricting officers' ability to carry guns during certain hours had reduced the force to feeling like "rent-a-cops" in a "Mickey Mouse operation."[15]

When campus officers received negative press, campus police unions often led the response to defend their officers' actions. For example, the University of Pennsylvania police union (known as the FOP PA Lodge #113 or the Penn Police Association) responded harshly to criticism, such as when community members came forward with accounts of officers' harassment of and violence against Black and unhoused people.[16] In one such instance in 1993, the director of the University City Hospitality Coalition, David Lynn, reported an incident in which three white Penn police officers prevented him from observing the arrest and harassment of two Black men for "panhandling."[17] The Penn Police union president, Bill Kane, responded by running a letter in the student newspaper stating, "We, the officers of the UPPD, resent Mr. Lynn's implying that we have a race problem. We feel that he is the one with the problem."[18] Kane went on to argue, "We do the University's dirty work for it," and asked, "Need we remind [Mr. Lynn] of the 'harmless' street person who stabbed to death the young Drexel graduate?"[19] Campus police unions have gone to great lengths to publicly rationalize reports of their officers' violence by intimidating victims and stoking fears of campus "crime waves."

This section has shown that as campus police surveilled and suppressed unionization attempts by university employees and student workers, they simultaneously built their own powerful unions and professional associations to protect their interests and assert their legitimacy. The following two sections turn to the actions of campus police unions in the present, focusing on their relationship to labor organizing and university austerity measures.

CAMPUS POLICE ARE NOT IN OUR LABOR MOVEMENT

For many radical labor organizers and abolitionist scholars there is an inherent contradiction between carceral unionism and social justice unionism that is for the public good. Carceral unions may collectively organize and use the same framework as traditional organized labor, but their goals are *not* aligned with creating flourishing futures for all. As Kristian Williams observes, police "organize as *police*, not workers."[20] In 2020, the *Guardian* released an investigative report documenting how police unions regularly "spend tens of millions of dollars annually to influence law enforcement policy and thwart pushes for reform."[21]

The foundations of policing itself is rooted in using state power to maintain chattel slavery and protect private property rights.[22] Policing, as Alex S. Vitale writes, is about state violence: "The suppression of workers and the tight surveillance and micromanagement of Black and brown lives have always been at the center of policing."[23] Enacting this core power of the state requires labor in the form of rank-and-file officers, such as those represented by campus police unions and other carceral unions. As Micol Seigel argues, "It takes work to represent and distribute state violence."[24] Social justice unionism is and should not be aligned with the kind of labor that carceral unions seek to protect.

Another point to emphasize is policing's often antagonistic relationship with organized labor. Simon Balto notes that the suppression of union organizing was fundamental to the founding of police departments across the United States, writing that a "primary purpose was to suppress labor militancy."[25] In the university context, campus police unions have prohibited their own members from engaging in forms of solidarity: for example, the Penn police union's bylaws in the late 1980s "[prohibited] their employees from supporting other union labor actions."[26] Moreover, campus police unions often enjoy special treatment by administrators as compared to other forms of campus organized labor.[27] For example, universities regularly bargain with campus police unions but refuse to recognize the unionization attempts of graduate students.[28]

Despite ample evidence that carceral unions protect violent structures and oppose worker organizing, the mainstream labor movement has been reluctant to challenge the power of carceral unions (and alienate their dollars and members). In 2020, the AFL-CIO started a discussion on the responsibility of unions to challenge "mass incarceration," but it has not yet ended its affiliation with the International Union of Police Associations or rejected the membership and dues of policing and corrections unions.[29] This hesitant and preliminary shift within the AFL-CIO builds on a longer history of anticarceral and abolitionist unionism.[30] In higher education, a particular area of focus moving forward should be the unions—such as large state public employee unions—that currently represent a large number of different university employees *including* campus police. In the struggle for thriving universities, academic labor unions need to deepen and build coalitions, but not with campus police and other carceral unions.

One of the most significant outputs of campus police unions in recent years is the creation of extensive job protection policies. A report by the UAW 2865 details one of the many methods campus police unions use to create job security: FUPOA has created a provision in its contract called the "discipline and dismissal" article, which allows "an officer charged with racial profiling or using excessive force ... to review their accuser's testimony before formulating their response."[31] Even campus police chiefs such as Ken Peak at the University of Nevada, Reno, have complained that these unions "make the attempt to terminate even the most deserving employee a trial by ordeal."[32] In 1989, Peak noted that "for as little as $12 dues per month," officers who had caused serious harm were able to receive what he called "pampered treatment" by campus police unions. When he tried to fire an officer who "had besmirched the uniform and code of ethics," the union treated him as a "persona non grata."[33]

These job protections are so robust that they have kept campus officers employed even when they are repeatedly reported for alarming and violent behavior. For example, the union representing the Florida International University police protected Officer Frederick Currie from being fired multiple times after several "incidents of domestic violence and an arrest for child abuse" and a "psychological evaluation that found him 'unfit for duty.'"[34] The union supplied him with arbitrators that successfully overturned each of the university's attempts to terminate his employment. After Currie was reinstated to his position in 2003, he sexually assaulted a young woman while on patrol, for which he was ultimately fired and sentenced to prison.[35]

The stringent employment protections afforded to campus police by their unions (compounded by the further protections of qualified immunity discussed by Dr. Vanessa Miller in this volume) provides officers with a degree of job security similar to tenure. This highlights a tension within the university labor context, namely, how to balance the need to advocate for strong job protections—especially for contingent and adjunct faculty, staff, and service workers—with the need to eliminate positions predicated on causing harm.

CARCERAL CAMPUS UNIONS CRACK THE FACADE OF AUSTERITY

In 2018 and 2019, teachers' unions in Chicago, Los Angeles, and West Virginia went on strike (including wildcat strikes in so-called right to work states where strikes by state employees are illegal) not only for improved wages and benefits but also for expanded public housing and against school closures. Standing in stark contrast to this organizing for the public or common good, the police often enforce organized abandonment. Ruth Wilson Gilmore explains that organized abandonment entails state and capital disinvestment in "adequate income, clean water, reasonable air, reliable shelter, and transportation and communication infrastructure" and their replacement with "policing and prison."[36] For example, police regularly arrest and ticket people for hopping turnstiles on increasingly expensive and broken-down subways and other public transit systems. As Micol Seigel writes, police are violence workers, and systems of organized violence abound in spaces of organized abandonment.

In the university and college context, despite engineered austerity—shrinking faculty hires, dissolution of entire academic departments, privatization of janitorial services, and perpetually rising tuition and fees—campus police budgets continue to grow. A 2018 article in the *Chronicle of Higher Education* referred to policing as the "hottest" job market on campus: police hires increased 30 percent between 2017 and 2018 as campus police annual budgets reached the multimillions.[37] Publicly available financial information for FUPOA reveals that it had just under $800,000 in assets during the 2020 fiscal year, which is larger than the assets retained by even some city police unions.[38] The expansion of policing in times of public retrenchment is not contradictory but rather in line with the logic of austerity regimes.[39] Campus police are regularly called to respond to issues that result from universities' failure to provide living wages, mental health support, and other essential services. As Michael Arceneaux has written, the system of policing is not broken but rather "working as it was designed."[40]

We contend that this design is oppositional to the interests of social justice unionism and public education. Academic labor unions must move beyond bread-and-butter demands to embrace a framework of social justice unionism that opposes austerity policies and organized abandonment. Campus police enforce these policies while expanding their size and scope in the forgotten places of neoliberal education reform.

Studying campus carceral unions, including their history, structure, and political strategies, is a necessary part of understanding their power. By naming the ways that campus police unions further austerity, oppose labor organizing, and naturalize state violence, organizers can more clearly assess the terrain of struggle and build abolitionist campaigns, as many are already doing. Harnessing the power of organized labor to challenge carceral unionization is nascent, but underway. We flag several promising pathways that highlight the work of graduate students and K-12 labor movements.

Graduate student labor unions have been at the forefront of challenging the naturalization of policing on campuses. In particular, several graduate labor unions included demands to defund police even before the 2020 rebellion: In 2018, in Davis, California, the campus-based labor union UAW 2865, representing the Coalition of Graduate Employee Unions, passed a proposal calling for police disarmament and demilitarization.[41] The work of Blu Buchanan and Amara Miller with Disarm UC also led to the Local 2865 "calling for the disaffiliation of AFL-CIO from police unions."[42] The Professional Staff Congress union representing City University of New York employees and faculty members passed a similar resolution calling for the AFL-CIO to cut ties with the International Union of Police Associations.[43] In 2020, the Graduate Employees' Organization at the University of Michigan in Ann Arbor demanded a 50 percent cut to the Division of Public Safety and Security budget and that the university "cut all ties with police, including Ann Arbor Police Department (AAPD) and Immigration and Customs Enforcement (ICE)."[44]

Recent developments suggest that unions in higher education are continuing to build on the work of graduate students. In 2021, the largest union of University of California employees, the AFSCME Local 3299, passed a resolution in response to what they noted was years of "[being assaulted] by UCPD during strikes & actions," including the serious injuries experienced by a Black union member, David Cole, during his arrest at a Berkeley protest in 2018.[45] The resolution specifically noted that "police associations have inserted themselves into the political process and continue to have undue influence on policies that affect the whole community" and called for "the dismantlement and dissolution of the [UCPD]."[46]

Postsecondary educational labor organizing must also pay attention to (and learn from) K-12 educational labor movements, which have long and radical histories and are creating opportunities to fight for and win abolitionist demands.

In Chicago, Caucus of Rank and File Educators (CORE) brought new vigor to the Chicago Teachers Union (CTU) in 2010 by centering the leadership and analysis of an intergenerational group of women of color. With leadership from CORE, over the last decade the CTU has consistently built power with Black and Brown communities to reject austerity and create a culture of political education. In 2012, the CTU demanded that the city administration create "sanctuary schools" by banning ICE, offer more affordable housing, and provide nurses and libraries in every public school.[47] These demands advanced an abolitionist agenda even though the CTU does not describe itself in these terms.

At colleges and universities across the United States—as well as in nations such as Greece and South Africa—students are organizing to remove police from campus and dismantle the carceral and colonial relationships between universities and the places where they are built. Founded in the wake of the 2020 rebellion, the Cops Off Campus Coalition was created to scale up this organizing and build movement infrastructure. In addition, Critical Resistance recently released a guide to discerning the difference between reformist and abolitionist reforms of campus police.[48] These are just a handful of the many projects that are developing to build campuses and communities without police. As these movements grow, understanding the power of campus police unions is integral to dismantling the larger carceral structure.

NOTES

1. Danielle Douglas-Gabriel, "Graduate Strike at UC Santa Cruz Leads to Arrests," *Washington Post*, February 14, 2020; Vivian Ho, "UC Santa Cruz Fires 54 Graduate Students Participating in Months-Long Strike," *Guardian*, February 28, 2020.

2. Nicole Karlis, "Emails Show UC Santa Cruz Police Used Military Surveillance to Suppress Grad Student Strike," *Salon*, May 18, 2020.

3. "About Us," Federated University Police Officers Association, https://federateduniversitypoa.org/about/who-we-are.

4. "Turning Frustration into Motivation," *PORAC Law Enforcement News*, https://federateduniversitypoa.org/news/porac-s-new-hq-porac-director-profile/?id=47062baa-2570-4e55-913e-2ddebecd9680.

5. "Turning Frustration into Motivation."

6. For more on the history of campus police, see Roderick Ferguson, *We Demand: The University and Student Protests* (Oakland: University of California Press, 2017); Dylan Rodríguez, "Beyond 'Police Brutality': Racist State Violence and the University of California," *American Quarterly* 64, no. 4 (2012): 301–13; Sunaina Maira and Julie

Sze, "Dispatches from Pepper Spray University: Privatization, Repression, and Revolts," *American Quarterly* 64, no. 4 (2012): 315–30; John Sloan and Bonnie Fisher, *The Dark Side of the Ivory Tower: Campus Crime as a Social Problem* (New York: Cambridge University Press, 2010); and Yalile Suriel, "What SUNY Albany Tells Us about the Policing of University Space," *Activist History Review*, December 4, 2019, https://activisthistory.com/2019/12/04/what-suny-albany-tells-us-about-the-policing-of-university-space/.

7. University Police Association 1972, AS.004, Box 7, Central Records Unit, University Archives, University of California, Irvine.

8. Brent Mitchell and Geoff Taubman, "U. Police Consider Contract," *Daily Pennsylvanian*, July 28, 1988, https://dparchives.library.upenn.edu/?a=d&d=tdp19880728-01.2.6&srpos=2783&e=-------en-20--2781-byDA-txt-txIN-campus+police------; Bret Parker and Brent Mitchell, "U. Police to Vote on Contract," *Daily Pennsylvanian*, September 8, 1988, https://dparchives.library.upenn.edu/?a=d&d=tdp19880908-01.2.2&srpos=2794&e=-------en-20--2781-byDA-txt-txIN-campus+police------.

9. "Labor Union Contacts," *Stony Brook University Employee and Labor Relations*, https://www.stonybrook.edu/commcms/employee-labor-relations/union.php.

10. Zach Schwartz-Weinstein, "Beneath the University: Service Workers and the University-Hospital City, 1964–1980" (PhD diss., New York University, 2015).

11. Bert Rinkel, "They Run a Tight Ship: Student Freedom at Central Missouri State College," *Kansas Free Press*, January 15, 1966, 6, https://jstor.org/stable/community.28038718.

12. Mitchell and Taubman, "U. Police Consider Contract."

13. Con Hitchcock, "New University Measures to Begin This Fall," *Chicago Maroon*, September 30, 1969, http://campub.lib.uchicago.edu/view/?docId=mvol-0004-1969-0930;query=campus%20security#page/6/mode/1up; "SIU Campus Police Join Janitor Strike," *Chicago Tribune*, October 7, 1977, C6; Dwayne Sye, "Yale Administrators, Union in Standoff over Contracts," *Daily Pennsylvanian*, January 22, 1992, www.thedp.com/article/1992/01/yale_administrators_union_in_standoff_over_contracts; Mitchell and Taubman, "U. Police Consider Contract"; Brent Mitchell, "Public Safety Rejects Contract, Strikes," *Daily Pennsylvanian*, August 4, 1988; "Both Police, Teamsters Have Picketed University," *Daily Pennsylvanian*, August 4, 1988.

14. Kristen Grabarz, "Penn Police Ask Gutmann for Apology after 'Die-In,'" *Daily Pennsylvanian*, December 13, 2014, www.thedp.com/article/2014/12/penn-police-respond-to-gutmann-die-in.

15. Bob Bramley, "Smith Won't Ease Brookdale Police Gun Restrictions," *Daily Register*, March 24, 1977.

16. For in-depth research on the University of Pennsylvania campus police, see Matt Johnson's chapter 6 in this volume on the history of this department.

17. Charles Ornstein, "U. Police Mistreatment Alleged," *Daily Pennsylvanian*, January 27, 1993.

18. Bill Kane, "Standard Procedure," *Daily Pennsylvanian*, February 1, 1993, https://dparchives.library.upenn.edu/?a=d&d=tdp19930201-01.2.24&srpos=3753&e=-------en-20--3741-byDA-txt-txIN-campus+police------.

19. Kane, "Standard Procedure."

20. Kristian Williams. *Our Enemies in Blue: Police and Power in America* (Oakland, CA: AK Press, 2015).

21. Tom Perkins, "Revealed: Police Unions Spend Millions to Influence Policy in Biggest US Cities," *Guardian*, June 23, 2020.

22. Rachel Herzing, "Big Dreams and Bold Steps toward a Police-Free Future," *Truthout*, September 16, 2015, www.truthout.org/articles/big-dreams-and-bold-steps-toward-a-police-free-future/.

23. Alex S. Vitale, *The End of Policing* (London: Verso, 2017), 27.

24. Micol Seigel, *Violence Work: State Power and the Limits of Police* (Durham, NC: Duke University Press, 2018), 11.

25. Jeremy Scahill, "Occupied Territory: Why Chicago's History Matters for Today's Demands to Defund Police," *Intercept*, July 4, 2020, https://theintercept.com/2020/07/04/chicago-police-simon-balto-intercepted/.

26. Geoff Taubman, "Strike Confuses Unions, but None Honor pickets," *Daily Pennsylvanian*, August 4, 1988, https://dparchives.library.upenn.edu/?a=d&d=tdp19880804-01.2.17&srpos=2788&e=-------en-20--2781-byDA-txt-txIN-campus+police------.

27. UAW 2865 Research Working Group, "Policing in the University of California: Racialized Policing and Ties to the Prison Industrial Complex," UAW 2865, February 2021, 7, https://uaw2865.org/wp-content/uploads/2021/02/Policing-in-the-UC-%E2%80%93-UAW-2865-Research-WG-Report.pdf.

28. Amy Littlefield, "Union Busting in the Name of God," *Nation*, April 13, 2020.

29. Kenneth Quinnell, "Get to Know AFL-CIO's Affiliates: International Union of Police Associations," AFL-CIO, September 23, 2019, https://aflcio.org/2019/9/23/get-know-afl-cios-affiliates-international-union-police-associations. Notably, the FOP, with approximately 325,000 members, is not a part of the AFL-CIO and therefore by choice not affiliated with the broader organized labor movement.

30. Ruth Wilson Gilmore, *Abolition Geography: Essays towards Liberation* (London: Verso, 2022), 350.

31. UAW 2865 Research Working Group, "Policing in the University of California," 7.

32. Ken Peak, "Changing Times and Future Expectations," *Campus Law Enforcement Journal* 19, no. 6 (1989): 22.

33. Peak, "Changing Times and Future Expectations," 22.

34. Anthony Cormier and Matthew Doig, "Special Report: How Florida's Problem Officers Remain on the Job," *Herald-Tribune*, December 4, 2011, https://www.heraldtribune.com/article/LK/20111204/News/605219990/SH; Ben Wieder, "Miami VA Hired Cop Turned Sex Offender," *Miami Herald*, May 10, 2021, www.miamiherald.com/news/local/crime/article251077129.html.

35. Wieder, "Miami VA Hired Cop Turned Sex Offender."

36. Ruth Wilson Gilmore and Chenjerai Kumanyika, "Ruth Wilson Gilmore Makes the Case for Abolition," *Intercept*, June 10, 2020, https://theintercept.com/2020/06/10/ruth-wilson-gilmore-makes-the-case-for-abolition/; Ruth Wilson Gilmore, *Golden Gulag: Prisons, Surplus, Crisis, and Opposition in Globalizing California* (Berkeley: University of California Press, 2007), 76–77.

37. Chris Quintana, "Among the Hottest Job Markets on Campus: Police Officer," *Chronicle of Higher Education*, May 14, 2018, www.chronicle.com/article/Among-the-Hottest-Job-Markets/243405?cid=wsinglestory_6_1a.

38. "Federated University Police Officers Association (FUPOA)," Cause IQ, www.causeiq.com/organizations/federated-university-police-officers-association,731680114/.

39. Alex Vitale and Scott Casleton, "The Problem Isn't Just Police–It's Politics," *Boston Review*, July 1, 2020, https://bostonreview.net/articles/alex-vitale-scott-casleton-problem-isnt-just-police-its-politics/.

40. Michael Arceneaux, "The System Isn't Broken. It's Working Exactly As Designed," *Splinter News*, June 17, 2017, https://splinternews.com/the-system-isnt-broken-its-working-exactly-as-designed-1796195604.

41. UAW 2865 Research Working Group, "Policing in the University of California."

42. Blu Buchanan and Amara Miller, "#DisarmUC: Disrupting the Arms Race," *Critical Times* 3, no. 3 (December 1, 2020): 551–58, https://read.dukeupress.edu/critical-times/article/3/3/551/170838/DisarmUCDisrupting-the-Arms-Race.

43. James Dennis Hoff, "CUNY Union Calls to Kick Cops out of the AFL-CIO," *Left Voice*, June 29, 2020, www.leftvoice.org/cuny-union-calls-to-kick-cops-out-of-the-afl-cio/.

44. "GEO'S Demands for a Safe and Just Pandemic Response for All," Graduate Employees' Organization, www.geo3550.org/2020/09/04/geos-demands-for-a-safe-and-just-pandemic-response-for-all/.

45. Melissa Morris, "AFSCME Local 3299 Files Unfair Labor Practice Charge against UC," *Daily Bruin*, March 26, 2019, https://dailybruin.com/2019/03/26/afscme-local-3299-files-unfair-labor-practice-charge-against-uc; "AFSCME 3299 Resolution on Police and University Policing," AFSCME 3299, February 1, 2021, https://afscme3299.org/blog/resolutiononucpolicing/.

46. "AFSCME 3299 Resolution on Police and University Policing."

47. Elizabeth Todd-Breland, *A Political Education: Black Politics and Education Reform in Chicago since the 1960s* (Chapel Hill: University of North Carolina Press, 2018).

48. "Policing & Militarism on Campus: Reformist Reforms vs. Abolitionist Steps," *Critical Resistance*, https://criticalresistance.org/resources/policing-militarism-on-campus-reformist-reforms-vs-abolitionist-steps/.

PART II
CHALLENGING THE NARRATIVE OF CAMPUS POLICING

5

LOCKING THE GATES

Yale University and Police Power
in the Postindustrial City, 1959–1976

JACOB ANBINDER

One day in January 1976, an undergraduate at Yale University opened the door to her dorm room to find a stranger lurking inside. He attempted to rape her, she later told police, when the telephone started ringing, startling the man and causing him to flee. It was the fifth assault of a Yale student by someone outside the university in as many months.[1] The following day, university secretary Henry Chauncey ordered a makeshift wooden barricade with a small door built within Phelps Gate, a stately brownstone archway separating Yale's main quad from the city green. An officer of the Yale Police Department (YPD) was to check the identification cards of anyone wishing to enter; those wishing to leave would have to telephone the YPD in advance. All other entryways, save one, were blocked. A special "extra" edition of the *Yale Daily News* applauded Chauncey's plan while also insisting that more had to be done. The only "complete solution," its editors wrote, would be permanent placement of "uniformed security personnel" at all dormitory entrances.[2]

Chauncey was aware of the possibility of stronger surveillance measures but also knew they would invite their own problems. In particular, a stronger police presence would invite criticism from students of color, who would inevitably bear the burden of having a stricter cordon around the campus. "The biggest problem is the question of stopping blacks," Chauncey had told Lou Cappiello, Yale's police chief, the previous semester. Less than a week after the construction of the barrier, in fact, fourteen Black undergraduates signed a petition accusing the YPD of demanding to see identification from Black students more often than from white students. The national press, too, believed that the events at Yale symbolized a broader trend in American race relations. A columnist for the *Baltimore Sun* castigated the "young liberals and the student activists of yesteryear" who once "broke bread with their black brethren" but were now the main advocates for a "Yale backlash." A reporter from the *New York Times* likewise wrote of a "reappraisal of the conventional 'liberal' attitudes" that had once characterized Yale. "We all of us look at a black person across the street now and say, 'my god!'" a Yale affiliate told her. "We still don't want it to be a fortress," another student added, "but we realize there's something to protect us from."[3]

As the *Sun* and *Times* journalists noted, the university's decision was, to some observers, the latest proof that whatever solidarity undergirded the political movements of the 1960s had given way to the cynical, atomized attitude that defined the 1970s. At the municipal level, the Phelps Gate barrier symbolized a new low for a city experiencing white flight, state and federal disinvestment, the decline of industrial employment, persistent Black poverty, and other aspects of the "urban crisis." Within the university, the debate over how crime should change campus life shed light on ongoing efforts by relatively new groups of Yale students—above all, women and African Americans—to demand a voice in university policy and lay claim to the protections, privileges, and rights they believed Yale more willingly afforded their white, male classmates.[4]

THE COMPLEX HISTORY OF THE YALE POLICE DEPARTMENT

Historians have devoted substantial attention to the societal changes that imbued the Yale lockdown with significance. At their confluence, however, lay an institution that has received little scholarly attention at all: the university police. Despite a wealth of recent research on the rise of the "carceral state" and the expansion of police power that helped bring it about, the simultaneous transformation of campus security guards into modern police officers has not yet been given similar attention.[5] Examining the changes that took place within the YPD in the 1960s and 1970s, this chapter encourages historians to consider the development of substantial private or semi-private police forces as a core aspect of universities' evolution in the middle of the twentieth century, thus linking education history, urban history, and the history of crime and punishment.

Focusing on Yale and New Haven reveals a complex history in which campus police evolved as a distinct kind of law enforcement, with tactics and priorities that deviated from those of its municipal counterparts. "Universities pay their police to prevent trouble before it starts," Yale security director John W. Powell told an audience of his colleagues in 1967. "They are not interested in how many arrests are made."[6] At the same time, Yale and its relationship with New Haven were not isolated from emergent trends in urban crime control and the rapid evolution in this era of the relationship between law enforcement and national politics.

THE MODERNIZATION OF THE YALE POLICE DEPARTMENT

When Chauncey ordered the Phelps Gate barricade built in 1976, he and his colleagues believed that they were responding to a short-term crime wave. But the organization tasked with enforcing the new policy—the YPD—owed its development to a longer and broader series of events. In 1959, a pair of incidents led administrators to conclude that the university would be best served by incorporating law enforcement more formally into its organizational structure.

It began with a snowball fight. At 10:00 p.m. on March 12, the chimes of the campus bell tower played the Yale fight song. It also signaled for a melee to begin. The YPD, aware of the tradition, locked the gates of the quad, but students nevertheless began to spill out into the streets through an exit that the police had neglected to shut. One snowball smashed a bus window, hurting a woman inside. A squad of New Haven police officers soon arrived and arrested twenty-five students. Two days later, the students and police clashed again at New Haven's St. Patrick's Day parade, which passed down a public street that ran through the middle of the campus. Police, "swinging nightsticks and charging students in massed battalions," according to the *Yale Daily News*, moved on the crowd. A city fire engine that was in the parade procession began spraying the students with water. Sixteen were arrested, and Yale president A. Whitney Griswold placed the entire undergraduate campus on a "general probation." Following the incident, he also commissioned an outside consultancy to study the YPD, which had seemed feckless to the point of negligence during both the initial snowball fight and the subsequent confrontation at the parade. In their assessment of the YPD, the consultants concluded that while the department was large, with a force appropriate for a city of twenty-five thousand people, it was not well-run. The YPD had "little in the way of lines of authority," they wrote, and there was no standard equipment; officers were expected to provide their own guns, handcuffs, and batons while on duty. Moreover, its obligations to the university and to students sullied its reputation in the eyes of the New Haven police, whose officers saw the YPD's weak response to the St. Patrick's Day incident as proof that its conflicting obligations to the university and to the law prevented it from operating effectively.

The consultants recommended that Yale reorganize the force along the lines of a municipal police department, with better-paid and trained officers; implement a hierarchical rank structure consisting of patrolmen, sergeants, and deputy chiefs; and develop a regular system of reports. The chief of police, the consultants wrote, should also be allotted Yale football tickets to hand out to key New Haven police officers with whom he wanted to curry favor. In addition, they advised that the university procure its own weapons. Such a suggestion surely troubled many faculty members who read it, but the consultants argued that Yale had little choice. "Police work today is classified as a profession," the study concluded, and only professionalization would help "inculcate in the student leaders the need and responsibility" of cooperating with the YPD and preventing future incidents.[7] In sum, a YPD that worked with and resembled its municipal counterpart would, in the consultants' view, improve town-gown relations. Such rhetoric anticipated the calls for modernization and professionalization of police departments that would define the federal War on Crime initiative a few years later. It reflected a broader confidence that an injection of technocratic expertise and training into law enforcement would better serve the needs of those being policed.[8]

MODERNIZING THE YPD AND EXPANDING YALE'S COMMUNITY FOOTPRINT

The modernization plan began during the summer of 1959 as most undergraduates left New Haven. The YPD and New Haven police set up a "liaison arrangement" to repair the relationship between the agencies, which the consultant's report had described as one of "outright hostility." Along with New Haven College, the two departments cosponsored a nighttime associate degree program in police science and administration. All three institutions lent instructors so that participants, mostly New Haven policemen, would learn not just the latest policing techniques but also rhetoric, psychology, sociology, government, and English composition. Yale's director of information, the son of a New Haven police commissioner, gave weekly talks to New Haven police officers throughout the fall and winter of 1959 with the intent of demonstrating that the myth of Yale as a "rich man's university" was "absolute bunk."[9]

Yale also examined ways it could involve itself in addressing pressing social problems in New Haven. Students from the Yale Hillel, for example, set up after-school classes at an elementary school in Dixwell, a predominantly African American neighborhood a few blocks north of the university. Their offerings ranged from "Great Figures in American History" to "How to Read a Newspaper" to "Civil Rights," the last of which taught sixth-graders how to hold a model filibuster. An article in the *Yale Alumni Magazine* reported on this unusual turn of events. "Strange as it may seem," it said, "there are times when the Yale undergraduate, tired from raising his glass on high and unable to play another hand of bridge, decides to abandon his normal schedule to do 'some good' in the community of New Haven."[10] The programming Yale students put together might have been unexceptional, but the role that administrators conceived for the university was particular to New Haven's political economy. If Yale was to involve itself in the life of the city, it would do so on its own terms, largely with students' volunteer labor, and act not as a cash cow for the city but as an auxiliary provider of services that cash-strapped New Haven found difficult to offer.

The YPD was a case in point. When its chief retired in 1960, the university decided not only to replace him but also to create a superior position. The title, security director and associate dean of students, was clear evidence of the more integrated role envisioned for the YPD in the university structure. The man Yale chose for the job was John W. Powell, a native of the New Haven suburbs who had matriculated at Dartmouth then briefly taught high school before joining the Federal Bureau of Investigation (FBI) in 1942, where he had worked ever since. Upon taking office, Powell declared the era of coddling undergraduates—at least as far as the YPD was concerned—to be over. "The Yale student is just like any other citizen," he told the *Yale Daily News*. "If he breaks the law, he will be punished for it."[11]

Powell's appointment reflected a broad national consensus on the positive attributes of the FBI. In 1965, a Gallup poll found that 96 percent of Americans had a "very favorable" or "favorable" opinion of Powell's former employer. Building on this goodwill, Powell saw himself as a national advocate for the professionalization of the campus police in an era of growth for the field. Between 1960 and 1967, the number of police officers employed by American educational institutions doubled, and "many of the universities and colleges look to us for guidance" when it came to policing, Powell proudly told Yale's provost. He became an active member of the National Association of College and University Traffic and Security Directors and was commissioned by the University of Rochester to conduct a study of its police force.¹²

RESISTANCE FROM WITHIN

While outside groups commended Powell's police work, navigating the treacherous political terrain within the university proved more difficult. Despite the St. Patrick's Day incident and other student run-ins with law enforcement, professors and a few administrators remained unconvinced about the need for a "professionalized" YPD. Some of Powell's more academically inclined colleagues saw him as an intellectual lightweight incapable of finding common ground with them. "He is almost constitutionally unable to pick up the phone and 'gossip,'" Chauncey wrote. Others were bothered by Powell's attempt to lay claim to the privileges of academia by virtue of his title. Speaking at an annual meeting of university police officers in Palo Alto, he called on administrators to view campus police chiefs "the same as the head of any administrative department or chairman of an academic department." Academics were "far too lenient on student offenders," he said, and "a weak, 'wishy-washy' dean is soon detected by a student body." His address, applauded in California, played less well back East. "I fear that he will go on feeling frustrated if his goal really is for him to be a real, rather than a wishy-washy dean," wrote Georges May, the dean of the undergraduate college. "He appears to be in sympathy neither with what most of us understand as a College education, nor with the new generation of young Americans."¹³

It was not clear, in fact, that Powell even sympathized with his own officers. Patrolmen suspected that a modernized YPD would impinge on their "discretion," which they considered a sacred right. In this respect, the politics within the YPD mirrored similar conflicts happening in much larger police departments in this era, including in New York and San Francisco. YPD officers particularly disliked Powell's rule that any policeman who drew his weapon would face disciplinary action if he could not prove that his own life had been in danger. Yale administrators received several anonymous complaints about the policy, presumably from disgruntled YPD officers. The gun rule made officers "fools in everyone's eyes," one wrote. "If Yale wants security GET RID OF POWELL and get someone who can do the job."¹⁴

These discrete criticisms of Powell—that as a buttoned-up G-man he understood neither campus culture nor police culture—intersected not long after his arrival. In November 1962, the *Yale Daily News* ran a special two-part exposé on the changes Powell had implemented at the YPD, made possible in part by documents leaked to student journalists by frustrated members of the rank-and-file. The centerpiece of the *Daily*'s reporting was the discovery that Powell, in classic FBI fashion, kept an array of meticulously organized confidential files, including one titled "Subversive Organizations, Activities and Individuals." The revelation roiled the Yale campus and spread beyond New Haven as well. Asked whether the Harvard Police Department kept similar records, its chief assured the *Harvard Crimson* that he did no such thing. While some members of the Yale faculty defended Powell, the overwhelming feeling was that the YPD's reformer-in-chief had crossed a line. Twenty professors signed a letter demanding that Powell clarify the purpose of the "subversive file," and he was subjected to a public dressing-down from provost Kingman Brewster, who became president of the university the following year.[15]

In the wake of the *Yale Daily News* exposé, the administration organized a police oversight board of faculty members. But the committee proved largely ineffectual and indifferent, perhaps because its chairman was the British historian Basil Henning, one of Powell's staunchest defenders. In 1965, Yale renewed Powell's contract with little fanfare but also no mention of approbation, and the remaking of the department continued apace.[16] While the YPD's force actually shrank by four officers between 1960 and 1967, the number of cases it handled increased by 50 percent. The department's reports did not list expenditures, but it is safe to say that the YPD's budget increased during this time as well. Yale's "general costs"—the line item covering operational expenses not associated with a particular school—grew from $6 million to nearly $23 million over the 1960s. With a reliable source of funding, and having rid the YPD of its "alcoholics and undesirables," as Powell described, the department could now operate more efficiently than ever before.[17]

CONTEXTUALIZING CHANGE IN THE YALE POLICE DEPARTMENT

The YPD's era of modernization had depended on a confluence of national political opinion favorably disposed toward law enforcement, a local politics open to the prospect of Yale involving itself more in New Haven's affairs, and a university whose administration believed (briefly, at least) that its students needed tough love. Powell, moreover, figured prominently in discussions on other campuses as an evangelist for the Yale model of campus policing, as evidenced by his advisory work, frequent speeches, and prominence in trade literature. In just a few years in the late 1960s, however, each of these individual dynamics evolved dramatically, arguably eliminating the rationale that had brought about Powell's reform efforts. But there would be no meaningful attempt to bring back the old YPD. Instead, as the university began to admit women and people of color in far greater numbers than ever before, the modern force Powell had built was redeployed to help incorporate these new groups of students into the life of the university. In some ways, this new mission was a recapitulation of the YPD's much older mission of protecting students from the city's harms—the objective that had been in officers' minds when they had locked the gates of the quad in March 1959 to prevent the undergraduate snowball fight from spilling over onto city streets. Ultimately, however, the reorientation of the department ran into problems, many of which were of its own making and reflected a misunderstanding or willful ignorance on the part of the university of the consequences of wielding law enforcement power.[18]

CHANGES IN THE CAMPUS AND NEW HAVEN POLITICAL CULTURE

It is difficult to overstate the broad sweep of changes in campus culture that took place at Yale in the late 1960s. In 1966 Yale adopted a need-blind admissions policy for the first time, hired its first African American admissions officer, and instituted its first policy of race-based affirmative action. Just six Black men had graduated from Yale in 1966; the freshman class that entered in 1968 had ninety-six African Americans. The average standardized test score among undergraduates rose, as did the number of high schools from which Yale accepted students. More upperclassmen began living off campus rather than in the residential colleges—a better bargain for students who were on average less wealthy than their predecessors. Finally, in the fall of 1969, Yale enrolled women in its undergraduate college for the first time—588 women, to be exact, including 42 African Americans. Some of these new groups of students brought to New Haven a species of left-wing politics molded more by the failures of the social movements of the early 1960s than by their successes, and they were more skeptical of reformist solutions to major social problems.[19]

Powell was ill prepared for this shift. Despite his public humiliation by Brewster regarding the "subversive file," the head of the YPD had grown even more insistent that the greatest threats to the nation's campus police forces were college students themselves. "Universities are now faced with 'beatniks' and the unshaved, unwashed, unpressed, and unemployed . . . who oftentimes live like parasites on the universities themselves," he told the 1967 meeting of the International Security Conference in Los Angeles, as well as a "growing homosexual problem which is practically condoned by some college administrators." Faculty members at Yale condemned the speech. "Governor Reagan must have loved it," wrote art historian Vincent Scully, referring to the tough-on-crime campaign that had won the actor the California governorship. The *Yale Daily News* printed a memorable poem, written by "Powell," in a parody issue of the newspaper:

> Buzz-a-fuzz, Buzz-a-fuzz
> Yale University
> Winced when I made a great
> Speech in the West
> Lots of our students are
> Conspiratorial,
> And those who complain are
> Under arrest.

The most telling response, however, came in a rebuke from Yale provost Charles Taylor at a meeting in New Haven of Powell's beloved College and University Security Association the following month. In a brief address, likely with Powell in the room, Taylor not only disputed Powell's opinion of college students but denied that the FBI veteran was even responsible for the amelioration of town-gown relations that was his main point of pride. It was students, Taylor argued, who were today "more highly motivated, more responsible, and more sensitive to social problems," who deserved the bulk of the credit. Having lost his base of support within the administration, Powell resigned the following year.[20]

THE NEW PRESENCE OF BLACK POWER DYNAMICS

The timing of Powell's departure makes its causes easy to misconstrue. In the first half of 1968, harsh law enforcement tactics on college campuses became a topic of national conversation after deadly police violence at South Carolina State University in February and unrest at Columbia University later in the spring. But criticisms of the YPD had already been mounting, led by incoming cohorts of Black students who had begun to organize around dual goals: economic and social justice for African Americans in New Haven and nationwide, and equitable treatment of them by the Yale administration. In 1967, several of them formed the Black Student Alliance at Yale (BSAY).

Policing was a theme that united the BSAY's critiques of the university, the city, and the country. In May 1967, sixty-two Black students signed a petition that called the YPD "a chronically unpleasant 'fact of life.'" Black students were asked, "What are you doing here?" on a regular basis by the overwhelmingly white campus police, they said, whereas white students were rarely stopped. In internal correspondence, administrators largely sympathized with the students' complaints. "It is obvious that we cannot continue a policy which results in the repeated interrogation of our own students," wrote Taylor, even if it meant YPD officers had to memorize the faces of every Black person at Yale. "In other words," he concluded, "we must bend over backwards not to offend the understandably sensitive feelings of the Negro members of our community."[21]

Consistent with nationwide trends in Black political thinking in the late 1960s, however, the BSAY was unimpressed by the supposedly enlightened Yale administration. Pressure on the administration to address the BSAY's criticisms increased when Glenn deChabert, one of its founding members, was arrested in the fall of 1969 by New Haven police on charges of disorderly conduct following an off-campus party sponsored by the organization. Two weeks later, 120 Black Yale students met with the university's trustees. Their demand was simple: Yale must take the lead in advocating for reform within the New Haven police, which they accused of harassing Black Yale students and Black New Haveners in general. As a key part of the local Democratic machine's system of patronage, the New Haven police remained disproportionately white. A study in 1973, for example, found that only 13 percent of New Haven police officers were Black in a city whose population was 26 percent African American. The administration's response was sympathetic but limited in its conception of Yale's role in addressing the problem. Shortly after the meeting, Brewster wrote to deChabert proposing two main solutions. First, the YPD would work to hire more Black officers. Second, Yale would establish a grievance procedure for students to report police brutality. A student would have the choice of a faculty member from the university police board or a trustee of Yale's Black cultural center to act as an investigator. If the complaint was against a Yale police officer, the university could pursue disciplinary measures. If the complaint was against the

New Haven police, Brewster promised that the university would send a report of its investigation to the department. In such cases, he cautioned, "obviously it is not within my authority to compel any action."²²

THE YPD AND COEDUCATION

Black men were not the only group of Yale students making demands of the administration. Welcoming the (largely white) first class of undergraduate women to campus involved a fundamental reconsideration of the university's mission. It was also a massive logistical undertaking that included changes to the role of law enforcement on campus. "There must be security" for the new women, Chauncey told the student newspaper in 1968 but emphasized it was "more from local undesirables than from Yalies." Among the physical changes that took place to the campus, the building designated as the women's dorm for first-year students was outfitted with new locks and twenty-four-hour security posts. The YPD offered to train students in using mace, and its annual reports began to document the specific locations where rapes occurred—a level of detail not afforded to other violent crimes. A nighttime shuttle bus service, intended to serve women, was inaugurated, and the first female YPD officer was hired in 1972. The department began to describe itself as a "preventative agency and not merely a corrective one," and instructed YPD officers—who had generally preferred plainclothes service—to make themselves "reasonably conspicuous" while on patrol.²³

The YPD was, in certain important ways, guiding the university toward a future in which the lines between the campus and the city would be drawn more visibly as a result of coeducation. Yet it would be inaccurate to say that women at Yale necessarily agreed with the YPD's move toward stricter policing. Some believed the university should incorporate women into campus life on equal terms and resented the idea of special treatment by the campus police or anyone else in the administration. Almost immediately after women arrived at Yale, for example, complaints emerged about the difficulties caused by the university's conservative approach to housing them on campus. A study of Yale commissioned by Dartmouth, which was preparing to become coed, found that men and women disliked the level of scrutiny the YPD gave visitors to the women's dorms and had a "strong preference" to live closer together.²⁴

YPD AND THE POLITICS OF PROTEST

To an extent, dissatisfaction with the YPD stemming from students' everyday experiences thus existed across multiple minority groups on campus. For a brief moment in May 1970, the university attempted to achieve a police response that would be at once inclusive, protective, and supportive of a structural critique of the New Haven police specifically and American society generally. It had become clear to Brewster and other Yale administrators that the New Haven police were engaged in a large, illegal wiretapping operation that included Yale's telephone lines, which perhaps brought to Brewster's mind memories of admonishing Powell for the YPD's own surveillance efforts eight years earlier. The issues of police surveillance and police treatment of African Americans in New Haven came to a head in 1970, when several members of the local Black Panther Party were arrested and charged with the murder of another Panther using evidence gathered from a wiretap. In protest, left-wing groups from Yale and across the country planned a rally in downtown New Haven for May 1, 1970.[25]

The role of the police in Yale's approach to the protest was telling. There was no on-campus police violence of the kind that had occurred at Columbia two years earlier. Nor, notably, would Yale limit access to its facilities—a lesson Brewster learned from a rally the month before in Cambridge, when Harvard had incited a confrontation between protesters and police by locking the gates of Harvard Yard. In particular, Phelps Gate, which faced the city green where the protesters planned to gather, was to remain open at all costs. Chauncey set up an emergency command post at another Yale building near the green, with bunks for rotating shifts of YPD officers and a temporary bank of fifty telephones with lines to other important Yale offices. The plan worked well. When New Haven police officers and National Guard troops began launching canisters of tear gas at demonstrators on May 2, the crowd of protestors retreated to the Yale quad, where Chauncey had ordered first-aid and rest areas set up.[26]

Yale's handling of the May Day rally demonstrated how the YPD had both evolved and embedded itself in the university's approach to on- and off-campus issues. Under Brewster, the YPD no longer acted as an auxiliary of municipal government but rather as an institution with a separate mission, more skeptical of the New Haven police and the city's political leadership. For the moment, Yale could maintain a welcoming posture toward the May Day demonstrators and, implicitly, the worldview of BSAY leaders like deChabert. The question of women's safety on campus in the early and mid-1970s, however, would test the extent to which Yale's leaders were intent on reducing the role of policing within the university.

Undergraduate women arrived at Yale as New Haven's two-decade economic decline deepened into a true collapse. By 1972, there were half as many industrial workers in New Haven as in the late 1950s, while the city's traditionally low crime rate soared past the national average for small cities. By 1974, one professor wrote that women in his classes "did not know any female graduate student who had not been assaulted at least once on the street." Moreover, the professor said, they dreaded asking the YPD to intervene for fear they would be branded as "alarmist, a neurotic, or a trouble-maker."²⁷

"SECURITY" AS THE NEW OPERATIONAL ROLE OF THE YPD

Yale's solution revolved around "security," a useful bit of jargon that began to appear frequently in the administration's correspondence and publications beginning in the 1970s. The notion of *security* was, for Yale, an attempt to reconcile the demand for protection from crime with the demand for a relatively noninvasive campus police department. It called for new measures that would physically isolate the campus from the city without necessarily increasing the visibility of the YPD. Perhaps even more importantly, it advocated for a new mindset among students, faculty, and administrators: a prudence—or perhaps a paranoia—about college life which implied that the city was characterologically different from the campus. "Being a part of the Yale community does not guarantee immunity from crime," read a YPD pamphlet given to incoming students in the mid-1970s, which warned that most crimes in New Haven were committed by teenagers who "may easily pass for students." The pamphlet suggested that students "report all strangers loitering" near buildings, to never sleep in an unlocked room, and to take their room keys with them in the showers. "Too often young people fail to report an offender because they are too kind-hearted," the YPD warned. The university began to implement a universal photo identification card system for the first time, while Chauncey convened an ad hoc committee on security to determine ways students could be made aware of the threat of crime "all the time."²⁸

Yet this shift in the YPD's mission almost immediately ran into problems. As many African Americans at Yale doubtless predicted, the idea that the YPD could increase student awareness of security without also encouraging racism proved to be too optimistic. "'Security consciousness' on campus has done absolutely nothing to increase the safety of women on campus," a Black student wrote to the *Yale Daily News*. "But, what it has done is to create an adverse situation for the black males on campus." Even the university's staunchest security advocates recognized that isolation from the city did not on its own terms represent a long-term solution. "Unless we . . . begin confronting and dealing with the causes of crime, in terms of attitudes and University policies which foster poor relationships between Yale and New Haven," Chauncey's committee concluded, "then any measures of physical security will eventually lose their effectiveness and purpose, and we will not have made any progress at all."[29]

IN ITS EXPOSÉ OF POWELL'S "SUBVERSIVE FILE" IN 1962, the *Yale Daily News* asked of the university, "Does the Yale campus police organization have to be run like the FBI?" Over the course of the 1960s and 1970s, the university's answer to this simple question proved surprisingly complicated. Though the dim view Powell took of students won him few fans at Yale, his expansive vision of campus police endured long after his departure. Rather than scale down the YPD, Yale administrators attempted to reshape it in a manner that reflected the changing composition of the student body and its demands. Once admitted to Yale, women and African Americans worked to instill in the university's leadership the idea that their presence on campus did not constitute the end of Yale's commitment to a more equitable university, city, and nation. The role of law enforcement in college and city life was central to their claims.

In some important respects, the university's approach succeeded. Yale avoided hosting the kinds of police brutality that occurred on several other college campuses in the 1960s and 1970s, and in 1970 the President's Commission on Campus Unrest applauded the YPD's handling of the May Day demonstrations.[30] Yet, the embedded presence of a modern, professional police force on the campus also created a form of path dependence, as a result of which Yale's leaders tried to grapple with an era of rapid change in town-gown relations by redefining the mission of the YPD rather than rejecting the idea that the university ought to wield police power altogether. Their inability to conceive of a university that would not rely on its police force to manage students' relationship with the city at large made women's requests for "security" seem diametrically opposed to African American students' requests for respect and equal treatment, when there was never anything inherently contradictory about such demands as expressed by students themselves. Ultimately, the Phelps Gate barricade showed that administrators would not hesitate to use the YPD to wall off the university from New Haven if they believed doing so was necessary to protect some students—even if it meant endangering the civil liberties of others.[31]

The choices Yale made in this era with regard to its police department still reverberate. As members of Chauncey's security committee noted, the steps the university took to isolate itself from New Haven in the mid-1970s were intended to lead to a more comprehensive attempt to address the root "causes of crime." Instead, they established a firm notion in some students' minds of the purpose that campus police exist to serve. When students rape their classmates today, such cases are adjudicated through byzantine internal processes—if they are adjudicated at all. When a Black graduate student takes a nap in a common area of her dorm, the YPD is called.[32]

NOTES

1. Lou Cappiello to Robert Fogelin, January 22, 1976, and Lou Cappiello to Robert Fogelin, January 23, 1976, Folder "Security 1974–1976," Box 23, Series 2, RU 52, Records of the Secretary's Office 1909–1975, Yale University Library, New Haven, CT; Mary Breasted, "Yale Shuts Gates to Curb Assaults," *New York Times*, February 5, 1976, 60.

2. Anonymous letter to Kingman Brewster Jr., February 11, 1976, Folder "Campus Police 1975–1976," Box 364, Series 3, RU 11, Kingman Brewster Jr. Presidential Records, Yale University Library; "Not Enough," *Yale Daily News*, January 24, 1976, 1; Jennifer Myers, "Old Campus Reacts to Last Week's Crime," *Yale Daily News*, January 26, 1976, 4.

3. Henry Chauncey to Eugene Waith, December 16, 1974, Folder "Security 1974–1976," Box 23, Series 2, Records of the Secretary's Office 1909–1975, Yale University Library; Henry Chauncey to Louis Cappiello, n.d., Folder "Security 1974–1976," Box 23, Series 2, Records of the Secretary's Office 1909–1975, Yale University Library; Christine B. Hall, "Locking the Gates at Yale Is an Ominous Sign," *Baltimore Sun*, February 15, 1976, K5; Breasted, "Yale Shuts Gates to Curb Assaults," 60.

4. The analytical lens of the "urban crisis" was first proposed in Thomas J. Sugrue, *The Origins of the Urban Crisis: Race and Inequality in Postwar Detroit* (Princeton, NJ: Princeton University Press, 1996). Sugrue himself was expanding on the "second ghetto" thesis put forth by Arnold Hirsch, *Making the Second Ghetto: Race and Housing in Chicago, 1940–1960* (New York: Cambridge University Press, 1983), and the concept has since been expanded upon and revised by several historians, notably Robert Self,

American Babylon: Race and the Struggle for Postwar Oakland (Princeton, NJ, 2003); and Kim Phillips-Fein, *Fear City: New York's Fiscal Crisis and the Rise of Austerity Politics* (New York: Metropolitan Books, 2017).

5. See, for example, Elizabeth Hinton, *From the War on Poverty to the War on Crime: The Making of Mass Incarceration in America* (Cambridge, MA: Harvard University Press, 2016); Heather Ann Thompson, "Why Mass Incarceration Matters: Rethinking Crisis, Decline, and Transformation in Postwar American History," *Journal of American History* 97 (December 2010): 703–34; Vesla Weaver, "Frontlash: Race and the Development of Punitive Crime Police," *Studies in American Political Development* 21 (Fall 2007): 230–65; C. Michael Otten, *University Authority and the Student: The Berkeley Experience* (Berkeley: University of California Press, 1970), 206; Michael Clay Smith, *Coping with Crime on Campus* (New York: American Council on Education, 1988), 1–9; Diane C. Bordner and David M. Petersen, *Campus Policing: The Nature of University Police Work* (Lanham, MD: University Press of America, 1983), xi; John W. Powell, *Campus Security and Law Enforcement* (Boston: Butterworth, 1981), 4–5; Micol Seigel, "Objects of Police History," *Journal of American History* 102 (June 2015): 155; Jim Shea, interview by Jared Brown, in *The Punitive Turn: New Approaches to Race and Incarceration*, ed. Deborah E. McDowell et al. Charlottesville: University of Virginia Press, 2013), 272.

6. John W. Powell, "Professionalizing the College Security Department," speech to the International Security Conference, Los Angeles, CA, February 22, 1967, Folder "Police Department—University 1967," Box 169, Kingman Brewster Jr. Presidential Records, Yale University Library.

7. A. Whitney Griswold, "President's Statement," *Yale Daily News*, March 15, 1959, 1; Confidential Research Associates, *Yale University Police Department—A Study* (Stamford, CT, 1959), 1–7, 12–18, 27–28, 47, 70, Folder "Police Department, University Study on, 1959," Box 170, Series 1, MS 255, Alfred Whitney Griswold Personal Papers, Yale University Library.

8. Hinton, *From the War on Poverty to the War on Crime*, 96–102.

9. Confidential Research Associates, *Yale University Police Department—A Study*, 33; Miscellaneous items, Folder "'Town and Gown': Police Science and Administration Program, n.d.," Box 282, Series 3, Reuben A. Holden Secretarial Records 1901–1971, Yale University Library; Reuben Holden to James W. Cooper, July 17, 1959, Folder "Town and Gown Meetings 1959–1960," Box 282, Series 3, Reuben A. Holden Secretarial Records 1901–1971, Yale University Library; Episode transcripts of *Yale, Your Neighbor*, Folder "Town and Gown: Yale Your Neighbor Radio Station WELI 1961," Box 282, Series 3, Holden Papers, Reuben A. Holden Secretarial Records 1901–1971, Yale University Library.

10. John Bowers to C. Hamilton Sanford, October 11, 1955, Folder "Campus Police (1954–1960)," Box 26, Alfred Whitney Griswold Personal Papers, Yale University Library; A. Whitney Griswold to Francis McManus, October 14, 1955, Folder "Campus Police (1954–1960)," Box 26, Alfred Whitney Griswold Personal Papers, Yale University Library; Richard Stewart, "Special Report on New Haven: Juvenile Delinquency: The Problem," *Yale Daily News*, November 17, 1959, 1; Hinton, *From the War on Poverty to the War on Crime*, 18–21, 38; "Voluntary, After-School 'Clubs' Promote Learning," *New Haven Register*, May 22, 1960, 28; Monroe E. Price, "Undergraduate Yale," *Yale Alumni Magazine*, May 1960.

    11. Mark Oppenheimer, "Suzi at Yale," *Tablet*, August 21, 2017, https://www.tablet mag.com/sections/news/articles/suzi-at-yale-2; "On Powell," *Yale Daily News*, February 25, 1960, 2; Van V. Burger Jr., "Profile: Transplanted Special Agent," *Yale Daily News*, February 25, 1960, 2.

    12. Darren K. Carlson, "American Still Have Moderately Favorable Opinion of FBI," July 18, 2001, http://news.gallup.com/poll/4696/americans-still-moderately-favorable -opinion-fbi.aspx; James S. Kakalik and Sorrel Wildhorn, *Special Purpose Public Police* (Santa Monica, CA:Rand Corporation, 1971), 37; John W. Powell to Charles Taylor, June 30, 1964, Folder "Police Department University 1964," Box 169, Alfred Whitney Griswold Personal Papers, Yale University Library; Various, Folder "Police Board: University 1965" and Folder "Police Department University 1966," Box 169, Griswold Papers, Alfred Whitney Griswold Personal Papers, Yale University Library.

    13. Henry Chauncey to Charles Taylor, April 1, 1965, Folder "Police Board: University 1965," Kingman Brewster Jr. Presidential Records, Yale University Library; John W. Powell, speech to National Association of College and University Traffic and Security Directors, Palo Alto, CA, June 30, 1965, Folder: "Police Department University 1964," Box 169, Henry Chauncey to Charles Taylor, April 1, 1965, Folder "Police Board: University 1965," Kingman Brewster Jr. Presidential Records, Yale University Library; Georges May to Henry Chauncey, July 5, 1965, Folder: "Police Department University 1964," Box 169, Henry Chauncey to Charles Taylor, April 1, 1965, Folder "Police Board: University 1965," Kingman Brewster Jr. Presidential Records, Yale University Library.

    14. Marilynn S. Johnson, *Street Justice: A History of Police Violence in New York City* (Boston: Beacon, 2003), 233–34; Agee, *Streets of San Francisco*, 10–13, 38–43; Miscellaneous anonymous letters, Folder "Police Department University 1966," Box 169, Alfred Whitney Griswold Personal Papers, Yale University Library.

    15. Robert G. Kaiser, "John Powell: A G-Man Comes to Yale," *Yale Daily News*, November 20, 1962, 1; Robert G. Kaiser, "Dissension in the Ranks," *Yale Daily News*, November 21, 1962, 1; Robert G. Kaiser, "Faculty Reacts Against Powell's Subversive File," *Yale Daily News*, November 28, 1962, 1; Robert G. Kaiser, "Campus Policemen See Need

for New Changes," *Yale Daily News*, November 29, 1962, 1; Kingman Brewster, "From: Brewster to Powell, Subject: Police Authority," *Yale Daily News*, December 3, 1962, 1; "Tonis Avoids FBI Methods Used at Yale," *Harvard Crimson*, November 27, 1962.

16. John W. Powell to Kingman Brewster, December 22, 1964, Folder "Police Department University 1964," Box 169, Kingman Brewster Jr. Presidential Records, Yale University Library; Andrew Patterson to Charles Taylor, October 19, 1964, Folder "Police (Campus) 1964–1967, RU 126, Yale College Records of the Dean, Yale University Library; Charles Taylor to John W. Powell, May 13, 1965, Folder "Police Department University 1964," Box 169, Kingman Brewster Jr. Presidential Records, Yale University Library.

17. New Haven Preservation Trust, *New Haven Modern*, http://newhavenmodern.org/all-buildings?dir=desc&order=date; Beverly Waters, Office of Institutional Research, Yale University, *Operating Expenditures by School/Category*, https://oir.yale.edu/sites/default/files/pierson_update_1976-2000.pdf; Yale Police Department, "Yale Police Department Annual Report 1964–1965," p. 5, Folder "Police Department University 1964," Box 169, Kingman Brewster Jr. Presidential Records, Yale University Library; John W. Powell to Charles Taylor, December 21, 1967, Folder "Police Board University 1967," Box 169, Kingman Brewster Jr. Presidential Records, Yale University Library.

18. Kakalik and Wildhorn, *Special Purpose Public Police*, 50–52; Geoffrey Kabaservice, "The Birth of a New Institution," *Yale Alumni Magazine*, December 1999, http://archives.yalealumnimagazine.com/issues/99_12/admissions.html.

19. Nancy Weiss Malkiel, *"Keep the Damned Women Out": The Struggle for Coeducation* (Princeton, NJ: Princeton University Press, 2018), 58; Henry Louis Gates Jr., *Are We Better Off?*, www.pbs.org/wgbh/pages/frontline/shows/race/etc/gates.html; Kabaservice, "The Birth of a New Institution"; Beverly Waters, Office of Institutional Research, Yale University, *Yale College Students Housed in Undergraduate Dormitories, 1950–1999*, https://oir.yale.edu/sites/default/files/pierson_update_1976-2000.pdf; Leslie Miller-Bernal and Susan L. Poulson, *Going Coed: Women's Experiences in Formerly Men's Colleges and Universities, 1950–2000* (Nashville, TN: Vanderbilt University Press, 2004), 120; "Yale Chaplain Urges Students to Ponder Spurning the Draft," *New York Times*, October 13, 1967, 1; David Mislin, "Anti-War Protests 50 Years Ago Helped Mold the Modern Christian Right," *The Conversation*, May 2, 2018, https://theconversation.com/anti-war-protests-50-years-ago-helped-mold-the-modern-christian-right-90802.

20. John W. Powell, speech to the International Security Conference, Los Angeles, CA, February 23, 1967, Folder "Police Department—University 1967," Box 169, Kingman Brewster Jr. Presidential Records, Yale University Library; "New Entry," *Yale Daily News*, May 6, 1967, 2; Charles Taylor, speech to College and University Security Association, New Haven, CT, March 1967, Folder "Police Department—University 1967," Box 169, Kingman Brewster Jr. Presidential Records, Yale University Library; Vincent Scully

to Kingman Brewster, February 23, 1967, Folder "Police Department—University 1967," Box 169, Kingman Brewster Jr. Presidential Records, Yale University Library; "Security Head Leaving Yale," *New York Times*, March 26, 1968, 28.

21. Petition of "Black Upperclassmen," May 11, 1967, Folder "Police (Campus) 1964-1967," Box 49, Yale College Records of the Dean, Yale University Library; Charles Taylor to John W. Powell, May 16, 1967, Folder "Police (Campus) 1964-1967," Box 49, Yale College Records of the Dean, Yale University Library.

22. "BSA Raps 'Oppression,' Calls for Class Boycott," *Yale Daily News*, March 12, 1968, 1; Tom Warren and John Coots, "Head of BSAY Arrested in City Unrest Saturday," *Yale Daily News*, September 29, 1969, 1; "Student Strike at Law School Centers on Police Harassment, Governance," *Yale Alumni Magazine*, November 1969, 20; Lee Brown and Glen Tagatz, "Minority Employment in the New Haven, Connecticut, Police Department," Folder "New Haven Police Advisory Committee," Box 6, Records of the Secretary's Office 1909-1975, Yale University Library; Kingman Brewster to Glenn deChabert, October 16, 1969, Folder "Security 1974-1976," Box 23, Records of the Secretary's Office 1909-1975, Yale University Library.

23. Jeffrey Gordon, "Chauncey on Coeds: Anti-Feminism, Dorms," *Yale Daily News*, November 27, 1968, 1; Cresap, McCormick & Paget, *Coeducation Report*, Folder "Coeducation Report—Cresap, McCormick & Paget," Box 5, Records of the Secretary's Office 1909-1975, Yale University Library; Yale Police Department, *Yale Police Department Annual Report 1971-1972*, 12-22, Folder 467, Box 25, Series 1, RU 12, Office of the President, Yale University, Annual and Special Reports, Yale University Library.

24. Cresap, McCormick & Paget, "Coeducation Report," iv-22; Hillel Weinberg et al., to James Mau, November 22, 1974, Folder "Security 1974-1976," Box 23, Records of the Secretary's Office 1909-1975, Yale University Library.

25. Paul Bass and Douglas W. Rae, *Murder in the Model City: The Black Panthers, Yale, and the Redemption of a Killer* (New York: Basic Books, 2006), 120-21; Yohuru R. Williams, *Black Politics, White Power: Civil Rights, Black Power, and the Black Panthers in New Haven* (St. James, NY: Brandywine Press, 2000), 99-100, 135.

26. Bass and Rae, *Murder in the Model City*, 122-23, 137, 144, 158-59.

27. Eugene Waith to Hanna Gray, November 28, 1974, Folder "Security 1974-1976," Box 23, Records of the Secretary's Office 1909-1975, Yale University Library; Bass and Rae, *Murder in the Model City*, 362, 387; Donald Ploch to Henry Chauncey, January 27, 1976, Folder "Security 1974-1976," Box 23, Records of the Secretary's Office 1909-1975, Yale University Library; Unsigned memo, April 20, 1976, attached to Henry Chauncey to Leonard Sperry Jr., April 23, 1976, Folder "Security 1974-1976," Box 23, Records of the Secretary's Office 1909-1975, Yale University Library.

28. Yale University Police Department, "Security at Yale and Related Services," 1975-1976, Folder "Campus Police," Box 5, Records of the Secretary's Office 1909-1975,

Yale University Library; Henry Chauncey, memorandum to the "university community," September 10, 1976, Folder "Security 1974–1977," Box 23, Records of the Secretary's Office 1909–1975, Yale University Library; Henry Chauncey to Susan Dobrof et al., November 11, 1975, Folder "Security 1974–1976," Box 23, Records of the Secretary's Office 1909–1975, Yale University Library.

29. Wayne Stephens, "Partial Security," *Yale Daily News*, February 20, 1976, 2; Open letter to Kingman Brewster Jr. and Lou Cappiello, February 2, 1976, Folder "Security 1974–1976," Box 23, Records of the Secretary's Office 1909–1975, Yale University Library; University Committee on Security, "Residential College Gate Hours," Folder "Security 1974–1976," Box 23, Records of the Secretary's Office 1909–1975, Yale University Library.

30. The President's Commission on Campus Unrest, *The Report of the President's Commission on Campus Unrest* (Washington, DC: US Government Printing Office, 1970), 44.

31. The President's Commission on Campus Unrest, *The Report of the President's Commission on Campus Unrest*, 44.

32. Tyler Kingkade, "Yale Fails to Expel Students Guilty of Sexual Assault," *Huffington Post*, August 1, 2013; Christina Caron, "Yale Police Are Called over a Black Student Napping in Her Building," *New York Times*, May 10, 2018, A21.

6

ANTI–SEXUAL ASSAULT ACTIVISM AND THE LEGITIMACY OF CAMPUS POLICE IN PHILADELPHIA

MATT JOHNSON

As of 2022, the University of Pennsylvania (hereafter, Penn) employed 121 police officers, making it the second-largest campus police force among private universities in the United States.[1] Fifty years ago, when campus police first appeared at US colleges and universities, Penn administrators would not have imagined a force this size. In the early 1970s, executive administrators, the campus security director, and a strong contingent of students and faculty didn't think the police force should grow beyond its then twenty officers. Anything larger, they thought, would compromise the intellectual atmosphere of the university and stress an already stressed budget. What happened?

In this chapter, I argue that anti–sexual assault activism helped justify and legitimize the expansion of campus police at Penn. This student-led movement to push the university to address sexual assault helped undermine the most influential rationales that limited the size of the campus police force. Particularly important in this process was the racialized image of sexual assault, which painted Black men who lived in the surrounding community as sexual predators preying on white women on campus.

This research expands our understanding of the increasing presence of police on higher education campuses in the 1960s and 1970s. Through early work on campus policing, we know those decades represented a turning point during which campus administrators saw campus police as a mechanism for controlling student bodies.[2] My work departs a bit by exploring why campus police were able to gain both legitimacy and longevity in higher education. To figure out why strong and sustained student movements against campus policing did not gain a national presence until relatively recently, scholars need to recognize that postsecondary administrators hoping to control students were not the only people invested in university-employed police officers. The story of Penn's campus police offers insight, as it reveals how grassroot student, faculty, and staff activism pushed reluctant Penn administrators to increase both the size and purpose of the campus police force.

This chapter also shows that universities are important sites to understand the relationship between feminist activism and the rise of the carceral state. Scholars such as Aya Gruber have revealed how feminist activists, trying to address violence against women, helped justify more policing and create more punitive laws that landed people in prison for long periods. The relationship between these feminist actors and the carceral state were not always comfortable or even desired initially. Even if it was a reluctant relationship, though, various factors led activists to see policing and punitive policies as one of the answers to violence against women.[3] But there were competing visions of policing and incarceration among feminist activists. Many Black feminists, in particular, developed an anticarceral feminism in the 1970s that, in the words of scholar Emily Thuma, "pointed to the carceral state as a source of further harm rather than safety and redress."[4] Looking at universities helps uncover which feminist vision had privileged access to powerful institutions that could strengthen or challenge the growing carceral state in the 1970s.

LIMITING POLICE GROWTH

Penn's campus police force has an unusually long history, as Penn hired its first sworn officers in the 1930s. The department, though, grew slowly in the subsequent decades. By the early 1970s, Penn's campus police force was small compared to some of its urban peers. Harvard, for example, spent almost twice as much ($1.2 million) on its security force and employed twenty more security professionals despite the fact that Harvard's student body was about one-third the size of Penn's.[5]

The number of officers on Penn's campus remained comparatively small even as concerns about crime more broadly grew in the 1960s. Nationally, the FBI reported skyrocketing crime rates that contributed to rising levels of fear of crime in the United States.[6] That fear resonated among people at Penn, as reports of crime on campus grew dramatically. Importantly, changing demographics of the

West Philadelphia neighborhoods surrounding Penn's campus exacerbated those fears. Immediately after World War II, Black working-class folks began to move into these previously white working-class communities. In one of these census tracts, the Black population grew from 30 percent in 1940 to 91 percent by 1960.[7]

The fear that followed these changes unleashed a vocal contingent of faculty, staff, and students who called for more police and security guards both on and off campus.[8] Letters from faculty and staff about thefts and assaults in academic buildings poured into university administrators' mailboxes; some of the letters included long, itemized lists of missing equipment.[9] One department chair reported that staff were quitting out of concern for their safety at work.[10] After a graduate student was stabbed in front of his West Philadelphia home, an archaeology professor suggested that [then] President Harnwell organize privately hired "block-sitters" to stand on "every other corner" on the west side of campus.[11] Students, too, complained about thefts in dormitories and feared for their safety when off campus. Embedded in all this fear was an assumption about who were the threats to safety. Students, faculty, and staff weren't criminals. They were under siege by Black criminals living close to campus and needed more protection. Hiring more police and security was the consistent suggestion in correspondence to administrators.

Penn administrators sought to respond to this pressure *without* expanding the campus police force. To do this, in 1969 then Penn president Gaylord Harnwell turned to Henry S. Ruth, a law school faculty member who later would become special prosecutor in the congressional investigation of the Watergate scandal. When Harnwell called on Ruth, he had just returned from serving as deputy director of President Lyndon Johnson's Commission on Law Enforcement and Administration of Justice.[12] Ruth, not surprisingly, saw more policing as the answer to crime. Administrators strongly supported Ruth's proposed solutions that asked the city to use its resources to address crime around campus. Ruth facilitated new relationships between Penn and the City of Philadelphia Police Department that resulted in increased patrols and the addition of "stake-out teams" in the neighborhoods around campus. Ruth also pressured the local district attorney's office to more aggressively prosecute anyone arrested around campus. Assistant District Attorney James Fitzgerald began closely overseeing the prosecution of anyone arrested for a major crime in Penn's policing district. The district attorney's office even contemplated opening a neighborhood office close to campus.[13]

Penn leaders were also quite receptive to Ruth's proposals for new infrastructure, especially since adding more lighting, security cameras, and emergency phones was a relatively inexpensive way to show that the university was taking action to alleviate a sense of fear. Penn installed sixty new spotlights on campus along with blue-light emergency telephones that directly connected callers with the campus police. Within a few years, ninety of these emergency telephones dotted the campus.[14]

Penn administrators were *less* receptive to Ruth's proposal to hire more campus police officers. The problem was money. Beginning in the 1950s, President Harnwell wanted to raise Penn's status as an Ivy League institution. The university had been a regional university that was not known for its intellectual rigor. World War II and the subsequent federal investment in defense research helped change that. Millions of federal research dollars began pouring into the university's science, technology, engineering, and medical departments. The influx of federal dollars resulted in the expansion of, and upgrades to, Penn's research infrastructure to support ever more projects. As Penn's prestige grew, the university's student population also grew and became less regional, which then meant more dormitories, classrooms, faculty, and staff were needed. Harnwell was especially focused on buying land and constructing new buildings, which turned out to be an expensive undertaking.[15] By the late 1960s and early 1970s, Penn's administrators faced a budget shortfall, which translated in part to controlling security costs.[16]

There is much irony in the fact that land acquisitions stressed the university's budget to the point that administrators tried to limit the growth of campus police. Like several of its peer institutions, Penn's leaders originally saw the Black displacement that came through land acquisition as a security strategy.[17] In February 1958, a Korean graduate student, In Ho Oh, studying political science at Penn was murdered just blocks from campus. Eleven Black teenagers were arrested. The story gained national attention in *Time* magazine and was quickly turned into a short film.[18] By June, President Harnwell brought together leaders of West Philadelphia's higher education and medical institutions. The nonprofit corporation then laid out its vision of redevelopment for West Philadelphia. The statement released after its first meeting in June did not hide its intentions. "We face the potential of an ever increasing and encroaching area of residential slums," and "we face the alternatives of ignoring the succession of land uses and population changes," the statement read. The leaders at the first meeting concluded that they needed to assume "leadership in creating and maintaining a desirable neighborhood in which our institutions can flourish."[19] In the case of Penn, In Ho

Oh's murder provided the initial spark that helped administrators link university land expansion with a desire to expand security. In light of the recent murder and the growing population of Black people in West Philadelphia since World War II, "population changes" and "desirable neighborhood" became thinly veiled references to the perceived need to displace Black people to "improve security."

Beginning in 1965, Penn also guaranteed mortgages for faculty and staff to move into the neighborhoods surrounding campus.[20] When Penn suspended the program due to financial constraints in the summer of 1973, the university was holding almost 150 mortgages.[21] Harnwell didn't hide Penn's vision of displacing Black people and replacing them with white faculty and staff. As more Penn faculty and staff moved into the surrounding neighborhoods, Harnwell wrote, "the neighborhoods will gradually take on the characteristics we all wish [them] to have."[22] This took place in several cities across the country, and as historian Margaret O'Mara concluded, city and university officials used "university-centered real estate development to eliminate poor and black areas and create a physical barrier between the white, professional community of scholars and the working-class, black West Philadelphia."[23]

With these financial constraints, administrators tried to control the campus community's expectations of Penn police. As was often the case elsewhere, the main purpose of Penn's campus police was to protect university property. Administrators and security directors were not shy of reminding the campus community about this limited role. For example, in 1961, police captain George Barcus explained in the student newspaper, "We are not a police organization, nor are we a detective bureau. Our job is, primarily, to protect the buildings and grounds of the university."[24] If campus police leaders wanted more responsibilities, they could have used concerns about crime to argue for more officers, but security directors consistently reported that they had enough officers to fulfill the department's mission.[25]

Administrators also suppressed crime data in order to limit pressure to hire more campus police. The department briefly published weekly crime statistics in 1972, but police officials quickly reversed course because they believed the data stoked an irrational fear of crime "causing more harm than good." A campus expert on criminology agreed. Fear of crime, he argued, already "runs in excess of reality."[26]

Interestingly, notions of personal responsibility and victim blaming also served as a powerful tool in resisting a larger campus police force. This was especially powerful in cases of property crime. People who opposed police expansion argued that students had a burden to protect their property—careless actions should not justify more police. Most property crime, opponents of police expansion argued, stemmed from students who failed to lock their dorm/apartment doors or left expensive items in their cars. Campus police joined this argument, suggesting that students were responsible for protecting their own property.[27] Even in cases of violent attacks, though, some students suggested that violence could be prevented if people would be more vigilant and report suspicious people. Campus police could not "be everywhere at once," a student leader of a group studying campus safety explained.[28]

Opponents of expanding the campus police department also challenged their peers to recognize that crime should be expected on an urban campus and in surrounding areas. It was not as if students didn't fear crime. Many of them saw the surrounding Black community as a threat to their safety and property. In the 1960s and 1970s, the overwhelming majority of Penn's students were white and brought with them assumptions about both Black people and urban spaces.[29] But while some students responded to every assault or burglary by calling for more police, a strong contingent of students saw crime as a tradeoff for the experience of living in a vibrant city—an experience that would likely be compromised by more police on campus. If their peers wanted the safety of a rural or suburban setting, they could go experience that "stale" environment.[30]

Students who pushed back against calls for more police also embraced a particular understanding of the causes of crime that stressed environmental factors, especially poverty. These students recognized that the university's own decisions, such as real estate investments that led to Black displacement, created some of these environmental factors. Emphasizing environmental factors never insulated Black people from blame, but it redirected solutions away from incarcerating Black people to fixing environmental problems that led to crime. To these students, more police was not the answer to crime. Penn administrators and Penn students were involved in community programs meant to address crime by providing safe spaces for youth to participate in social activities and get help in school through tutoring services. While these programs revealed the limited understanding of environmental solutions, they still show how Penn administrators and students used their environmental understanding of crime to seek solutions that didn't increase police presence.[31]

Concerns that too many campus police officers would hinder the educational purpose of a university also led to rationales against police expansion. Universities and colleges were unique places, the argument went, that had to be policed differently than other urban spaces. The director of Penn's security, Donald Shultis, agreed. He frequently reminded people who called for more officers that "it would be a simple matter to provide total security, but you wouldn't like the things we'd have to do to get it. On the College Green where we teach and learn, we like to minimize the presence of guards." Faculty, in particular, deemed gun-carrying police officers a special threat to freedom of thought.[32]

Concern about the impact of policing on Black students and people living in surrounding neighborhoods also appeared in critiques of hiring more campus police officers. Black students, for example, offered public accounts of police harassment they had experienced. They argued that Penn police officers often confused Black Penn students with members of the surrounding community and frequently stopped and detained them when investigating campus crimes. Black activists, in particular, saw the campus police as a racist organization. Black students who were part of the House of the Black Family, a Black social center set up as a nonprofit to lease property from Penn to avoid violating Title VI of the Civil Rights Act of 1964, experienced the consequences of harassment by campus and city police. In 1970, Penn's police captain, George Barcus, joined Philadelphia police on a raid of the House of the Black Family after Penn officials charged that members had firebombed a university building.[33] The rationales and financial constraints of the 1960s and early 1970s worked together to create a powerful group of opponents to expanding Penn's police force.

ANTI–SEXUAL ASSAULT ACTIVISM AND POLICE LEGITIMACY

By 1973, anti–sexual assault activism started to chip away at the power of forces opposed to hiring more campus police at Penn. Sexual assault was rarely discussed among administrators or reported in the student newspaper during the 1960s. Part of this likely resulted from a culture of silence and shame, along with a criminal justice system that made convictions unlikely. The emerging women's liberation movement challenged that culture and the criminal justice system that largely supported it. With the help of women's growing representation on campus that made it easier to organize, activists expanded the definitions of sexual assault and reinterpreted its causes while also pushing for new solutions that held offenders and enablers accountable and empowered women to defend themselves.[34]

In the early 1970s, three feminist groups operated on campus: Penn Women's

Liberation (PWL), Penn's Women's Studies Planners, and Women for Equal Opportunity at the University of Pennsylvania (WEOUP). PWL created consciousness-raising groups. WEOUP, mainly made up of Penn faculty and staff, fought against the university's employment discrimination against women. Penn's Women's Studies Planners had been working together since 1971 to create a women's studies department. None of these groups had organized to push the university to address sexual assault before 1973.

That changed when six women associated with Penn were sexually assaulted in one week. It's difficult to overstate the fear that resulted from so many assaults in a short period. No place on campus seemed safe as the assaults occurred in dorm rooms, parking garages, dark alleys, and offices. Still, existing organizations at Penn didn't immediately organize to push for change. Robin Morgan, the well-known feminist activist, helped these organizations come together to fight against sexual assault. She visited campus just over a week after the most widely publicized sexual assault, where five men attacked two nursing students. Morgan devoted part of her public address to sexual assault, which she called "an act of political terrorism," and pushed women at Penn to organize for better security and support for survivors.[35]

Less than a week after Morgan's visit, two hundred women, including students, faculty, and staff, occupied College Hall and demanded the university take steps to address campus sexual assault.[36] Part of their vision did not involve policing. For example, activists called for an escort service so women didn't have to walk home alone. They wanted self-defense classes. They wanted a women's center that would serve as a safe place for women to organize against sexual assault and provide counseling for survivors. And the sit-in activists wanted administrators to spend more money on lighting, alarms, and emergency phones around campus. But sit-in activists also believed that policing had to be a vital part of any solution.[37]

Campus activists' call for more police wasn't inevitable. In the early 1970s, there were competing visions of the role policing and incarceration should play in addressing sexual assault. Black feminists, especially those organizing in working-class communities, led the way in establishing an anticarceral feminism that saw policing and incarceration as a part of a larger system of anti-Black and sexist violence. The carceral state, then, could never be part of the solution.[38] The predominantly white, middle-class women organizers at Penn didn't bring the same level of concern about the harm adding police officers could do in a predominantly Black urban space. That's not to say that feminist activists at Penn were always comfortable with policing or that they never thought about the negative consequences Black people might experience through increased police contact. It is to say that any discomfort or concerns didn't stop Penn activists from seeing policing as part of the solution in addressing sexual assault.

The rejection of anticarceral feminists' visions influenced the future of policing at Penn, as sit-in activists' calls for campus police expansion proved harder to oppose than past calls. Sexual assault challenged the typical liberal environmental interpretations of crime. Poverty, racism, and real estate initiatives that led to displacement didn't seem to explain why men sexually assaulted women. The absence of environmental explanations proved important because environmental interpretations of crime helped students to imagine solutions that didn't involve policing.

Sit-in activists tried to offer an alternative environmental explanation for sexual assault that failed to take hold at Penn. The only way to eradicate sexual assault, activists argued, was to address what they called the "culture of sexism." This environmental interpretation led to some solutions that didn't involve police. The women's center, along with the women's studies program that activists were also involved in building, was part of a larger vision of "confronting, analyzing, and attempting to eliminate sexism," which would reduce the likelihood of sexual assault.[39] But this framing was met by a backlash from too many men on campus for feminists' environmental interpretation to gain widespread popularity. "The next time a woman is faced with the situation where a man wants to rape her," a male Penn student commented, "the female should launch into a 'political' lecture on sexism in America and educate the poor male about his degenerate beliefs. I dare say the results would be interesting."[40] Other students criticized anti-sexual assault activists for making sexual assault "political."[41] Men on campus preferred nonenvironmental explanations that relieved themselves from any responsibility for sexual assault. Instead, they blamed evil monsters, a problem that only policing and incarceration could address. The backlash shows how Penn activists' fight against sexual assault could be co-opted to produce even more dangerous framings of criminality that would increase support for more policing.

Sit-in activists also lost the battle to frame the purpose of the police. For sit-in activists, policing actually offered an opportunity to empower women and challenge sexism. Sit-in activists rejected any call for men to protect women, which included the all-male police force. When a criminologist on campus suggested that police needed to "saturate the area" to protect Penn's "high population of vulnerable girls," sit-in activists responded forcefully.[42] Women on campus had spent years fighting *in loco parentis*, and they didn't want to support another organization based on some of the same principles. But activists believed the campus police could be reformed to become a feminist organization. Women simply needed to control the police and serve as police officers and leaders. As one of the sit-in activists explained, the demand for more female officers was "a response to the felt need of women to take responsibility for our own lives and for the conditions in which we live." The sit-in activists, though, didn't just want more female officers; they wanted more control of the police department itself. Policing could never be a tool of women's empowerment if women didn't have oversight power and a role in shaping the mission and practices of the police. They wanted a woman to replace the police captain, Donald Shultis, and envisioned a committee composed of women on campus that had the "power to implement and supervise University security policy."[43]

This, too, was met with opposition. Shultis kept his job, and he initially hired only one woman to the police force. Women also didn't gain any significant oversight control over campus police. It remained a male-led organization that saw its new purpose as "protecting women." Despite their inability to achieve the desired change, feminist activists didn't turn against campus policing. They continued to see the campus police as an important tool in fighting sexual assault.[44]

UNDERMINING EFFORTS TO LIMIT POLICE GROWTH

Consider how these developments helped undermine the forces that wanted to limit campus police expansion. When feminists' alternative environmental interpretation of sexual assault failed to gain widespread acceptance, more popular interpretations took hold. These interpretations saw people who attacked women as evil monsters who could only be dealt with through more policing and incarceration. And when feminist activists continued to support more policing when they lost battles to exercise control over campus police, they empowered a pro-policing group on campus that cared little about women's liberation.

The 1973 sit-in also undermined other key strategies used by people who wanted to limit the number of campus officers. Opponents of police expansion were reluctant to tell women that sexual assault was just something that should be expected in a city and a justifiable tradeoff for living in a vibrant urban environment. Anti–sexual assault activism also challenged another popular strategy in opposing police expansion: victim blaming. At least in published venues, students were much less likely to blame women for being victims of sexual assault than they were to blame students who were victims of robbery or theft. In fact, victim blaming provided the final spark that led to the sit-in. Initially, anti–sexual assault activists didn't plan to take over part of a building. They first went to Shultis to express their concerns. He suggested that women should wear less provocative clothing. As one of the activists remembered, a sixteen-year-old undergraduate stood up and told Shultis, "I can walk buck naked down this campus and your job is to protect me." The women in Shultis's office helped take over College Hall soon thereafter. Without victim blaming, blame became hyperfocused on the people who assaulted women, especially Black men.[45]

The racialized imagery of sexual assault on Penn's campus likely offered women some protection against victim blaming. No crime at Penn was more racialized than sexual assault. The image of Black men preying on white women was so dominant that when a group of white men who reportedly resembled students sexually assaulted a woman in public, folks standing on the street claimed that they didn't call the police because the men didn't look like rapists.[46]

The image of Black men preying on white women activated a deeply rooted trope in US history: it was the responsibility of white men to protect white women from Black sexual predators. It wasn't women's responsibility to protect themselves, as it was students' responsibility to protect their bikes and stereos. It helped that white men were never publicly portrayed as sexual predators on campus in the early 1970s. Victim blaming would have been much more likely if white men were portrayed as the villains.

Racialized imagery sometimes turned to biological explanations: Black men had an uncontrollable urge to have sex with white women. A local white resident in West Philadelphia wrote in response to sexual assaults on campus: "The appeal of white skin to black youths is often uncontrollable."[47] The student newspaper was never so direct, but writers often left it to the reader to imagine why Black men, and only Black men, were the reported perpetrators of sexual assault against white women on campus.

Concerns about the negative impact police would have on Black students and people living in surrounding neighborhoods had been an important piece of the opposition to campus police expansion. But Black men on campus were often left to voice these concerns alone in the aftermath of the sit-in. Gerald Early, the future historian and then an undergraduate student reporter, took sit-in activists to task for this. "When one is forced to conjure up a picture of a rapist," Early wrote in Penn's newspaper, "that picture is probably not going to be a blond-haired, blue-eyed gentleman wearing a business suit." Early accused "white middle-class ladies of women's lib crying 'stop violent rape'" of trying to "keep Black men in their place." At no time, Early claimed, did white anti–sexual assault activists show concern about the violence Black women faced at the hands of white men.[48] Another student echoed Early, claiming that the calls for tighter security following recent sexual assaults was actually an excuse to "wage an attack on the black people at the University and in the community."[49] The racialized imagery of sexual assault at Penn had real consequences for Black men in West Philadelphia.

Sit-in activists immediately challenged Black students' critiques. They took special exception to the idea that feminist activists calling for more police could be lumped together with some of the architects of mass incarceration, such as President Richard Nixon and Philadelphia mayor and former police commissioner Frank Rizzo. In other words, they contended that there were noble reasons to expand policing that were not motivated by racism and the desire to put more people in prison. One sit-in activist argued that Early's claims of racism suggested that he had been "victimized by . . . propaganda."[50]

Sit-in activists initially tried to distance themselves from people like Nixon and Rizzo by pushing back against the racialized imagery of sexual assault and showed some concern about the consequences their calls for more security would have on Black men. They claimed in 1973 that "protecting women does not mean violating the rights of black male students or men in the community." When a fraternity member suggested that men patrol campus to protect women, a sit-in activist criticized his "machismo band of fraternity men" that fantasized about "protect[ing] white women from black men." But empathy and fear are like oil and water. As police harassment of Black men ramped up, white feminist activists didn't protest police practices.[51]

Beyond a few statements, sit-in activists didn't take any concrete steps to prevent police harassment of Black people. Consider, for example, their plans for "community control" of campus police. Sit-in activists criticized Penn campus police as an autonomous organization with no oversight and accountability. They envisioned more "community" control over the goals and policies of Penn's police. But when sit-in activists envisioned the people who would provide this oversight to determine how and where the police would operate, activists only thought about the faculty, staff, and students at Penn. Even though they realized Black men who weren't employed or enrolled at Penn would suffer the consequences of increased patrols, activists didn't think these Black men should have a voice in how those patrols should operate. Black women were also left out of the conversation—the same Black women who helped create an anticarceral feminism in the 1970s.[52]

Anti–sexual assault activism also compromised administrators' interests in controlling costs by limiting the purpose and size of the police force. Campus leaders had tried to limit the purpose of campus policing to control students' expectations of Penn police officers. Campus police would respond to reports about violent crime, but actually protecting students from violence wasn't the force's primary responsibility. Anti–sexual assault activism called on Penn police to take on that new responsibility. Part of their strategy was, as one activist put it, to "attack the University in a soft spot: its wallet."[53] Survivors of sexual assault then began suing the university for its negligence in protecting women from sexual assault, creating financial consequences for refusing to expand the campus police force and its responsibilities.[54]

Activists also believed that testifying about sexual assault in media outlets would lead administrators to calculate the potential cost of losing current and prospective students because of Penn's reputation as a place that failed to protect women from sexual assault. Administrators were already concerned about this. In 1969, the admissions dean reported to President Harnwell that "the criminal acts that have occurred in the campus area do have a deleterious effect on the ability of this University to attract a highly qualified undergraduate student body." Through phone calls from concerned parents and prospective students, as well as through recruitment visits outside the state, the dean reported that Penn's reputation as "a center of criminal activity" was spreading. Publicity about sexual assault on campus during the sit-in only amplified these concerns. Internal documents show administrators scrambling to figure out how to prevent Penn from gaining a reputation as a dangerous place for women. More policing, in the minds of administrators, had now become the answer.[55]

Sit-in activists also challenged the university's efforts to suppress crime data. Recall that limiting public access to crime data was an administrative tactic to reduce pressure to expand campus policing. Sit-in activists accused Penn leaders of suppressing crime data "in order to preserve its image and to avoid losing applicants." They called for transparency about crime, asking for regular public releases of crime statistics. This created serious problems for administrators because the stories about crime became less anecdotal. Proponents of campus policing had relied on single stories of assaults and theft, but they usually disappeared from the student newspaper in a day or two. Regularly released data provided an endless supply of evidence that made it easier for students, faculty, and staff to claim that the size of the campus police department was insufficient.[56]

Activists in the 1973 College Hall sit-in ended up winning many concessions from the university. Penn hired a female police officer who would specialize in working with sexual assault victims. An escort service transported students across campus and to their off-campus homes. Officers became more active in patrolling parts of campus where women were thought to be especially vulnerable. However, the protest didn't immediately lead to an explosion in hiring. The women who led the 1973 sit-in likely never imagined a police force of more than one hundred officers. It would take decades for the department to grow to its current size. But the protest left a legacy at Penn that made it more difficult to stop the police department's growth. The sit-in helped expand the expectations that students had of campus police and legitimized the police as the proper organization to turn to for protection. It changed the way campus police were evaluated—now being held accountable for sexual violence on campus, not just property crime. It created consequences for administrators who wanted to limit the role and size of the police force. And it helped criminalize the surrounding Black community in new ways, creating more urgency to control the perceived threat Black men posed to the campus community. Together, these changes created a powerful set of expectations, incentives, and consequences that would be hard to unravel.

Over the next decades, police expansion became a circular story, as more university police officers became the default answer to any public outcry to address violent crime on or around campus. In response to every well-publicized sexual assault or homicide, administrators immediately offered more police officers as a solution. Opponents to police expansion faded and wouldn't gain a strong voice on campus again until the Black Lives Matter Movement emerged forty years later.

AS HISTORIANS INVESTIGATE MORE CAMPUSES around the country, they need to ask how anti–sexual assault activism fits into the story of campus policing. Penn's urban campus and proximity to Black communities make this story a powerful and insightful case study into the many dynamics shaping campus police expansion. But as we look across the country and find all the peculiarities that come with different environments, we're faced with a tough question: why does a strong contingent of administrators, faculty, and students see more campus police as a solution? Concerns about sexual assault will likely emerge as an important factor that ties our stories together.

As the scholarship of campus policing continues, historians should also address a question that was outside the scope of this chapter: why, given the poor record of campus policing in addressing sexual assault, did policing remain the solution to sexual assault for decades? In the context of sexual assault, the history of campus policing is a story of failure. Key to unlocking the legitimacy of campus police is figuring out why an organization that consistently fails is so difficult to challenge and abolish.

NOTES

1. "Penn Police Department," May 5, 2023, www.publicsafety.upenn.edu/about/uppd/#:~:text=The%20University%20of%20Pennsylvania%20Police,full%2Dtime%20sworn%20police%20officers; Kelly Heinzerling, "With 120 Officers, Penn Has the Largest Private Police Force," *Daily Pennsylvanian* October 8, 2017, www.thedp.com/article/2017/10/with-120-officers-penn-has-the-largest-private-police-force-in-pennsylvania.

2. See, for example, Diane C. Bordner and David M. Peterson, *Campus Policing: The Nature of University Police Work* (New York: University Press of America, 1983); and Seymour Gelber, *The Role of Campus Security in the College Setting* (Washington, DC: US Government Printing Office, 1972).

3. Aya Gruber, *The Feminist War on Crime: The Unexpected Role of Women's Liberation in Mass Incarceration* (Berkeley: University of California Press, 2021).

4. Emily Thuma, *All Our Trials: Prisons, Policing, and the Feminist Fight to End Violence* (Urbana: University of Illinois Press, 2019), 14.

5. Mitchell Berger, "Gang Rape Prompts Questioning of University Security Measures," *Daily Pennsylvanian*, July 1, 1973.

6. For a critique of these statistics, see Michelle Alexander, *The New Jim Crow: Mass Incarceration in the Age of Colorblindness* (New York: New Press, 2010), 51.

7. Margaret Pugh O'Mara, *Cities of Knowledge: Cold War Science and the Search for the Next Silicon Valley* (Princeton, NJ: Princeton University Press, 2005), 156.

8. Jan Lief, "History Fellows Discuss Safety after Recent Murder in Area," *Daily Pennsylvanian*, February 5, 1969.

9. These letters are available in the Hackney Administration Records, Box 442, Folder 6, University of Pennsylvania Archives, hereafter (UPA).

10. Russell P. Sebold to Robert H. Dyson, November 18, 1969, Sheldon Hackney Administration Records, Box 442, Folder 6, UPA.

11. George F. Bass to Gaylord P. Harnwell, December 17, 1968, Sheldon Hackney Administration Records, Box 442, Folder 6, UPA.

12. "Ruth to Coordinate Anti-Crime Program," *Daily Pennsylvanian*, January 21, 1969.

13. Joseph T. Looby to Donald K. Angell et al., March 6, 1969, Sheldon Hackney Administration Records, Box 442, Folder 6, UPA.

14. "GSA Council Offers Safety Regulations," *Daily Pennsylvanian*, January 30, 1969; Clarence Greene, "Safety Efforts Increased, U. Business Manager Says," *Daily Pennsylvanian*, March 21, 1969; University of Pennsylvania News Bureau Release, April 3, 1973, Martin Myerson Administration Records, Box 311, Folder 6, UPA.

15. John L. Puckett and Mark Frazier Lloyd, *Becoming Penn: The Pragmatic University, 1950–2000* (Philadelphia: University of Pennsylvania Press, 2015), 25; Margaret O'Mara, *Cities of Knowledge*, 145–51.

16. Peter Eglick, "Univ. Security Force Adds Student Guards," *Daily Pennsylvanian*, July 1, 1970.

17. For examples of similar strategies at other universities, see Eddie Cole, *The Campus Color Line: College Presidents and the Struggle for Black Freedom* (Princeton, NJ: Princeton University Press 2020), 70–118; and Stefan Bradley, *Upending the Ivory Tower: Civil Rights, Black Power, and the Ivy League* (New York: New York University Press, 2018), 167–96.

18. "Cities: Hands Dripping Blood," *Time* magazine, May 12, 1958; *An Epistle from the Koreans*, dir. Lloyd Young (Burbank, CA: Film Productions, International, 1959).

19. Quoted in Puckett and Lloyd, *Becoming Penn*, 96.

20. Phyllis Kaniss, "U. May Reinstate Low Interest Mortgage Systems for Employees," *Daily Pennsylvanian*, October 1, 1970.

21. Mitchell Berger, "Problems of Urban Living Confront Faculty Residents in U. City Neighborhoods," *Daily Pennsylvanian*, October 8, 1973.

22. Gaylord P. Harnwell to Richard C. Clelland, January 21, 1969, Sheldon Hackney Administration Records, Box 442, Folder 6, UPA.

23. Margaret O'Mara, *Cities of Knowledge: Cold War Science and the Search for the Next Silicon Valley* (Princeton, NJ: Princeton University Press, 2005), 158.

24. Edward I. Savitz, "Captain Barcus Defined Duty of Campus Guards to Univ.," *Daily Pennsylvanian*, February 9, 1961.

25. "Finding Dead Man and Carrying Guns Revealed as Forming Part of the Life of the Campus Guards," *Daily Pennsylvanian*, March 9, 1938; Barbara Slopak, "Barcus Likes His Cops Middle-Aged and Well 'Settled,'" *Daily Pennsylvanian*, September 16, 1968.

26. Mitchell Berger, "Security Office Discontinues Release of Crime Statistics," *Daily Pennsylvanian*, December 1, 1972.

27. Dave Berk, "Shultis, Robinson Detail New Security Steps at 'Lunch Rap,'" *Daily Pennsylvanian*, October 19, 1971, 3.

28. "Security," *Daily Pennsylvanian*, November 9, 1971; Chat Blakeman, "Security Investigation Has Poor Attendance," *Daily Pennsylvanian*, April 1, 1971.

29. Wayne Glasker, *Black Students in the Ivory Tower: African American Student Activism at the University of Pennsylvania, 1967–1990* (Amherst: University of Massachusetts Press, 2002), 20.

30. John Riley and Jeff Rothbard, "Campus Security," *Daily Pennsylvanian*, February 10, 1969.

31. "Almost Every Home In Area Is Affected by Youth Programs," *Philadelphia Inquirer*, October 3, 1962; "Slum Residents Are Assisted by Community Involvement Council," *Daily Pennsylvanian*, August 25, 1967; "Fraternities Begin Program of Constructive Pledging through Welfare Projects," *Daily Pennsylvanian*, February 19, 1962; Stephen H. Kneisel, "1960 a Year of Stress, Tragedy . . . and Then Mobilization," *1960 Annual Report of the Crime Prevention Association*, Gaylor Harnwell Administration Records, Box 125, Folder: Crime Commission of Philadelphia, Inc., 1960–1965, UPA

32. Mitchell Berger, "Committee Protests Cops' Guns at Trial," *Daily Pennsylvanian*, October 13, 1972; Anne O'Connell, "Shultis, Police Discuss Safety," *Daily Pennsylvanian*, October 28, 1970.

33. Gary Hicks, "The Arrest of William Bradley," *Daily Pennsylvanian*, November 17, 1971; Glasker, *Black Students in the Ivory Tower*, 88–89, 96–97.

34. Gruber, *The Feminist War on Crime*; Catherine O. Jacquet, *The Injustices of Rape: How Activists Responded to Sexual Violence, 1950–1980* (Chapel Hill: University of North Carolina Press, 2019); Nancy A. Matthews, *The Feminist Anti-Rape Movement and the State* (New York: Routledge, 1994).

35. "Improving Campus Security," *Daily Pennsylvanian*, March 26, 1973; Betsy Sandel and Susan MacDonald, "Women's Movement: Many-Faceted," *Daily Pennsylvanian*, July 1, 1973, 29; Mitchell Berger, "Five Youths Questioned in Connection with a Series of Rapes around Campus," *Daily Pennsylvanian*, March 23, 1973.

36. Liz Stein and Peter Ginsberg, "200 Women Stage Sit-in, Demand Rape Protection," *Daily Pennsylvanian*, April 4, 1973.

37. Marilyn Murphy, "Women Plan College Hall Protest; Meetings, Sit-In Set for Tuesday," *Daily Pennsylvanian*, April 2, 1973.

38. For an excellent history of anticarceral feminism, see Thuma, *All Our Trials*.

39. Betsy Sandel and Susan MacDonald, "Women's Movement: Many-Faceted," *Daily Pennsylvanian*, July 1, 1973.

40. Frank T. McDevitt, "Solving the Rape Problem," *Daily Pennsylvanian*, April 30, 1973.

41. An activist explains this criticism in Donna Lamb, "Rape Sit-In: New Breed of Activism," *Daily Pennsylvanian*, April 24, 1973.

42. Susan MacDonald, letter to the editor, *Daily Pennsylvanian*, April 26, 1973.

43. Lamb, "Rape Sit-In," 4.

44. Liz Stein, "Fulfills Majority of Sit-In Agreement," *Daily Pennsylvanian*, September 7, 1973.

45. Jiahui (Emilee) Gu, "When Women's Rights Are at Stake, Carol Tracy Takes a Stand," *34th Street* November 9, 2021, www.34st.com/article/2021/11/carol-tracy-feminism-abortion-women-rights; Carole Tracy, interview by the author April 22, 2022.

46. Amy Borrus and Peter Grant, "Gang Rape of University Student Reported Saturday near Hi-Rise," *Daily Pennsylvanian*, October 11, 1976.

47. Gerard H. Bye to Martin Myerson, March 22, 1973, Martin Myerson Administration Records, Box 311, Folder 12, UPA.

48. Gerald Early, "Day in the Life: Rape and the Black Woman," *Daily Pennsylvanian*, November 6, 1973.

49. Maria T. Elmo, letter to the editor, *Daily Pennsylvanian*, April 4, 1973.

50. "Early's Views on Rape and the Black Woman Criticized," *Daily Pennsylvanian*, November 13, 1973.

51. Marilyn Murphy, "Women Plan College Hall Protest; Meetings, Sit-in Set for Tuesday," *Daily Pennsylvanian*, April 2, 1973; Ruth Weil, letter to the editor, *Daily Pennsylvanian*, May 1, 1973; "Early's Views on Rape and the Black Woman Criticized," *Daily Pennsylvanian*, November 13, 1973.

52. Lamb, "Rape Sit-In," 3.

53. Lamb, "Rape Sit-In," 3.

54. Stephen B. Burbank to Joseph H. Foster, May 2, 1978, Martin Myerson Administration Records, Box 311, Folder 3, UPA.

55. George A. Schlekat to Gaylord P. Harnwell, February 12, 1969, Sheldon Hackney Administration Records, Box 442, folder 6, UPA; Val Carlson to President Martin Myerson, Re: Maureen K. Carlson, November 3, 1977, Martin Myerson Administration Records, Box 311, Folder 2, Management and Finance, Office of Public Safety, 1975–1980 (II), UPA; Carol Tracy to Mr. Stephen B. Burbank, January 13, 1978, Martin Myerson Administration Records, Box 311, Folder 3, UPA; Stephen B. Burbank to Joseph H. Foster, May 2, 1978, Martin Myerson Administration Records, Box 311, Folder 3, UPA.

56. Marilyn Murphy, "Women Plan College Hall Protest; Meetings, Sit-In Set for Tuesday," *Daily Pennsylvanian*, April 2, 1973.

7

THE WAR ON DRUGS MEETS CAMPUS POLICE

YALILE SURIEL

On December 4, 2012, two campus police officers working undercover at the University of Massachusetts at Amherst (U-Mass Amherst) caught Logan Sinacori, a sophomore student, selling LSD. Typically, a student caught with drugs would be arrested and charged with unlawful possession of a controlled substance and/or referred to the university judicial system, whose sanctions include suspension, an educational outcome, and/or community service. Additionally, at U-Mass Amherst, university policy dictated that if a student under the age of twenty-one was caught with drugs or alcohol, parental notification would automatically take place. That night, however, campus police officers decided to go in another direction. The two undercover campus officers told Logan that if he became a "confidential informant" (CI) for them and "gave up a higher-level dealer," they would not charge him with a crime or tell his parents. Logan, scared of facing drug charges and getting into further trouble, took the deal and wore a wire. The result was his former roommate being arrested and charged with various drug offenses. In the aftermath, Logan told childhood friends how bad he felt about the situation, stating in texts: It is "kinda hard to live with myself. . . . [T]hat was honestly the worst day of my life. . . . I feel like I lost a brother and it [is] all my fault. Kinda wish I was just behind bars right now."[1] He eventually also admitted to friends, "I'm a heroin addict," and stated he was planning to seek help when the semester ended. Ten months after becoming a CI for campus police, he was found dead from a heroin overdose.[2]

Logan's story provides a small but powerful glimpse into the CI programs run by campus police departments at public and private colleges and universities across the country. It also sheds light on how such programs can interfere with the resources that an institution of higher learning has in place for its students struggling with substance abuse. In an effort to grow in power and legitimacy, as well as engage in "proactive crime-fighting," campus police developed CI-type programs and did so largely hidden from public view. Investigations into Logan's death revealed that U-Mass's CI program had been in place for at least ten years and that similar programs exist at the University of Wisconsin, Whitewater; University of Illinois at Urbana-Champaign; Virginia Commonwealth University, and many others.[3] Importantly, while these programs and practices are relatively new, they are nonetheless connected to a much longer history grounded in the federal War on Drugs and informed by the continued desire of campus police to attain legitimacy and power. To truly understand the trajectory of campus police forces, we must therefore ask how the War on Drugs of the 1970s shaped higher education.

This chapter argues that the War on Drugs was a critical force in making campus police what they are today. There are two major ways that the War on Drugs shaped the formation of campus law enforcement. First, through their eventual collaborations with municipal police on drug matters, campus police began to be perceived as more "professional," that is, more capable, trained, legitimate, and connected to the broader policing apparatus. Since their institutionalization in the 1960s, campus officers and their commanders continually looked for ways to acquire the "recognition and legitimacy" their off-campus counterparts enjoyed. Campus officers complained that members of law enforcement more broadly "tended to ignore the campus policeman. . . . [T]hey tended to look at us in the same way they would a plant guard."[4] The War on Drugs thus became one of several critical influences in the larger project to secure campus police legitimacy. Second, as drug raids by county and municipal police on college campuses grabbed national headlines, postsecondary administrators turned to campus police as a way to comply with public calls to eliminate the "illegal drug sanctuaries," that colleges were feared of becoming while simultaneously protecting the school's brand.

These shifts in their functional role often led campus police officers to decry a double standard in which campus police were asked to insulate students from punitive drug enforcement in order to avoid media attention but were also working with municipal police to arrest nonstudents for the same behaviors. Ultimately, this chapter seeks to bring some clarity to the tensions that the War on Drugs produced between university administrators and campus police, as well as highlight the relationships it cultivated between campus and municipal departments.

INVESTIGATING THE DRUG PROBLEM

The idea that colleges and universities were serving as sanctuaries for rampant illegal drug activity was one that was percolating across the country for many years prior to the official declaration of a war on drugs by the U.S. government. All the talk of drug use prompted flurries of investigations by journalists and postsecondary institutions who were hoping to get a sense of how widespread drugs might be on their campuses. As colleges and universities undertook efforts to identify the problem, what they actually found were contradictions.

Newspapers across the country and the Food and Drug Administration (FDA) spoke about the "frightening reports of widespread, fast-growing use of hallucinogenic drugs on college campuses."[5] However, upon closer investigation, reporters and administrators admitted that what they found were "contradictory answers."[6] For example, in a spread appearing in May 1966, reporters for the *Austin American* interviewed campus police, students, and administrators. One student told reporters that although "the exact number is hard to say . . . anyone who tries to say [the drug problem] doesn't exist [here] is closing his eyes to it," referring specifically to lists on bulletin boards where one could solicit LSD.[7] Chief Allen Hamilton of the UT Austin Campus Security told reporters he kept a "running file" on suspected illegal drug activity on and around campus. However, the 1965–66 list to date only included forty-four names, with fewer than half of them being the names of current students, members of the faculty, or staff. Chief Hamilton stated, "When you have no more evidence than we have turned up[, drug possession and use] can't be treated as widespread on this campus."[8] The dean of students, Jack Holland, concurred, stating, "If we have a problem with drugs on this campus we are not aware of it."[9] The dean of men, Dr. Lawrence T. Franks, stated, "If we went around turning up stones and looking behind bushes we might make the mistake of attaching undue interest to it. . . . [T]he number of cases we have had involving drugs is infinitesimally small—I'm speak[ing] about less than five."[10]

Contradictory answers were also found at the University of Minnesota. In November 1967, the *Minneapolis Star* launched a five-part investigative series to figure out exactly how widespread was the use of drugs at the University of Minnesota. Concerns over alleged campus drug use had been growing across the country, but exactly how widespread was the drug use in the campuses closest to home remained a mystery to most. The fact that "several University of Minnesota students were arrested after drug raids by police and federal agents" touched off "a new round of questions about the extent of drug use at the university."[11] The *Minneapolis Star* reporters interviewed young people around the campus who admitted to using psychedelics but spoke of a "paranoia on the West Bank of campus" with users simultaneously "wanting to 'turn on' the world, but fearing the police" after the recent raids.[12] However, when asked particularly about the University of Minnesota, a federal narcotics official stated, "For all the talk that goes around, the University of Minnesota still remains a beer and hot dog campus."[13] One University of Minnesota police officer also characterized claims of rampant drug use among students "just gross exaggerations."[14] More often than not, campus police admitted that while there might be a drug problem at "colleges and universities," from what they could tell, it was not very prevalent at *their* institutions.

Prior to President Nixon's official declaration of a "War on Drugs," colleges and universities often dealt with student experimentation with drugs through educational programs. For example, in 1968 Colgate University formed a committee to establish university policy toward drug use. Members of the committee discussed both the "beneficial and harmful" effects of drug use in order to shape drug education programming. After a year of research, which included discussion sessions with students living in residence halls, they published their conclusions in the *Journal of the American College Health Association*. Administrators at Colgate University worked to not be in violation of state and federal drug laws while simultaneously trying to avoid becoming utterly consumed by the issue. They understood that they could not actively allow campus space to be a sanctuary for drug use but did not want to divert all of their resources to the task of enforcement. This resulted in Colgate taking the position that "the university will abide by the federal and state laws on drugs, but will not act as an additional enforcement agency."[15] In practice, this policy translated to the university's student judicial system handling campus drug cases, insisting that the results of their reviews remain an internal matter, and refusing to turn over their information to civil authorities.[16] In cases where civil authorities searched or arrested students on drug charges, the university would see to it that "the appropriate legal safeguards for the students are secured" by ensuring that no information about the case was released to third parties without first informing the student.[17]

During the 1970s, administrators tended to carefully navigate the tension that existed between maintaining university autonomy and the desires of law enforcement to investigate student drug use. Administrators like Allan Cohen at the University of California, Berkeley, reminded his colleagues in an article appearing in the *Journal of College Student Personnel* that "in drug education and counseling, the promise of confidentiality is a powerful ally."[18] Cohen further suggested that "if there is an undesirable possibility of confiscation of files, you might refrain from making written evidence of the student's drug involvement. Both Colgate and Berkeley placed an emphasis on developing library collections that allowed students to do their own research on the consequences of drug use.

This lack of aggressive enforcement deeply irked municipal police, who often laid the blame on "ineffective" campus police departments. Spokespeople for municipal police would tell the press that "campus officers are soft on drug traffic."[19] Perhaps the most notable case of this occurred at the University of Wisconsin, Madison (UW-Madison), in 1969.[20] Campus police at UW-Madison conceded they were "simply not equipped to become investigators of the drug scene" but that they help local police "when they can."[21] It was thus not uncommon during this era for campus and municipal police officers to be at odds, particularly when municipal police perceived campus officers as having little authority and characterized them as little more than "conservation warden[s]" at a state park.[22] This would be a claim that campus officers across the country would spend the better part of a decade trying to combat by developing stronger connections to state, county, and municipal policing networks.

Interestingly, the extension of the war on drugs to higher education became the most visible and contentious at the institutions where campus police were viewed as weak. It was at these institutions that municipal police repeatedly conducted drug raids to correct what they felt was an inability or unwillingness by administrators and campus officers to keep students' protests, rebelliousness, and drug use in check. One police intrusion in particular would prove especially influential in the trajectory of campus policing expanding its connections to broader law enforcement.

On par with many postsecondary institutions around the country, Stony Brook University (SBU) wished to stay true to the principles of academic freedom by avoiding external police presence on their campus. Therefore, it was no surprise that when county police officials asked campus administrators for permission to put undercover officers on the campus in 1968, their request was denied. The dean instead instructed campus security officers to report drug-related incidents internally and not to the county police.[23] Subsequently, in the predawn hours of a cold January morning in 1968, 198 Suffolk County Sheriff's Office deputies conducted a major drug raid that resulted in the arrest of thirty-eight people, including twenty-one students. Some administrators and students complained about the decision to conduct this raid at 5:00 a.m., thereby waking students during final exams week and employing "methods normally [reserved] for desperate criminals about to escape."[24] More importantly, this police action garnered national headlines and resulted in a probe by the state legislature into whether university administrators were "defying law enforcers."[25] State senators believed the university to be in a state of "near-anarchy" and challenged administrators on whether they were actually capable of "cleaning up their own houses."[26]

In the aftermath of the Stony Brook drug raid, two things happened. The first was that across the country, campus police, who had already been fighting for increased police powers, began to collaborate more closely with local law enforcement, especially in drug enforcement efforts. In the SBU case, written guidelines were developed to systematize the process of turning over any student or staff member found in possession of drugs to the sheriff's office.[27] SBU police officers hoped that the drug raid would lead to a "strengthening of campus police powers" and "greater authority to enforce the law on campus."[28] Additionally, the chancellor of the State University of New York (SUNY) called for an extra $975,000 in funding "to improve security on university campuses" including the hiring of 122 security personnel for the fifty-seven campuses then comprising the SUNY System.[29]

The second consequence from the Stony Brook drug raid was that a clear message was sent to colleges and universities across the country when it came to the issue of drug enforcement. As Charles Olton, former history professor and dean of students at Union College, wrote in 1969: "In the aftermath of the notorious drug scandal at the Stony Brook campus . . . colleges throughout [the] northeastern United States began to take a second look at themselves and their attitudes and ideas on the subject of drug use."[30] There was a strong sense that "what happened at Stony Brook could have happened at dozens of other ill-prepared colleges and universities" and that dealing with this issue now has a "new urgency."[31] It was of the utmost importance that institutions make clear to students that illegal activity would not be tolerated on campuses and that if students were honest about needing counseling, schools would do their best to help. In the end, the Stony Brook drug raid would foreshadow an era of increased campus police cooperation with a broader police network that would take place as the War on Drugs continued to intensify.

THE WAR ON DRUGS

After years of growing panic over the growing presence of illegal drugs in the United States, President Richard Nixon, in a speech to Congress in 1971, officially announced the federal government's War on Drugs. This initiative profoundly shaped the legal system in the form of new laws that harshly punished not only the manufacture and distribution of illegal drugs but their possession as well. New York's Rockefeller Drug Laws, for example, imposed very long *mandatory minimum* sentences on those convicted of selling 57 grams of any controlled substance (including marijuana), and Michigan's "650-Lifer" law called for life imprisonment for those convicted of possessing 650 grams or more of any opiate. State laws such as these quickly proliferated, and with these policy changes soon came a massive explosion in US incarceration rates increasingly characterized by massive racial disparities along with the militarization of the police who were now being equipped with tanks, helicopters, and military-grade weaponry to conduct drug raids.[32]

Historians such as David Farber have explained how, "since the Nixon era, politicians have generally used drug war rhetoric to demonstrate their willingness to 'get tough' on people they deem to be marginal."[33] Indeed, the War on Drugs itself has been enmeshed with broader "War on Crime" politics of the 1960s and 1970s that targeted political and countercultural movements, particularly those occurring on college campuses. While it has been well established that the national War on Drugs was a reaction to antiwar protests, Black Power, and feminist ideas, less discussed is the idea that the War on Drugs was also a response to "stop the constant disruption" to campus life in the 1960s and 1970s, an important site of organizing for these and other political movements. In histories of higher education, the War on Drugs has largely remained a footnote, merely indicating that the federal initiative was partly a reaction to the diversification and rebelliousness of the youth culture found on college campuses. This chapter addresses this oversight by providing a small excavation of how the nation's War on Drugs transformed institutions of higher learning in fundamental ways by legitimizing the role of newly formed campus police forces.

For institutions of higher learning, the War on Drugs presented administrators with yet another dilemma to grapple with at the dawn of the 1970s. Administrators had desperately hoped they were approaching the end of massive unrest and disruption that marked the previous tumultuous decade of the 1960s. Overwhelmed with protests that demanded universities cease their complicity in Vietnam-era war efforts, empire building, and racism, riddled with bomb threats, and still reeling from the long, turbulent demise of *in loco parentis* in 1961, administrators continued to wrestle with how to exert control over students.³⁴ The war on drugs would introduce yet another element that administrators had to learn to navigate in an era where their traditional mechanisms of control had been eliminated. While national and state reports painted campuses as providing "sanctuaries" for illegal behavior including drug use, Boards of Trustees, local community, parents, alumni, donors were using the rhetoric of the War on Drugs as a weapon against youth and loudly calling for students to be put in their place.³⁵

THE WAR ON DRUGS ENTERS INSTITUTIONS OF HIGHER LEARNING

Advocates of punitive drug enforcement called for more drug raids and undercover activity to root out drugs, drug dealers, and all other troublemakers. Undercover activity by city and county police and the FBI publicly justified these actions as "the only practical way to enforce drug laws and to keep watch on radical campus activities . . . that might trigger disturbances in the surrounding community."³⁶ Although many campus police officers did not see drugs as the most important issue (instead citing campus thefts, protests, and bomb threats as priorities), campus police still saw collaborations with other branches of law enforcement as a path toward increasing their own legitimacy.³⁷ It was not uncommon for campus officers to use a moment of student protests to threaten to walk off the job if they were not granted expanded powers.³⁸ In some circumstances, this collaboration took the form of conducting co-beat patrols, as was the case with the University of Minnesota Campus Police Department (UMPD) and the Minneapolis Police Department (MPD) in 1974. In other circumstances, it took the form of creating narcotic squads, as was the case at Michigan State University.

Funded by the Law Enforcement Assistance Administration (LEAA), officers of the Michigan State University Department of Police and Public Safety (MSUDPPS) had been part of a larger Metro Narcotic Investigation Squad since 1969.³⁹ The squad consisted of two county officers, two municipal officers, a member of the Michigan State Police, and the MSUDPPS. By 1970, the frequency of these meetings increased, resulting in more activity. As MSUDPPS officer Haywood Julian stated, "When we get involved in the investigation of drugs, it might spread from campus to East Lansing, Lansing, and the whole general area,"⁴⁰ adding that a student might go to East Lansing (home to MSU) to sell, or nonstudents might enter the campus to sell. This type of crossover in jurisdictions required collaboration among the various agencies and officers involved.[41] These collaborations proved foundational in subsequent lobbying for the expanded jurisdictional scope of campus police off campus grounds.

Collaboration *between* police forces was not just encouraged by advocates of punitive drug enforcement, it was also supported with federal LEAA funds, and advocated for by the International Association of College and University Security Directors (IACUSD), who in 1970 made clear at their annual conference that "cooperation with local police is one of the most important functions of campus security."[42] Even at campuses where the relationship between campus police and external law enforcement was driven by hostility, there was still a sense that strict enforcement of laws was needed within university space.[43] By 1971, it was clear that the tide had dramatically turned. The belief that institutions of higher learning would not "serve as an additional enforcement agency" (as some institutions had articulated earlier) had severely faded. In one example, at Pennsylvania's Lehigh University, the president and dean made clear to students and the public that "the university is not a sanctuary for students from city police for any infraction of the law."[44] If students are arrested by town officials, they added, "town discipline applies."[45] While they agreed that student drug users caught on campus would be subject to university discipline, it was clear that the pressure to enforce drug laws had moved the needle on how detached the university could be from law enforcement.

It did not take long for campus police to loudly call for the increased police powers they were enjoying *within* campus spaces to be extended *beyond* university gates into the surrounding community. Equipped with these enhanced powers, campus police began to decry what they referred to as a "double standard of justice" in which university-affiliated individuals were given special treatment (e.g., referred for university discipline), whereas an unaffiliated individual would be subject to full prosecution under the law for the same violation. As the director of the MSUDPPS made clear, this practice was "a continued [holdover] of *in loco parentis*" that "promulgated a double standard of justice" and was "significantly worsening town-gown relations."[46]

Campus police understood that college administrators looked to them to handle these issues in a way that prioritized avoiding bad publicity for the institution. However, while a previous generation of campus security might have been on board with that to a large degree (especially when the student body was largely male, white, and elite), this new generation of campus police officers saw students and their protests as extremely out of line. The campus police officers of the 1970s were not the same as the security guards of the 1940s and 1950s; newer officers instead sought police legitimacy and therefore saw any practice of shielding or educating students as hypocrisy.

College administrators, wanting to insulate the War on Drugs from their campuses and the bad publicity that would emerge, started pointing to the outside community as the source of the drug problems schools were experiencing, and insisting that campus police focus their energy on arresting individuals not affiliated with the university. For example, in 1972, Charles LeMaistre, chancellor of the University of Texas System (one of the largest public higher education systems in the country), asked campus law enforcement, "What about the area surrounding the campus?" LeMaistre held that "this is the environment in which drug traffic flourishes. The perimeter of the campus has become the marketplace of the peddlers, the pushers, and the instigators of the drug problem."[47]

Ultimately, in the 1970s a central tension emerged that was most evident when it came to drug enforcement on campuses: institutional administrators, wanting to use campus police to shield the school from bad publicity, knocked heads with campus police officers, who pushed for the elimination of any double standard that protected students from punitive prosecution for drug offenses. Furthermore, campus police were encouraged to enforce drug laws in the surrounding community, on nonaffiliated individuals, based on the argument that it was "outsiders" who caused trouble for the campus community.

THIS CHAPTER has explored some of the tensions that the War on Drugs produced on college campuses. At different moments throughout the 1970s, college administrators and campus and municipal police had differing perspectives on how to best enforce emerging federal and state drug laws. Campus police saw tough enforcement of emerging drug laws as opportunities to collaborate with municipal police, earning them more resources, power, and legitimacy. College administrators, who originally wanted to avoid becoming an additional police agency, were faced with increasing drug raids that captured national headlines, leaving them with bad publicity. In response, administrators pushed for campus police to be able to independently handle drug raids as much as possible and keep results of the raids confidential, and urged officers to look outward to the local community to exercise their newly enhanced police powers. Indeed, in their continued search for legitimacy, power, and prestige, campus police forces were fundamentally shaped by the historical application of the War on Drugs to college campuses.

The legacy of these decisions continues to shape drug enforcement on campuses and their surrounding communities. For example, in 2015 four Wesleyan University students were "arrested in connection to a 'bad batch' of 'Molly' (also known as Ecstasy) that sent ten students to the hospital."[48] The story led to reporting that highlighted how "small, private liberal arts colleges tend to have low number of arrests, even with proportionately high numbers of disciplinary referrals."[49] In just one example, at Colgate University, 245 students in 2012 and 2013 were referred for disciplinary action for drug abuse violations, and 6 were arrested.[50] Time and again, numbers showed that "student arrests were in the single digits even if disciplinary referrals were in the hundreds."[51] However, this is not the case at large public institutions, where "arrested students actually outnumber students who are referred for disciplinary action." According to *Inside Higher Ed*: "Between 2011 and 2013, 537 students at the University of California at Berkeley were arrested for drug use on campus, and 254 were referred for disciplinary action. At the University of Georgia, 42 students received disciplinary referrals, while there were nearly 200 arrests."[52] All of this evidence generates further questions about campus police and drug enforcement. Furthermore, at present, the historical expansion of campus police jurisdictional authority into surrounding areas of campus has come under serious critique from activists concerned about the creation of spaces that are "doubly policed" by both municipal *and* campus police—despite residents having no affiliation with the university. Local residents have called attention to the way that university forces police working-class people of color while sheltering largely white, elite, student populations.[53]

NOTES

1. Gail Deutsch, Stephanie Fuerte, Jonathan Balthaser and Lauren Effron, "The Dangers of a College Student Becoming a Campus Police Drug Informant," ABC News, January 23, 2015, https://abcnews.go.com/US/dangers-college-student-campus-police-drug-informant/story?id=28357345; Suhauna Hussain, "When Colleges Use Their Own Students to Catch Drug Dealers" *Chronicle of Higher Education*, October 27, 2017.

2. Deutsch, Fuerte, Balthaser and Effron, "The Dangers of a College Student Becoming a Campus Police Drug Informant."

3. Deutsch, Fuerte, Balthaser and Effron, "The Dangers of a College Student Becom-

ing a Campus Police Drug Informant." Additionally, another story that received media attention is the 2013 case of Andrew Sadek, a student at North Dakota State College of Science who was caught selling eighty dollars' worth of pot on campus. He also became an informant, this time for a drug task force that involved several local police agencies including the campus police. He was found dead in 2014 (https://www.washingtonpost.com/news/the-watch/wp/2015/07/09/campus-cops-are-shadowy-militarized-and-more-powerful-than-ever/).

4. "Campus Security Men Examine New Status," *Los Angeles Times*, September 3, 1970.

5. Jim Berry, "The Campus Drug Problem," *Austin American*, May 1, 1966.

6. Berry, "The Campus Drug Problem."

7. Berry, "The Campus Drug Problem."

8. Berry, "The Campus Drug Problem."

9. Berry, "The Campus Drug Problem."

10. Berry, "The Campus Drug Problem."

11. "Drugs at U," *Minneapolis Star*, November 20, 1967.

12. "David Nimmer and John Greenwald, "More Raids Feared: Psychedelic Drug Users Are Uneasy," *Minneapolis Star*, November 24, 1967.

13. "Drugs at U."

14. "Drugs at U."

15. Robert Benion and John Martire, "An Educational Program on Drug Use," *Journal of the American College Health Association* 18 (April 1970): 271.

16. Benion and Martire, "An Educational Program on Drug Use," 271.

17. Benion and Martire, "An Educational Program on Drug Use," 271.

18. Allan Y. Cohen, "Psychedelic Drugs and the Student: Educational Strategies," *Journal of College Student Personnel* 10, no. 2 (March 1969): 96–101.

19. Gloria B. Anderson, "UW Campus Police Proposal Causes Rift," *Waukesha Daily Freeman*, May 28, 1969.

20. Anderson, "UW Campus Police Proposal Causes Rift."

21. Anderson, "UW Campus Police Proposal Causes Rift."

22. Anderson, "UW Campus Police Proposal Causes Rift."

23. Emmet O'Brien, "Legislature Opens SUNY Probe," *Press and Sun Bulletin*, January 24, 1968.

24. H. D. Quigg, "Pre-Dawn Narcotics Raid Exposed N.Y. University's Lack of Policing Procedures," *Tampa Tribune-Times*, February 18, 1968.

25. Quigg, "Pre-Dawn Narcotics Raid."

26. O'Brien, "Legislature Opens SUNY Probe."

27. Tom Renner and Robert Smith, "State U Agrees to Report Drug Use," *Newsday*, March 6, 1968.

28. Renner and Smith, "State U Agrees to Report Drug Use."
29. Renner and Smith, "State U Agrees to Report Drug Use."
30. Charles S. Olton, "Drugs and the Small College," *NASPA Journal* 8, no. 2 (1970): 83–89.
31. Olton, "Drugs and the Small College."
32. For works that tackle the war on drugs from a carceral state lens, see Michelle Alexander, *The New Jim Crow: Mass Incarceration in the Age of Colorblindness* (New York: New Press, 2010); Julilly Kohler-Hausmann, *Getting Tough: Welfare and Imprisonment in 1970s America* (Princeton, NJ: Princeton University Press, 2017); Caroline Jean Acker, *Creating the American Junkie: Addiction Research in the Classic Era of Narcotic Control* (Baltimore, MD: Johns Hopkins University Press, 2002); Donna Murch, "Crack in Los Angeles: Crisis, Militarization, and Black Response to the Late Twentieth-Century War on Drugs," *Journal of American History* 102, no. 1 (June 2015): 162–73; and Kathleen Frydl, *The Drug Wars in America: 1940–1973* (New York: Cambridge University Press, 2013).
33. David Farber, *The War on Drugs: A History* (New York: NYU Press, 2022), 6; Donna Murch, *Racist Logic: Markets, Drugs, Sex* (Cambridge, MA: MIT Press, 2019); Murch, "Crack in Los Angeles," 162–73.
34. For more on *in loco parentis*, see John Sloan, chapter 1 of this volume; and Philip Lee, "The Curious Life of In Loco Parentis in American Universities," *Higher Education in Review* 8 (2011): 65–90. For works that discuss student activism in relation to the military industrial complex, see Michael A. Bernstein, "The Uses of the University: After Fifty Years: Introduction," *Social Science History* 36, no. 4 (2012): 473–79; and Ethan Schrum, "To 'Administer the Present': Clark Kerr and the Purpose of the Postwar American Research University," *Social Science History* 36, no. 4 (2012): 499–523. For key works on the Black Campus Movement, see Ibram (Kendi) Rogers, *The Black Campus Movement: Black Students and the Racial Reconstitution of Higher Education, 1965–1972* (New York: Palgrave, 2012); Stefan Bradley, *Harlem vs. Columbia University: Black Student Power in the Late 1960s* (Urbana: University of Illinois Press, 2009); Martha Biondi, *The Black Revolution on Campus* (Berkeley: University of California Press, 2014); and Joy Ann Williamson, *Black Power on Campus: The University of Illinois* (Urbana: University of Illinois Press, 2003). For works on the demand of Chicano studies departments, see Michael Soldatenko, *Chicano Studies: The Genesis of a Discipline* (Tucson: University of Arizona Press, 2009); Mario T. Garcia and Sal Castro, *Blowout! The Chicano Struggle for Educational Justice* (Chapel Hill: University of North Carolina Press, 2011); Rodolfo F. Acuña, *The Making of Chicana/o Studies: In the Trenches of Academe* (New Brunswick, NJ: Rutgers University Press, 2011); and Carlos Muñoz, *Youth, Identity, Power: The Chicano Movement* (London: Verso, 1989). For the creation of Asian American studies departments, see Shirley Hune, "Opening the American: Mind

and Body: The Role of Asian American Studies," *Change* 21, no. 6 (November–December 1989): 56–63. For a particularly powerful reflection on this era of student activism, see Robin D. G. Kelley, "Black Study, Black Struggle," *Boston Review*, March 7, 2016.

35. See, for example, President's Commission on Campus Unrest, *The Report of the President's Commission on Campus Unrest* (Washington, DC: US Government Printing Office, 1970). Additionally, Emily Dufton's "Cannabis Culture Wars," in *The War on Drugs: A History* (New York: NYU Press, 2022), 160, explains how the battle over cannabis was waged by everyday citizens in the media, through social organizing, and lobbying.

36. Anthony Ripley, "Spies Cover the US Campus Scene," *Fresno Bee*, April 4, 1971.

37. Terry Ryan, "Campus Police Say Thievery Has Replaced Militancy as No 1 College Security Problem," *Red Bank (NJ) Daily Register*, December 20, 1972.

38. For insight into campus police unions, see chapter 4 of this volume.

39. The LEAA was a federal agency under the Department of Justice and administered millions of dollars in funds to state and local police agencies as part of the war on crime. For more on the LEAA, see Elizabeth Kai Hinton, *From the War on Poverty to the War on Crime: The Making of Mass Incarceration in America* (Cambridge, MA: Harvard University Press, 2016).

40. Helen Clegg, "Police Agencies Cooperate to Enforce Drug Laws," *Lansing State Journal*, March 15, 1970.

41. Clegg, "Police Agencies Cooperate to Enforce Drug Laws."

42. "Security Chiefs Meet Here: City, Campus Police Cooperation Urged," *Times Colonist*, June 19, 1970.

43. Associated Press, "Bill to Abolish Campus Police Is Rejected," *Oshkosh Northwestern*, January 15, 1970.

44. "Lehigh Studies Role of University Police," *Morning Calls*, January 11, 1971.

45. "Lehigh Studies Role of University Police."

46. Richard O. Bernitt, "Campus Law Enforcement: Town-Gown Relations," in *New Directions in Campus Law Enforcement: A Handbook for Administrators*, ed. O. Suthern Sims (Athens: University of Georgia Center for Continuing Education, 1971).

47. Charles LeMaistre, *The Challenge of New Directions in Campus Law Enforcement* (Athens: University of Georgia Center for Continuing Education, 1971).

48. Jake New, "What Happens on Campus Stays on Campus?," *Inside Higher Ed*, February 27, 2015, www.insidehighered.com/news/2015/02/27/how-institutions-handle-drug-violations-varies-greatly.

49. New, "What Happens on Campus Stays on Campus?"

50. New, "What Happens on Campus Stays on Campus?"

51. New, "What Happens on Campus Stays on Campus?"

52. New, "What Happens on Campus Stays on Campus?"

53. This phenomenon is powerfully described in more detail in chapter 3.

8

"THE KING OF STING"

A History of the UCLA Police Department

ANDREW PEDRO GUERRERO

Campus police are the "armed guards" of colleges and universities. They often hold state-sanctioned peace officer status, granting them the power to detain, arrest, and engage in legalized violence. In this way, they are virtually indistinguishable from their municipal counterparts.[1] The 2020 uprisings led to increased scrutiny of campus police, their role within universities, and the ways they reproduce racialized violence. Students across the nation called on campus administrators to defund, disarm, and disband their police forces. With intimate knowledge of racist policing on their campuses, students articulated new, more just visions of public safety.[2] Community members, organizers, and researchers have provided crucial insights into the destructive operations of campus police.[3] A growing body of scholarship has revealed the role of campus police in the territorial expansion of urban universities at the expense of Black communities.[4] Such critiques, together with efforts to defund and abolish campus police, have been particularly palpable at the University of California.[5]

The University of California Police Department (UCPD) is the policing arm of the University of California. The UCPD is a full-fledged policing agency with semi-autonomous departments operating at each University of California campus. The force operating at the University of California Los Angeles (UCLA PD) is the largest within the UCPD and the focus of this chapter.[6] By tracing the history of the department, this chapter demonstrates how the UCLA PD's pursuit of *guarding property*—the original mandate of *all* campus police—has criminalized people on campus and beyond. As the department's original objective, guarding property fundamentally shaped its initiatives and relationships with students, other law enforcement agencies, and the broader community.

This chapter first charts the origins of the UCLA PD and the events that shaped its objectives and authority. It then explores the ways that UCLA police cooperated with law enforcement agencies from the local to the federal level. By tracing this interagency collaboration, this chapter shows how campus police often circumscribed their supposed commitment to student safety in order to engage in off-campus drug and property investigations, enhance their status within law enforcement circles, and bolster departmental coffers. The roots of this story are found with a small group of men tasked with protecting campus property.

THE MAKING OF THE UCLA POLICE DEPARTMENT

UCLA's police force finds its origins in the "campus watchman" system. Established in the 1910s by Alfred E. Davie, the superintendent of the Grounds and Buildings Department, watchmen were charged with guarding university property. Holding ambiguous authority, they were known for their aggressive treatment of students.[7] In order to legitimize his campus watchmen in the eyes of students and guard rapidly expanding campus infrastructure, Davie replaced the watchmen with a police force in 1929.[8] Composed of former Los Angeles Police Department (LAPD) officers and cowboys, Davie's new force was "thoroughly serious in their intent" because the Westwood neighborhood was "so isolated that property and homes need special protection."[9] Though Davie's new campus guards did not wield full police powers, the student newspaper noted approvingly that they "know how to shoot revolvers."[10]

Nearly two decades after Davie's cowboys arrived on campus with guns at their hip, the State of California moved to formalize its campus police forces. In 1947, the California attorney general declared that the University of California system had "outgrown the need for a small security force" and implemented a plan to codify campus police powers. In what was later described as a "precedent-setting move," lawmakers modified the state's education code to grant the Regents of the University of California the authority to establish their own state police force.[11] Thus, the UCPD was born. Into the early 1960s, however, campus police continued to operate in a similar capacity to their watchmen predecessors. Administrators understood that custodial tasks—traffic regulation, ticketing, and addressing petty theft—fell under the domain of campus police, while the LAPD maintained authority over criminal matters.[12] In this period, university police forces occupied similar roles throughout the United States. However, student activism soon catalyzed structural reform.

Fully fledged campus police forces only proliferated following the mass student protests of the 1960s and early 1970s. In these years, legal and social change provided the groundwork for refashioned tools of campus suppression. Until the early 1960s, American universities exercised extensive disciplinary discretion over students under the legal doctrine *in loco parentis* (in place of the parent).[13] Student activism in the early 1960s, however, effectively ended this system and simultaneously prompted violent responses from law enforcement. In the face of increasingly large-scale protests and renewed concerns for student safety, university administrators began to reconsider the role of police on campus.[14] At UCLA, a series of LAPD scandals prompted such reform and set the stage for a fully fledged campus police force.

During the height of the antiwar protests in 1969, LAPD officers enrolled at UCLA as students to gather intelligence and disrupt student activism.[15] Embedding themselves within campus groups, undercover officers became prominent figures within antiwar groups, incited violence during protests, and wrote op-eds for the *Daily Bruin*, UCLA's student newspaper.[16] The day after the May 4, 1970, massacre at Kent State, the LAPD's increasing unpopularity was cemented when officers violently cracked down on student demonstrators and conducted mass arrests. LAPD's brutality led to many hospitalizations and garnered significant media attention.[17] Though UCLA police had previously conducted covert surveillance and responded to campus protests with violence, outrage over the LAPD's actions on May 5 finally pressured administrators to act.[18]

Like other universities in this period, administrators at the University of California came to recognize the counterproductive and often disastrous results of using outside law enforcement to subdue campus protests. They decided to rapidly expand their campus police capabilities to maintain order and curtail negative press and criticism from lawmakers. As UC Regent Norm Simon proclaimed, "I don't care if you give up foreign language departments, to me I think it's more important that we have campus police."[19] State lawmakers and university representatives pushed forward campus police reforms. State assemblyman Paul Priolo introduced a bill to standardize campus police training. Given that the UCPD was granted policing authority in 1947, he asked, "Why shouldn't the UCPD be forced to conform to the same standards?"[20] Although the original proposal was vetoed, Priolo's hopes were soon realized during a period of reforms that sought to address complaints from community members, administrators, and campus police themselves. By standardizing officer qualifications, legislators began to restructure the UCPD in the image of municipal police.[21] At the university level, a report sponsored by the University of California Regents surveyed UCPD forces throughout the state. Among other suggestions, the report echoed the desire to standardize training and education requirements, delineate jurisdictional lines, and establish the legal authority of campus police ascribed in law.[22]

Reforms provided UCLA police with an opportunity to assert their power on campus and contend with past scandals. In essence, professionalization amounted to a series of reforms designed to establish campus police legitimacy by directing resources to personnel and expanding their authority. As a result, the LAPD's presence on campus fell significantly. A decade after the 1970 student demonstrations, UCLA PD Officer Russ Duncan told the *Daily Bruin* that requesting LAPD assistance "would be a very rare occasion."[23] Campus police preferred to address campus unrest themselves. The LAPD agreed. "Society wants the university to have some independence from the municipal police," LAPD Officer Wallace Gray said. "We don't want to come on campus."[24]

Following the Student Protest Movement, campus police and administrators turned their attention to perceived threats coming from off campus. Universities had long employed security forces and police to assist in their urban renewal efforts. As Davarian L. Baldwin attests, universities have had destructive and extractive impacts on urban spaces, displacing Black residents to secure new spaces of operation.[25] Campus police have operated as one of the most visible and violent elements of university-community relations. At the University of Chicago, for example, campus police were instrumental in clearing urban infrastructure for development while criminalizing and removing Black residents.[26]

For the UCLA police, the 1980s represented a crucial period in which racialized threats emerged from poor and working-class Los Angeles neighborhoods. In the 1970s, three in every four UCLA students were white.[27] In the 1980s, however, students of color began to enroll at greater rates. In addition, local events attracted thousands of people of color from South Central and East Los Angeles. Citing "demographic changes" for rising crime, Chief John Barber contended that Westwood was "beginning to look a lot like Sunset in the 60s," replete with violent crime, houselessness, and juvenile gangs.[28] Campus police asserted that outsiders accounted for nearly 90 percent of all arrests.[29]

Effectively tasked with differentiating acceptable visitors and undesirables, campus police continually confronted the unhoused. John Barber identified "transients" who "drift on campus" after dark as a leading cause of crime.[30] In reality, the unhoused were stigmatized and targeted for merely existing on campus property. UCLA PD Officer James Alexander said that officers were "mainly looking for smell" in determining who to remove from campus.³¹ The UCLA PD also sounded alarms over the threat of "gang activity." In practice, such views amounted to targeting and harassing Black and Latine residents and students alike. During a 1986 student safety-awareness event, for example, then UCLA PD Officer Greg Allen discussed the "invasion" of gang members in Westwood. He warned, "If you see blue shoestrings you can be sure he's a gangbanger," and promised to deny them access at campus events.³² His remarks were met with outrage by Black students, with one contending that the UCLA PD contributed to an "atmosphere of paranoia" that positioned Black youth as criminals perpetually subject to monitoring and detainment. To Black students it was clear which communities were to be *protected* and which were to be *policed*. Such tactics were not limited to campus grounds. For example, UCLA police repeatedly worked with the LAPD to bar more than six hundred Black and Latine youth from the popular campus "Mardi Gras" festival in the mid-1980s.³³ Labeled gang-related, visiting teenagers were consistently targeted by campus police. In sum, as more unhoused residents and people of color occupied their jurisdiction, UCLA police moved to criminalize both by marking youth of color as "gang members" and hyperpolicing houselessness on and around campus.

The structure and priorities of the UCLA PD were shaped by its efforts to protect campus property and enforce a racialized and classist vision of order. Its development was particularly guided by its partnerships with, and emulation of, neighboring police forces. This history created the conditions for the UCLA PD's most ambitious and wide-ranging campaigns.

"THE KING OF STING"

President Lyndon B. Johnson's War on Crime initiatives expanded the role and power of police departments throughout the nation.³⁴ His administration established the Law Enforcement Assistance Administration (LEAA) to oversee the disbursement of federal funding to local police departments, which included funding for not only education and training but also new technologies and weaponry. These initiatives led to new mechanisms for monitoring and policing Black urban communities such as undercover fencing operations.³⁵ Early projects such as "Operation Sting" in Washington, DC, pioneered an investigative model that would soon be replicated by law enforcement agencies across the nation, including at UCLA.

In the early 1970s, UCLA administrators employed their police force to address a series of typewriter thefts. Two officers, UCLA PD Lieutenant Joe Ares and Sergeant Al Brown, initiated an undercover campaign to recover several electronic IBM typewriters. In 1975, as their operation gained momentum, they were chosen for their "exceptional investigative skill" by the US Department of Justice and LEAA to head a statewide initiative to recover stolen office property and awarded a $150,000 grant. The UCLA grant covered travel, equipment, and buy-money for undercover transactions. Their three-man squad spearheaded what was essentially a pilot program for a federal initiative to distribute similar property recovery grants to other states.[36]

Ares and Brown not only trained police from numerous states, but they also helped develop new methods of police investigation. The broader project's innovation was in its use of a vast Sacramento-based database of more than 180,000 serial numbers for electronic machines. Cross-listing this data with serial numbers from electronic repair shops, police located sellers and buyers and made arrests across the nation.[37] For federal officials, the methods employed by the UCLA police merited expansion. Brown touted their appointment as overseers of the California grant as part of an "effort to bring UCLA expertise" to agencies seeking investigative knowledge.[38] In fact, a primary goal of the project was to create a manual on property recovery investigations that would be distributed to thousands of law enforcement agencies throughout the country.[39] Produced by the Battelle Law and Justice Study Center of the California Department of Justice, *The Identification and Recovery of Stolen Property Using Automated Information System: An Investigator's Handbook* provided agencies with an overview of property recovery efforts, field investigation methods, and the serial number "match technique" at the heart of the recovery program.[40]

Ares described his on-campus investigations, which were cheaper to operate than a storefront, as a "mobile sting program."[41] To locate machines and identify potential buyers and sellers, Ares and his colleagues employed various tactics such as scanning local newspaper ads.[42] They concocted a fictitious typewriter repair shop and accompanying business cards. Once potential dealers were located, UCLA police sold them stolen IBM machines and then proceeded to make arrests for "receiving stolen property." Preempting criticisms of his officer's methods, UCLA PD Chief John Barber contended that "the operation is not police entrapment" because information gained through "informants, past records or stakeouts" provided grounds for suspicion of criminality.[43] While the project started as a means to retrieve stolen university property, its scope quickly grew far beyond these bounds. The UCLA PD seized more than $1 million in weapons and jewelry and collaborated with law enforcement agencies as far away as San Diego County.[44] The operation was considered a resounding success by police authorities and media outlets alike, as can be seen in a positive profile of Joe Ares and the IBM recovery project that aired on *60 Minutes* in 1980.[45]

Under the national coordination of Charles Wynne at the California Department of Justice, the LEAA provided the recovery project with more than $1 million in funding from 1976 to 1981. Wynne was hopeful that Ares's effectiveness would extend to officers across states. As the *Los Angeles Times* articulated, Joe Ares's UCLA team acted as the "enforcement arm of Wynne's operation."[46] For LEAA officials, the project's cost-effectiveness and upscaling potential were promising. Citing the recovery project's significance, James Golden of the LEAA declared it the "first attempt to determine the pattern of property recovery flow in law enforcement history." According to Joe Ares, it was the first time a university was funded for "criminal experiments."[47]

The property recovery project was an important income generator for the UCPD as the department faced statewide budget cuts in 1981. UCLA PD leadership launched a fundraising campaign to offset the upcoming state budget allocation. Joe Ares assured the *Los Angeles Times* that there was a "strong indication that private industry" would help to financially support the UCLA PD.[48] For example, IBM offered approximately $60,000 to fund Ares's property recovery project in a show of appreciation for recovering their machines.[49] The UCLA PD also sought to charge university programs "deemed to be self-supporting"—such as the medical center, family and married student housing, and student residence halls—for campus police services. In the fall of 1981, UCLA PD Chief John Barber, Joe Ares, and Charles Wynne traveled to Washington, DC, to seek federal support as well. They secured a $100,000 grant from the US Department of Justice's Office of Justice Assistance Research and Statistics (OJARS), which allowed Joe Ares to expand his "mobile sting" into a large brick-and-mortar fencing operation.[50]

In the months leading up to Barber's acquisition of the OJARS grant, Los Angeles–area detectives had been brainstorming new ways to confront theft in West Los Angeles. During informal luncheons, they explored different strategies for targeting "suspected criminals." The Westside Major Crime Violators Task Force emerged from these discussions. The task force was designed to be a multi-jurisdiction unit staffed with officers from the UCLA PD, LAPD, Beverly Hills PD, Culver City PD, Santa Monica PD, and the Los Angeles County Sheriff's Department.[51] It became one of the most prominent task forces in Los Angeles history.

Joe Ares and John Barber were foundational to the unit. With a budding reputation for his undercover work, Ares was appointed to the unit, and Barber's OJARS grant funded its first major investigation. The undercover sting became the Westside Task Force's primary mode of investigation, garnering its members widespread media attention. Each of their three major stings was supported by a state or federal grant ranging from $75,0000 to $100,000 and followed a similar model: establish a storefront equipped with surveillance and entice residents to deliver stolen goods. Agents then acted as scouts to establish a clientele base, often selling and buying stolen goods in view of their targets. At the end of each operation, Westside Task Force agents shut down their storefront as their former clients were arrested in a sweep of early-morning raids.

LAPD Wilshire Division Captain Joe De Ladurantey interviewed potential task force members by screening for those who had suspects in mind, but not enough capacity (or evidence) to make an arrest: "Who are the top ten burglars in your area, people you'd concentrate on if you had the time?" For Captain De Ladurantey, the Westside Task Force aimed to resurrect the "lost art" of investigation in which officers were granted the authority to pursue "known suspects."[52] A philosophy of prevention justified proactive policing. The Westside Task Force sought, as the *Los Angeles Times* elaborated, to understand "what crime the criminal is likely to commit, not which criminal is likely to have committed the crime."[53] To gain such understanding, task force agents worked with parole officers to identify hangouts and set surveillance. To build trust on the street, agents often befriended and played pool with their targets.

In July 1982, "Anything and Everything" opened its doors to the community. Westside Task Force agents posed as "wholesale brokers" who would buy just about anything; the storefront was adorned with a sign proclaiming, "If We Can Sell It, We'll Buy It."[54] As surveillance cameras recorded, patrons were prompted to speak openly about stolen goods. In making purchases, agents were persistent, even equipping their pawnshop with a "pickup service" to retrieve items from sellers unable to afford transportation.[55] Ares later commented to the *Daily Bruin*, "If it was stolen and it could be traced, we would buy it."[56] By the time the OJARS funds were exhausted, the operation had seized more than $23 million in goods and made 459 felony arrests. Known to officers as Operation Hornet's Nest, the task force carried out the largest sting in Los Angeles history.[57] LAPD Lieutenant and task force spokesperson Dan Cooke declared that he "knew of no sting operation so massive and successful as this one."[58] For the Los Angeles police, the task force model proved highly effective and efficient. According to the LAPD's 1982 annual report, temporary police transfers to meet defined objectives served as a cost-effective policing strategy. The Westside Task Force, the LAPD's most successful task force at the time, met or exceeded its initial objectives. With more task forces established than at any time in LAPD history, the report declared 1982 the "Year of the Task Force."[59]

Following a second sting in Santa Monica, task force agents set their sights on Beverly Hills. The Westside Task Force opened "Exclusive Import-Export Co." in 1985, and, like Ares's mobile sting at UCLA, they created business cards and placed advertisements in local newspapers.[60] At times, agents also placed orders to their connections on the street. For example, when local blouse manufacturer George Doonan suspected that his merchandise was being stolen, police tapped Westside Task Force agents. Exclusive agents reached out to clients to place an order for the type of blouses that Doonan produced. Soon, a familiar client arrived at the shop with Doonan's blouses. On April 1, 1986, "Exclusive Import-Export Co." shut down operations as officers raided the residence of its former patrons.[61] According to a task force spokesperson, the date was no accident. For this April Fool's Day, the *San Pedro News-Pilot* affirmed, the joke was on Exclusive's former clientele, who were awakened by police raids.[62] The early-dawn raids brought the total arrests made through Westside Task Force investigations to nearly two thousand.[63] Joe Ares's work with the Westside Major Crime Violators Task Force demonstrates the extent to which campus police ventured off campus to enhance interagency police relationships, increase their profile, and seize goods for their own benefit. In addition, the Westside Task Force served to *produce* crime, not necessarily reduce it.[64] For example, the unit selected front locations by identifying an area with a "high crime rate."[65] Beverly Hills is hardly awash in crime, yet the task force created new arenas of criminality by enticing locals to deliver stolen goods.

Joe Ares's successful property recovery operations propelled his career. Deemed an expert on sting and property recovery investigations, he led instruction in courses on fencing techniques to law enforcement agencies in at least twenty-nine states and worked as a private security consultant. UCLA police proudly touted Ares's credentials and interpersonal skills when he was honored by the International Association of Chiefs of Police (IACP) in 1987.[66] "He would have been a great parish priest [who] would have blessed criminals first and then probably arrested them. . . . He can cover any robbery, rape or assault, and has been in numerous shootouts," boasted UCLA's police chief.[67] Santa Monica Police Chief James F. Keane called him "one of the most innovative law enforcement officers" he had worked with and coined his nickname "The King of Sting."[68]

A History of the UCLA Police Department 117

Interagency task force investigations were supplemented by similar strategies on campus. By 1989, with the Westside Task Force's third sting complete and Joe Ares entering retirement, the UCLA PD was conducting two large undercover operations on campus *every year*. In 1989, for example, an undercover drug investigation led to the arrest of eight workers at the UCLA Medical Center. UCLA officers spent $25,000 to make drug purchases during the six-month investigation.[69] As the UCLA police became more deeply integrated into Los Angeles's broader policing apparatus, the department often sent officers to municipal departments to gain patrol and undercover experience.[70] UCLA police embraced the weaponry that typifies police militarization, equipping themselves with submachine guns in the mid-1980s.[71] In adopting such weapons, the department strove to be taken as seriously as their municipal police collaborators. In 1989, after years of lobbying UC administrators, they replaced their tan police outfits with dark blue uniforms. According to a campus police coordinator, the public learned to associate such uniforms with legitimate police officers through TV shows such as *Adam-12*.[72] The department also pioneered campus police programs, instituting the first university police K-9 unit in the nation. Combing through campus grounds, UCLA police believed their dogs provided officers a "psychological edge in fighting crime."[73]

Beyond campus, UCLA police continued to participate in local police task forces. Like the Westside Task Force, the El Segundo–based Westside Narcotics Enforcement Team (WESTNET) was created in 1989 to expand the jurisdictional capacity of local police.[74] The unit monitored suspected drug dealers, conducted extensive surveillance, and orchestrated numerous raids. Soon, LAPD Captain Tim Grimmond, WESTNET's head, reached out to UCLA police leader John Barber. Barber agreed for his officers to join in the summer of 1990, believing that participation in WESTNET would improve the department's approach to policing on campus.[75]

Perhaps more important than narcotics experience, UCLA police also sought the spoils of WESTNET investigations. With federal laws permitting police to keep the bulk of the assets seized in such investigations, participating officers were guaranteed a percentage of the goods and money acquired through seizures for their departments.[76] Officers reasoned that the potential cash rewards would fund overtime pay and allow the department to hire more officers. The loot was not insignificant. WESTNET had already seized goods worth millions, and just weeks after accepting Grimmond's offer, Barber's UCLA officers participated in one of the largest drug seizures in US history.[77] Such acquisitions more than covered the costs of operation, and by July 1990 each police department involved had acquired at least $250,000 through WESTNET raids and seizures.[78]

UCLA PD's participation in WESTNET proved to be an ample funding reservoir. Indeed, task forces may be viewed as one of the UCLA PD's primary strategies for securing supplemental revenue and serving as a buffer against fluctuations in state funding. Two years after joining WESTNET, UCLA police tapped into a $300,000 "narcotics-seizure fund" to accommodate budget reductions.[79] Just as in earlier years, financial opportunities made through undercover investigations provided the department with a valuable safety net. Thus, investigation seizures not only allowed the UCLA PD to acquire policing experience and solidify interdepartmental relationships but also to secure financial security independent of university funds.

THE UCLA PD EXPANDED from its origins as watchmen to replicate the same racist and classist policing that characterizes municipal departments throughout the nation. Departmental reforms in the late 1960s and early 1970s were followed by an era in which campus police engaged in extensive off-campus investigations. These operations worked to the department's professional and financial advantage. Arrests and seizures impacted thousands of people far beyond the grounds of UCLA's campus and, in turn, informed the tactics and practices that the department used on students and university employees. In conducting this work, the UCLA PD not only reproduced police violence in the service of the drug war and property protection but also helped innovate new methods of police investigation. UCLA officers were instrumental in crafting precedent-setting relationships between campus police, state and federal agencies, and the business sector. Such relationships provided campus police with crucial resources and career opportunities at the expense of thousands of Los Angeles residents.

In the 1980s, undercover investigations became a staple of the UCLA PD. Recent data demonstrates that, long after anxieties about gangs first began to shape their priorities, UCLA police continue to target Black residents: despite comprising only 2 percent of the Westwood population, Black residents make up 29 percent of all arrests.[80] This revealing data is the outgrowth of the pursuit of order and property protection that led to the professionalization of Davie's modest five-man police force. The mid-twentieth-century rise of campus police forces has widened the state's ability to monitor, detain, and incarcerate students and community members. Far too often, these agencies maintain authority that replicate the racialized class-based violence that has always guided American police departments.

NOTES

1. See, for example, Nicholas M. Perez and Max Bromley, "Comparing Campus and City Police Human Resource and Select Community Outreach Policies and Practices: An Update," *Policing: An International Journal* 38, no. 4 (2015): 664–74.

2. Julia Barajas, "At Some U.S. Universities, a Time to Rethink Cops on Campus," *Los Angeles Times*, July 9, 2020; Michael Sainato, "US Students Call on Universities to Dismantle and Defund Campus Policing," *Guardian*, June 24, 2020.

3. Sunaina Maira and Julie Sze, "Dispatches from Pepper Spray University: Privatization, Repression, and Revolts," *American Quarterly* 64, no. 2 (2012): 315–30; Dylan Rodríguez, "Beyond 'Police Brutality': Racist State Violence and the University of California," *American Quarterly* 64, no. 2 (2012): 303–13.

4. Davarian Baldwin, *In the Shadow of the Ivory Tower: How Universities Are Plundering Our Cities* (New York: Bold Type Books, 2021); Jordan Larson, "A Brief History of the UCPD," *Chicago Maroon*, May 25, 2012.

5. Felicia Mello and Vanessa Arredondo, "Students Push UC to Abolish Police Departments," *Cal Matters*, June 26, 2020, https://calmatters.org/education/2020/06/students-push-uc-to-abolish-police-departments/.

6. As of May 2022, campus police webpages note that the UCLA PD is staffed with sixty-four sworn officers, while UCPD Berkeley maintains forty-nine officers ("UCLA Police Department," *UCLA*, https://campusservices.ucla.edu/ucla-police-department#:~:text=UCLA%20Police%20Department%20(UCPD)%20provides,crime%20prevention%20and%20education%20programs; "Department Demographics," *Berkeley UCPD*, https://ucpd.berkeley.edu/department-demographics).

7. John Sloan. "The Modern Campus Police: An Analysis of Their Evolution, Structure, and Function," *American Journal of Police* 11 (1992): 85–104.

8. "Men Form Police Force; Former Cowboys Guard Buildings," *California Daily Bruin*, October 22, 1929.

9. "Men Form Police Force; Former Cowboys Guard Buildings."

10. Jeff Kibre, "Firing Line," *California Daily Bruin*, October 22, 1929.

11. Colvin Terry, "Policies, Problems of University Police Investigated," *Daily Bruin*, May 24, 1971; "Lynn Explains Campus Police," *Daily Bruin*, March 7, 1962.

12. Clyde Rexrode, "Campus Police–'Great White Father,'" *Daily Bruin*, April 13, 1951; Memo to Vice President Cunningham by Assistant to the Chancellor Charles E. Young, May 8, 1961, Box 48, 1957–1962; 1964–1970, Office of the Chancellor, Admin-

istrative files of Franklin D. Murphy, University Archives Record Series 401, UCLA Library Special Collections, University Archives, University of California, Los Angeles.

13. See John Sloan's chapter on *in loco parentis* in this volume.

14. Yalile Suriel, "Discipling the Nation: Teaching the History of Campus Police," *Metropole*, August 4, 2022.

15. Ann Rankin and Susan Sword, "Undercover Agents Identified on Campus: Three Committees Investigate Local 'Mod Squad,'" *Daily Bruin*, June 3, 1970; "Letters to the Editor," *Daily Bruin*, June 1, 1970; Ted Kozak, "Sounding Board," *Daily Bruin*, August 14, 1969.

16. Philip Hager, "Ruling in UCLA Undercover Case: State High Court Bars Police 'Snooping,'" *Los Angeles Times*, March 25, 1975; Chancellor's Commission on the Events of May 5, 1970, "Violence at UCLA: May 5, 1970," University Archives. Subject Files (Reference Collection), University Archives Record Series 746, UCLA Library Special Collections, University Archives.

17. Chancellor's Commission on the Events of May 5, 1970, "Violence at UCLA: May 5, 1970."

18. "ACLU Urges Student Review of UCLA Police," *Los Angeles Sentinel*, May 30, 1963.

19. Terry, "Policies, Problems of University Police Investigated."

20. Terry, "Policies, Problems of University Police Investigated."

21. The California Commission on Peace Officer Standards and Training (POST) included establishing minimum selection standards for peace officers. Campus police became required to pass a POST course in 1971 (see California Council on Criminal Justice, "1971 Annual Report," January 1972).

22. John Barber, "UCLA Police: A Role in Education," Box 78, Governmental Relations–Los Angeles City–1984 Olympics–Security, Office of the Chancellor. Administrative files of Charles E. Young, University Archives Record Series 594, UCLA Library Special Collections, University Archives, University of California, Los Angeles.

23. Jane Rosenberg, "Campus Municipal Jurisdictions: Just How Gray Is the Gray Area?," *Daily Bruin*, September 22, 1981.

24. Rosenberg, "Campus Municipal Jurisdictions."

25. Eddie Cole, "The Racist Roots of Campus Policing," *Washington Post*, June 2, 2021; Baldwin, *In the Shadow of the Ivory Tower*.

26. Jordan Larson, "A Brief History of the UCPD," *Chicago Maroon*, May 25, 2012.

27. Bridget Shackelford, "The Changing Face of UCLA Diversity," *Daily Bruin*, September 23, 2006, https://dailybruin.com/2006/09/23/the-changing-face-of-ucla-dive.

28. Jill Farhi, "LAPD Force Coming to Westwood, *Daily Bruin*, January 29, 1981.

29. In 1979, UCLA police contended that nonstudents comprised nearly 90 percent of all arrests (see Mary Astadourian, "Crime Rate Rises Here while Violence Drops,"

Daily Bruin, October 23, 1979). In 1987, campus police again maintained that over 95 percent of crime was attributable to outsiders (see Nicole Allesi, "UCLA Rape Frequency Ranks High among Universities," *Daily Bruin*, February 11, 1987).

30. Astadourian, "Crime Rate Rises Here While Violence Drops."

31. Gary Lee Seto, "Bums Simply People Who Never Learned to Wait," *Daily Bruin*, October 14, 1982.

32. TeriAnne Carpenter, "Westwood Street Gang Threat Rising," *Daily Bruin*, October 7, 1986.

33. Nathan Shapell, Haig G. Mardikin, et al., "Little Hoover" Commission on California State Government Organization and Economy, *A Review of Crime on University of California Campuses*, Report Library, Report #82, June 1987, https://lhc.ca.gov/sites/lhc.ca.gov/files/Reports/082/Report82.PDF; "Marian Bereiowitz, "Panel Hears Testimony on UC Crime," *Daily Bruin*, March 5, 1987; Connor Thompson, "UCLA Community Reflects on Loss of Mardi Gras Celebrations," *Daily Bruin*, February 9, 2016.

34. Elizabeth Hinton, *From the War on Poverty to the War on Crime: The Making of Mass Incarceration in America* (Cambridge, MA: Harvard University Press, 2016).

35. Hinton, *From the War on Poverty to the War on Crime*, 209–17.

36. Meryl Ginsberg, "Getting It Back: UCLA Team Might Have Key to Finding Stolen Typewriters," *Daily Bruin*, November 21, 1980.

37. Bill Farr, "Trail of Hijacked Typewriters Takes a San Diego Twist," *Los Angeles Times*, October 12, 1981.

38. Ginsberg, "Getting It Back."

39. Heidi Swanbeck, "Will IBM Pick up Tab for Crime Project?," *Daily Bruin*, August 13, 1981.

40. Mary V. McGuire and Marilyn E. Walsh, *Identification and Recovery of Stolen Property Using Automated Information System: An Investigator's Handbook* (Washington, DC: US Department of Justice, Office of Justice Programs, 1981), www.ojp.gov/ncjrs/virtual-library/abstracts/identification-and-recovery-stolen-property-using-automated.

41. Pat B. Anderson, "Police Hunt and Find a Peck of Typewriters," *Los Angeles Times*, November 2, 1980.

42. Jane Rosenberg, "UCPD Arrests Typewriter Thief," *Daily Bruin*, April 20, 1981.

43. Anderson, "Police Hunt and Find a Peck of Typewriters."

44. Paul Selleck, "11 Arrested in Office Machine Burglary," *Los Angeles Times*, May 18, 1979; Anderson, "Police Hunt and Find a Peck of Typewriters."

45. "IBM Caper," *60 Minutes*, November 23, 1980.

46. Farr, "Trail of Hijacked Typewriters Takes a San Diego Twist."

47. Swanbeck, "Will IBM Pick up Tab for Crime Project?"

48. Farr, "Trail of Hijacked Typewriters Takes a San Diego Twist."

49. Lee Goldberg, "UCPD Expecting Cuts in Funding for '81–'82," *Daily Bruin*, October 1, 1981.

50. Richard West, "459 Arrested in $23 Million Police 'Sting,'" *Los Angeles Times*, June 16, 1983.

51. West, "459 Arrested in $23 Million Police 'Sting.'"

52. Martina Hernandez, "5 West County Police Units to Join Crack Crime Ring," *Los Angeles Times*, December 5, 1981.

53. Eric Malnic, "L.A. Police Task Force's Start with a Criminal Instead of a Crime," *Los Angeles Times*, August 11, 1983.

54. West, "459 Arrested in $23 Million Police 'Sting.'"

55. Michael D. Harris, "In What Is Thought to Be the Largest Sting," United Press International, June 16, 1983.

56. Bart Ziegler, "UCPD Officer Recognized as One of Nation's Finest," *Daily Bruin*, January 15, 1988.

57. US Department of Justice, *Justice Assistance News* 4, no. 6 (August 1983); Russell Snyder, "More Than 300 Arrested in One-Year Police Sting Operation," *San Pedro (CA) News-Pilot*, April 4, 1985.

58. West, "459 Arrested in $23 Million Police 'Sting.'"

59. Board of Police Commissioners, *Los Angeles Police Department 1982 Annual Report*, www.ojp.gov/ncjrs/virtual-library/abstracts/los-angeles-police-department-annual-report-1982.

60. Robert Hallwacks, "Joke on Suspects in LAPD Sting," *San Pedro (CA) News-Pilot*, April 2, 1986.

61. "Huge LA Sting Nets 46 Suspects," *Roseville (CA) Press-Tribune*, April 2, 1986.

62. Hallwacks, "Joke on Suspects in LAPD Sting."

63. Jack Jones and Boris Varo, "'Sting' Raids Net 43 Theft Suspects across L.A. Area," *Los Angeles Times*, April 2, 1986.

64. This point is made by Gary Marx in his seminal *Undercover: Police Surveillance in America* (Berkeley: University of California Press, 1989). In addition, see Hinton, *From the War on Poverty to the War on Crime*, 209.

65. Ziegler, "UCPD Officer Recognized as One of Nation's Finest."

66. Nancy Graham, "Police: Covering Campus Crime Day and Night," *Los Angeles Times*, September 20, 1981.

67. Marison Mull, "Valencia Man: Prize Stinger," *Santa Clarita (CA) Signal*, November 15, 1987.

68. Ziegler, "UCPD Officer Recognized as One of Nation's Finest."

69. Nancy Reed, "8 UCLA Employees Arrested as Suspects in Drug Sales," *San Pedro (CA) News-Pilot*, January 17, 1989; Eugene Ahn, "UCLA Employees Arrested during Campus Drug Bust," *Daily Bruin*, June 26, 1989.

70. Terrence Duren, *University Sheepdog in Westwood, L.A.* (Page Publishing, 2017), 211–12.

71. J. Jioni Palmer, "Crime's Worst Enemy: Police Chief Captains a Tight Ship on Campus," *Daily Bruin*, September 22–25, 1997.

72. Eugene Ahn, "Into the Dark: University Police Sport New Navy-Colored Uniforms," *Daily Bruin*, August 10, 1989; Eugene Ahn, "Into the Dark: Blue Uniforms Add to Respect," *Daily Bruin*, September 25–28, 1989.

73. Brian Bossert, "Dog Ensures Residence Hall Safety," *Daily Bruin*, August 13, 1987.

74. Janet Rae-Dupree, "Area Police Drug Team Spreads Its Net Wider," *Los Angeles Times*, July 6, 1990.

75. Josh Romonek, "Six Police Officers Get the Ax," *Daily Bruin*, August 10, 1992; Kenneth Secskes, "UC Police Join Los Angeles Narcotics Squad," *Daily Bruin*, July 16, 1990.

76. Janet Rae-Dupree, "Area Police Drug Team Spreads Its Net Wider."

77. Janet Rae-Dupree, "Sylmar Drug Haul Is 3rd Largest in U.S. History," *Los Angeles Times*, Valley ed. July 27, 1990.

78. Rae-Dupree, "Area Police Drug Team Spreads Its Net Wider."

79. Romonek, "Six Police Officers Get the Ax."

80. Andrew Guerrero, Ary Sanchez-Amaya, Michelle Servin, Jai'Myah Henderson, Humberto Flores, and Moe Miller, *Policing UCLA: UCLA PD Arrests (2013–2018). No UCPD Coalition & The Million Dollar Hoods Project*, www.dropbox.com/s/2ruvr7al 62eyksa/Policing%20UCLA%20-%20No%20UCPD%20Coalition%20Report.pdf?dl=0.

PART III
CURRENT ISSUES IN CAMPUS POLICING

9

"YOU'RE NOT EVEN IN THE UNITED STATES. YOU'RE IN GEORGIA TECH."

Campus Police, Urban Governance, and the Creation of the Client-Student

STEPHEN AVERILL SHERMAN

On a fall afternoon in 2017 at the Georgia Tech campus, I met Mathilde, an undergraduate engineering student.[1] Mathilde was probably the most perceptive student I interviewed for a project I was conducting on policing and near-campus planning at Georgia Tech and Georgia State University (GSU). Prior to my asking her questions at our first interview, she asked me how a recent campus police shooting had changed my research.

On September 16, 2017, a few weeks after starting my research, a Georgia Tech Police Department (GTPD) officer fatally shot a student named Scout Schultz. Scout was in the middle of a mental health crisis and holding a pocket knife as they approached Officer Tyler Beck, who fired the deadly shots.

Like the thousands of other international students coming to US universities, Mathilde had to make sense of local police and university police. She wrestled with the idea that her campus police both go to great lengths to present themselves as friendly to students yet may also shoot and kill students. Campus police host orientations about personal safety, sometimes scaring students in the process, yet some of these students (like Mathilde) come from cities or countries with far more violent crime, or places where police more openly participate in organized crime.

Mathilde's process of acculturation into US university life is extremely common. In 2019, about 25 percent and 6 percent of Georgia Tech and Georgia State

University students were legally classified as "nonresident aliens," respectively. These percentages do not include the thousands of US nationals and in-state students who move to an urban campus and must also acclimate to a new environment. They also must make decisions about their personal safety while considering the role of campus police in their new communities. Only one of the forty-five students in my research at Georgia Tech and GSU was from Atlanta proper. What expectations of benefits and rights do these new Atlanta residents have as students? Does their relatively privileged status mean that they expect campus police will work at their behest?

Central to these questions is the concept of *citizenship*, as each question focuses on the claims to rights that students make, and the rights they expect from the state, or in this case their public universities.[2] Mathilde's experience illustrates three common themes within the literature on citizenship and policing: differential citizenship under neoliberalism, border policing, and citizenship as claims-making.

Mathilde was a "nonresident alien" undergrad at Georgia Tech. She was aware of how policing was different for Georgia Tech students relative to other Atlantans and keen to the ways students learned to expect specific benefits from "their" police. Mathilde grew up in a city in the Global South known for large-scale violence. So, when moving to Atlanta, she was surprised to hear her peers and the GTPD talk about Atlanta, a major US metro center, as a dangerous place. She recognized that students' fear of Atlanta contributed to undergrads living in a campus "bubble" and seeing themselves as separate from the rest of the city despite living essentially in the city center.

In a recent publication, I relate a vivid quote from Mathilde that clarifies how she saw policing at Georgia Tech relative to the rest of Atlanta, and how her ability to defer crisis judgments on the Georgia Tech campus shaped how she lived in the United States.[3] During our interview Mathilde spoke of her decision not to call 911 after finding an alcohol-poisoned and very ill peer on the dorm bathroom floor. She instead contacted local residence hall staff, who then contacted GTPD: "For me, I feel like it has to do with the whole bubble thing. I never even consider 911 as an option [because I am from a country where 911 does not exist]. Because at some point you're not in Atlanta. You're not even in the United States. You're in Georgia Tech. . . . It's kind of amazing how just going one block from here can change your whole outlook on the world." In this quote Mathilde makes explicit a sentiment I found to be common among not only international students but students more broadly. Students at both campuses, to varying extents investigated in this chapter, believed that being university students gave them a certain "protected" status. Students felt like they had different rights outside of campus. On and off campus, different agencies mediated their attempts to invoke state power.[4] Students saw their tuition payments as a fee-for-service exchange that led to their possessing a unique bundle of rights and entitled them to make claims about how public safety and policing *should* occur for them. A coordinated group of agencies, including campus police but also counselors, residence hall staff, and others, performed public safety labor for tuition-paying students like Mathilde's drunk dorm mate. However, Georgia Tech's student body is significantly wealthier and whiter than GSU's, which was paralleled in the demographics of this study's research sample;[5] this affected how students made claims to police. University police mediate students' geographies;[6] they shape the appeals students make to the state and the political rights students expect. In short, university police mediate citizenship and belonging in a US global city.

I aim for this chapter to be a provocation for scholars of policing to consider campus police as crucial not only to the fields of policing or US higher education but also to larger questions about citizenship and urban governance in contemporary cities. The rest of the chapter explores how campus police in the United States complicate, complement, and relate to larger debates about citizenship. I will introduce my broader project and reflect on methods before framing the specific theoretical understandings of citizenship and showing how my project sheds new light on these debates.

A NOTE ON METHODS

I am an urban planner. As part of my broader agenda, I research the economic and urbanization impacts of "eds and meds," the large not-for-profit hospitals and universities that often anchor regional economies.[7] Although an "eds and meds" economic development strategy is often associated with Rust Belt cities like Pittsburgh, where the University of Pittsburgh Medical Center became the largest employer after steel industry employment contracted, even Sun Belt regions like Greater Dallas–Fort Worth or Houston have major university systems or hospitals that are among the area's largest employers.

Unlike other major employers, urban universities and major hospitals have their own police forces.[8] This fact seems important. Yet in multiple scholarly accounts of university-based development and expansion found in my home discipline, it seemed police and public safety were broached but not elaborated upon.[9] News stories highlighted instances of racist university police abuse and painted university police as sentries guarding universities from intrusions by nonwhite neighborhood residents.[10] While this portrait of university police as sentries at the watchtower felt important, it was also incomplete. My own research on the University of Chicago's police, and that of historian Arnold Hirsch, suggested that urban university police acted as de facto care workers for anxious white neighborhood residents, university administrators, and students.[11] University police work is not just territorial but also performative and psychological;[12] officers' presence may signal to white people that an area is safe for property investment and development, and property investment and development are important things for an urban planner to research. Hence, the project I conducted in Atlanta.

To understand the performative and psychological aspects of university policing, I employed a qualitative research design that employed a mobile Geographic Information Systems (GIS) approach with students from Georgia Tech and GSU. Throughout the 2017–18 academic year, I flyered the university campuses in order to recruit forty-five students for two one-hour interviews. These interviews bookended a one-week period when students, using a smartphone app that tracked their movements, kept geo-logged textual and photographic notes on their impressions of policing during their campus lives. For their participation the students received fifty dollars. These notes and geo-logged waypoints informed our second interactional interview, as the data rested on the screen between us.[13] This adaptation of Kwan and Ding's geo-narrative approach centered both students' personal histories and the role of the police in their day-to-day lives as they moved on and off campus, though in the case of the Georgia Tech sample it was almost entirely "on campus."[14]

The two schools, located only 1.5 miles away from each other, are a rich two-case study on policing and urban development. While both are public "R1" research universities, Georgia Tech is located north of downtown in the Midtown neighborhood, a de facto second city center. Its campus has lawns and quadrangles, historical buildings, and manicured greenspaces. In contrast, GSU is a school with a plurality Black student body sited largely in repurposed office buildings in the heart of downtown Atlanta. GSU's campus is downtown. It includes many nonuniversity workers from nearby office buildings, tourists, and people experiencing homelessness, whereas Georgia Tech's campus is sequestered by major highways and thoroughfares in Atlanta's prosperous Midtown neighborhood. GSU graduates more Black bachelor's degree students than any major

DEMOGRAPHIC INFORMATION OF INTERVIEWEES

	Georgia Tech	Georgia State	Total
Total	25	20	45
Male	13	8	21
Female	12	12	24
White	11	5	16
Black	4	11	15
Latino	2	1	3
Asian	6	2	8
Mixed-race	2	1	3
US national	20	16	36
Foreign	5	4	9
Grad	8	3	11
Undergrad	17	17	34
Atlanta metro native	10	14	24

research university in the country, whereas Georgia Tech is a predominantly white, STEM-focused university which recruits students from a larger geography. I purposely replicated these universities' race and domestic/international demographics in my samples.[15]

Each university also employs its own fully sworn, fully armed police force of around seventy officers who have full arrest powers within five hundred yards of university property, per Georgia law. The police patrol a student body made up of different types of students, coming from different places, which, as I argue here, informs the type of claims students make to state power.

BRIEF PRIMER ON CITIZENSHIP: RIGHTS, BENEFITS, AND BORDERS

The neoliberal turn in Western governance has brought with it changes to how we understand citizenship. Central to this are the police. In searching for "actually existing neoliberalism," scholarly attention turns to the punitive rollout of new and violent forms of policing, securitization, and surveillance.[16] The focus is usually on private security, and the private forces securing elite spaces of consumption like downtown business districts, amusement parks, or shopping malls.[17] This private policing is reserved for fee-paying clients in these wealthier spaces. The neoliberal rollout of punitive policing extends to the public sphere, too, particularly in the excessive, revanchist disciplining of the urban poor and others left behind in the current economic order.[18] (Much of the recent critique on citizenship and policing has emerged from scholars of the Global South, despite [I argue] its application in Global North metro centers like Atlanta.[19]) The police response to claims of citizenship from below is often violent and results in criminalizing entire communities in the punitive neoliberal rollout.[20] Police and security agencies restructure cities with walls, CCTV, and "smart city" surveillance to contain these claims of rights and benefits from the urban margins.[21]

For migrants in these spaces, this may entail a "borderland condition" of migrants being at the whim of exceptional state power, where even in nonborder spaces migrants are subjected to a unique legal regime of enhanced surveillance and detention.[22] As a rejoinder to this condition, Monica Varsanyi proposed the idea of "unbounded" citizenship, that a person could obtain citizenship rights and protection from these legal regimes merely through residence in a city.[23] Varsanyi's point summarizes a major theme across scholarship, emphasizing how the question of citizenship is "rescaled" down from the nation state onto smaller scales.[24] Among these scales can be states, cities, and, for the purposes of this book chapter, urban university campuses.

GEORGIA TECH, GSU, AND POLICING THE NEOLIBERAL URBAN UNIVERSITY

The practice of policing at Georgia Tech and GSU resonates with certain insights about policing in neoliberal urban spaces. Within the context of campus policing at my field sites, two phenomena relate to this change of governance and citizenship: the extent to which policing is both a *differentiated public service* for fee-paying clients, and the extent to which policing is a *participatory governance activity.*[25]

Unlike the private security centered in many critiques of policing as a differentiated public service, campus police are usually public sector employees. In the United States, public universities' enrollments are exponentially larger than private universities'; the University of Central Florida alone enrolls about as many undergraduates as the entire Ivy League. It follows that most campus police are public sector, as noted in this volume's introduction. According to Bureau of Justice Statistics research of campus police at institutions enrolling more than 2,500 students during the 2011–12 academic year, there were more than three times as many public sworn campus police than private (11,248 sworn officers at public institutions versus 3,328 at private institutions).[26] This entails that campus police have close connections to "traditional" public police organizations. At Georgia Tech and GSU, the police went through the public police academy. Many department members, from the chiefs to entry-level patrol police, had served in nearby municipalities. The GSUPD chief during my research had most recently served as a zone commander (akin to a precinct chief) for the Atlanta police, while the GTPD chief had served in leadership positions in other public departments.

Students within the geo-narrative research recognized that policing was "different" for them, as a result of their status as fee-paying clients at a public university. The state has downloaded state-like functions onto smaller scales, like university communities, leading to different populations having different benefits from the state.

At both universities, students believed these campus police would be more lenient than the municipal police, though with notable differences across the two campuses. Participants frequently noted the campus police's public relations work and very visible acts of caretaking. "They're trying to [be] visible as really nice guys," said Anna, a Georgia Tech grad student, citing how GTPD officers sometimes give rides home to drunk students. "They're cops, and everyone's wary of cops. . . . But [the GTPD] have a snapchat. They want to be hip. They're trying to be nice," said a Georgia Tech undergrad. Yet within my sample of GSU students, a majority (17 of 20) cited previous negative experiences with law enforcement from any department. A few (4) had been arrested or received criminal citation, whereas no Georgia Tech student cited prior arrest, and far fewer cited poor prior experiences (9 of 25). Of those 4 at GSU with criminal sanctions, 3 were cited on campus for underage drinking or marijuana use by the GSUPD. Meanwhile, no

Georgia Tech student cited an arrest or sanction for drugs or alcohol. A Georgia Tech student cited a cop neglecting to sanction him for public alcohol consumption, instead asking the underage student to dump out his drink.

Yet even at GSU, there was a widespread belief that the university police were more deferential and friendlier than the Atlanta police or members of other municipal forces. "Cops are cops," to quote multiple students, but the GSUPD were generally seen as more benign than the Atlanta police. The police on campus seemed aware of students' criticisms toward them. Notably, in my interview with then-GSUPD chief John Spillane, he wore a suit and tie, because he was coming from teaching a class and preferred to teach while not in uniform, as he realized that students would find it intimidating. During the citizens police academy at Georgia Tech that I attended, officers were always either in uniform or in GTPD-branded clothing.

While university policing represents not only the segmentation of public services and public utilities, it also follows another trend in contemporary neoliberal governance: *citizen participation* in public service delivery.[27] As Mathilde's case made clear, nonpolice university staff in residence life, counseling, and other student service departments have a direct line to the university police. GTPD also employs multiple students to help monitor other students' social media, something which became particularly salient following Scout Schultz's death.[28] Students also help the police through capstones, research, internships, and other for-credit projects. Research on the coproduction of public safety between students and campus police does not account for situations when "student citizens" design police technologies.[29]

Georgia Tech is one of the country's most prestigious engineering-focused universities, and GTPD leadership proudly draws on the intellectual resources of the student body to develop new policing technologies, a point they emphasized during the citizens police academy. For example, Georgia Tech seniors, for their capstones, proposed a redesign of the new GTPD headquarters. Georgia Tech students have programmed crime mapping applications for the police and designed a system for logging drone flights around campus.[30] GTPD has sponsored "Living Learning Labs" projects to develop an "internet accessible platform to display cameras, patrol car locations, calls for service, and building floorplans to improve GTPD's situational awareness," which they then implemented at their headquarters.[31] My research at GSU did not yield any information about students performing intellectual labor for police, either because of lack of interest from both the police and students, or fewer STEM students from whom police could draw expertise.

BORDERS, MIGRANTS, AND CAMPUS COPS

What to make of international students, who are far more privileged than the type of migrants discussed in most critical social science literature on citizenship? What lessons from Georgia Tech and GSU may apply here, and how can a focus on university policing broaden these debates on migration, citizenship, and policing?

Universities may be one "rescaled" site where citizenship rights emerge. As tuition-paying residents of a university community, international students have healthcare and counseling benefits through student health, benefits which nonstudent US citizens do not have. They also are protected by a police force (ostensibly) focused on their unique needs. It is a funhouse-mirror distortion of the sort of "unbounded" citizenship proposed by Varsanyi, as through mere residence in a university community international students have certain rights, provided they can pay tuition.[32]

"Nonresident alien" students with F visas face the threat of deportation if they lose their student status or are charged with a serious crime. They are under a digital surveillance regime, in which registrations, address change notices, and other bureaucratic-surveillance tactics are a matter of course. The border goes from being a geographic line to something negotiated through university administrative offices.[33] Both schools in the sample enroll thousands of international students, with Georgia Tech enrolling a larger share. Within my research, 9 of 45 subjects were international students.

One student's (Karl) geo-narrative presents a case of how, even though they live under heightened scrutiny, international students may still expect the sort of curative, deferential policing that domestic students at Georgia Tech expect from campus police. Like many international students, Karl was from an upper-class household in the Global South. He told me that the fifty-dollar research participant stipend I paid him was the first time in his life he had earned his own money. He enjoyed smoking marijuana and drinking alcohol and chose to do these illegal activities on campus because he felt that GTPD were less likely to legally sanction him and threaten deportation. When he sent me his geo-logged information prior to his second interview, I noticed he made multiple visits to a forested area of the Georgia Tech campus.[34] I asked him why he went there, and he said that he chose to smoke marijuana on campus because he felt that if he were caught, the GTPD would not legally sanction him, whereas the Atlanta police would. "I don't fuck with the APD," was how he bluntly explained his choice. "When it comes to things that are illegal on campus . . . well, *there's that one shooting* [emphasis added], but I haven't heard about the campus police arresting people. They're there to keep decorum on campus. Assisting us in our daily lives." Like domestic students at Georgia Tech, the comparatively privileged university, he did not expect police to sanction him.

Other international students saw the campus police's added security as a benefit. Two Chinese students sampled cited how Chinese media closely covers crime in the United States, particularly crimes against Chinese students attending US universities, and that they themselves harbored worries about attending school in a large city like Atlanta. Speaking frankly during our interviews, one Georgia Tech graduate student and one Georgia State undergraduate from China both shared that they harbored worries attending school in a predominantly Black city like Atlanta (and at a predominantly Black university like GSU), given how both the Chinese and US media promote stereotypes about Black Americans being prone to violence. And their fears were assuaged by the large police presence they encountered on their campuses. I do not and will not generalize from this small sample, but it remains a point to explore how the university police work with and through these racist crime fears with their large international student bodies.

Perceived benefits like added security, or deferential policing, have an ambivalence for international students given their precarious immigration status and additional geopolitical factors. Chinese and Middle Eastern students in the United States have been subject to increased surveillance and spying.[35] No student in my sample reported additional state surveillance from US intelligence agencies, but I would not have expected them to honestly disclose this given that I was a white male stranger. Georgia Tech in particular has been the site of controversies surrounding accusations of Chinese student and faculty spying. In 2020, then secretary of state Mike Pompeo gave a jingoistic speech at the Georgia Tech campus, focusing on the alleged security threats of Chinese scholars in US universities.[36] No cabinet member felt compelled to give such a jingoistic speech at GSU, a non-STEM-focused university with a larger domestic and nonwhite student body.

There were only two Black international students in my 45-student sample, both from majority Black countries and one each enrolled at Georgia Tech and GSU. They both commented on the university police's diligence and care toward students at their respective campuses. One student noted how police offered rides to students late at night; however, both noted how news stories about racist policing in the United States led them to be cautious around officers. Again, this is too small a sample from which to generalize, but the case of Kofi

Adu-Brempong at the University of Florida, who was nonfatally shot by police officers there during a mental health crisis, brings to light how Black international students have unique challenges: their skin color may make them more prone to negative police attention, while they simultaneously have less experience with the customs and norms through which African Americans navigate encounters with the US police.[37]

A focus on university policing brings to light how policing migrants and borders involves not only regulating and sequestering poorer migrants but also managing relatively privileged international migrants at universities. They may receive deference but also surveillance. Focusing on punitive state power and extralegal detention within border and migrant policing, as has largely been the focus on research on borders and citizenship, may lead to scholars neglecting the ways that police, particularly university police, treat international students as protected citizen-subjects even as they receive additional surveillance from both university administrators and federal police agencies. Given that university administrators must approve all F visas, the role of policing international students is largely descaled from the nation-state to the university itself.[38] These additional agencies create additional tensions, leading to potential contradictions and paradoxes ripe for future research.

Although my research largely did not address intelligence and border policing, it did suggest that "international students" do not constitute a monolithic category and do not have a singular response to campus police. Students like Karl, when on campus, felt empowered to enjoy illegal drugs without sanction and possible deportation, whereas other international (and domestic) students saw the campus police as a bulwark against off-campus crime, falling back on racist anti-Black stereotypes in the process. Black international students had to learn strategies for not attracting police attention on the fly. Future research into international students and campus policing should note how the international diversity of US research universities means that there may also be diverse responses to campus police. The "benefits" of police services flow unevenly across a community.

MAKING CLAIMS OF STUDENTHOOD AFTER A POLICE KILLING

I want to conclude this chapter by emphasizing a theme—the "practice" of citizenship through making public claims of rights—as seen in light of the murder of Scout Schultz.[39]

After Officer Beck killed Scout, there were two notable gatherings: a small informal vigil near the murder site the day after their death, and a larger, university-sanctioned memorial the day after that. While the smaller Sunday event featured only a few mourners, the larger gathering on Monday was followed by a march to the GTPD station and a confrontation with officers in which someone set a cop car on fire and at least one officer suffered a head injury.[40] (I could not locate media stories of protestor injuries, though at least three were arrested that day.) During that protest, students received multiple text alerts telling them to stay away from windows and take shelter. I attended the vigil and protest at the GTPD station and interviewed students watching from the side. During one interview recording, one can hear explosions roughly twenty yards away, while the student I was interviewing shared stories about police being nice to him even as we watched a police car explode and burn.

In the days after the protests, students taped large signs reading "I [HEART] GTPD" across multiple dorm windows and wrote similar messages in sidewalk chalk around campus. As I attempted to solicit geo-narrative research subjects with flyers, I was competing for bulletin board space with an array of flyers, some in favor of defunding the GTPD and others thanking them for their service. Some students verbally thanked the GTPD even after an officer had shot and killed a peer of theirs. One geo-narrative subject admitted to this. I tried to imagine how a friend of Scout's would feel seeing "THANK YOU GTPD" scribbled in chalk on a sidewalk. GTPD officers themselves seemed wary of these gestures and asked students to remove these messages.

This student support for the GTPD spoke to the extent to which many students expected GTPD to work at their behest. They were "their" police. As I changed my interview schedule to address Scout's death and the campus-wide emergency after the protest, a recurring statement emerged. "It's a student [who was shot]," as if fatal police shootings happened in communities not like Georgia Tech. Underlying this logic is students having the expectation of benefits, which they earn through tuition payments, good academic standing, or other demographic factors.[41] Because GSUPD did not murder a student during my time there, I did not hear statements about GSU students' shock at a police murder. They largely seemed resigned to that sad reality: "Cops are cops." Notably, at least three people arrested during and after the protests at Georgia Tech were GSU students, one of whom took their own life shortly thereafter.[42]

These claims of studenthood, and studenthood leading to the expectation of certain rights and benefits, were not at the center of the protest against GTPD. At least according to the signs and chants, the protest centered on abolishing GTPD and/or protecting LGBT+ students.

There are two sets of claims being made. First, privately, students like those I talked to watching the protest and most geo-narrative participants made claims that their student status should lead to the benefits of deferential and curative policing. Second, publicly, protestors claimed that the police must be abolished and centered the importance of LGBT+ student health. When analyzing citizenship claims, one can examine how the state or state agencies, like police, respond to these claims.[43] In this case, the claims for abolition were met with university police violence, whereas private claims of privileged studenthood went unchallenged and were even perhaps affirmed. The university bolstered its mental health resources and some LGBT+ student resources after Scout's murder. One subject noted that, when she went to the student health office for a sickness after Scout's murder, her check-in questionnaire included an array of questions about her mental health. Across geo-narrative interviews, students continued to still see GTPD's work as deferential and curative, and as a bulwark against "people from Atlanta" (to repeat a phrase three students used), while dismissing Scout's death as "suicide by cop." The officer who shot Scout Schultz eventually returned to work.

A NOTE ABOUT PROVINCIALIZING FINDINGS

When you're on campus, you're not *really* in the United States: you have earned or paid for membership into a political community onto which many state-like activities—such healthcare, housing, and policing—have been rescaled. "Citizenship" at an urban university in a global city leads to specific rights, and the university police play a role in brokering these rights. University police are tasked with policing a certain substratum of urban residents who largely (though not entirely) expect police care, and who are seen as essential to urban "regeneration" policies. They are a protected class, yet this protection is uneven. Scout Schultz's murder and its aftermath is the cruelest reminder of this fact. Campus police services have unforeseen negative effects even for this "protected class."

Students make claims for different rights. They make claims for curative policing, or LGBT+ services, or police abolition, or additional security. As this study shows, the nature of these students' citizenship claims and expectations changes across and within campuses, and they meet different police responses. The expectation of the "benefit" of police also changed across campuses, and for different students depending on their country of nationality, race, and other factors. Most students expected deference, but this was not uniformly true. If the contemporary global, neoliberal urban university employs police to protect its students or its reputation, a careful study of these police through the lens of citizenship shows a clear finding: much like the benefits of traditional citizenship granted by nation-states, the "benefits" of university policing flow unevenly to the campus's student-citizens.

NOTES

1. All subject names presented in this chapter are pseudonyms, and I omit any potentially identifying information.

2. James Holston, "Contesting Privilege with Right: The Transformation of Differentiated Citizenship in Brazil," *Citizenship Studies* 15, no. 3–4 (June 1, 2011): 335–52, https://doi.org/10.1080/13621025.2011.565157.

3. Stephen Averill Sherman, "Where Are the Police in Urban Governance? Three Investigations of Police, Planning, and Governance in Central Atlanta," *Journal of Urban Affairs* (October 28, 2022): 1–16, https://doi.org/10.1080/07352166.2022.2115376.

4. Jeffrey T. Martin, "Calling the Police, More or Less Democratically," *Theoretical Criminology* 20, no. 4 (November 1, 2016): 462–81, https://doi.org/10.1177/1362480616659808.

5. See also Stephen Averill Sherman, "Policing the Campus: Police Communications and Near-Campus Development across Atlanta's University Communities," *Planning Theory & Practice* 23, no. 3 (March 29, 2022): 1–20, https://doi.org/10.1080/14649357.2022.2050281.

6. Mark Holton, "'I Already Know the City, I Don't Have to Explore It': Adjustments to 'Sense of Place' for 'Local' UK University Students," *Population, Space and Place* 21, no. 8 (2015): 820–31, https://doi.org/10.1002/psp.1866.

7. Carolyn Adams, "The Meds and Eds in Urban Economic Development," *Journal of Urban Affairs* 25, no. 5 (December 1, 2003): 571–88, https://doi.org/10.1111/j.1467-9906.2003.00003.x; Ira Harkavy and Harmon Zuckerman, "Eds and Meds: Cities Hidden Assets" (Washington, DC: Brookings, 1999), www.brookings.edu/research/reports/1999/09/community-development-harkavy-zuckerman.

8. Note that many major hospitals are university affiliated and have their own police. For example, the Emory University Hospital in downtown Atlanta is patrolled by the university's police.

9. See, for example, *Pushing Back the Gates: Neighborhood Perspectives on University-Driven Revitalization in West Philadelphia* (Philadelphia: Temple University

Press, 2012) on the University of Pennsylvania's recent efforts in West Philadelphia; or "Defining University Anchor Institution Strategies: Comparing Theory to Practice," *Planning Theory & Practice* 19, no. 1 (January 1, 2018): 74–92, https://doi.org/10.1080/14649357.2017.1406980.

10. Jonah Newman, "New Data Supports Old Accusations of Racial Profiling by University of Chicago Police Department," April 5, 2016, http://chicagoreporter.com/new-data-supports-old-accusations-of-racial-profiling-by-university-of-chicago-police-department/.

11. Stephen Averill Sherman, "From Revanchism to Inclusion: Institutional Forms of Planning and Police in Hyde Park, Chicago," *Journal of Planning Education and Research* 40, no. 2 (June 1, 2020): 139–50, https://doi.org/10.1177/0739456X19877683; Arnold R. Hirsch, *Making the Second Ghetto* (Chicago: University of Chicago Press, 1998).

12. Peter K Manning, "The Police: Mandate, Strategies, and Appearances," *Policing: A View from the Street* (Santa Monica, CA: Goodyear, 1978), 7–31.

13. Catherine Kohler Riessman, *Narrative Analysis*, Qualitative Research Methods series, no. 30 (Newbury Park, CA: Sage, 1993).

14. "Geo-Narrative: Extending Geographic Information Systems for Narrative Analysis in Qualitative and Mixed-Method Research," *Professional Geographer* 60, no. 4 (September 16, 2008): 443–65, https://doi.org/10.1080/00330120802211752.

15. Richard Fausset, "Georgia State, Leading U.S. in Black Graduates, Is Engine of Social Mobility," *New York Times*, May 15, 2018.

16. Neil Brenner and Nik Theodore, "Cities and the Geographies of 'Actually Existing Neoliberalism,'" in *Spaces of Neoliberalism: Urban Restructuring in North America and Western Europe*, ed. Brenner and Theodore, Antipode series (Malden, MA: Wiley-Blackwell, 2003), 2–32.

17. Faranak Miraftab, "Governing Post-Apartheid Spatiality: Implementing City Improvement Districts in Cape Town," *Antipode* 39, no. 4 (September 1, 2007): 602–26, https://doi.org/10.1111/j.1467-8330.2007.00543.x; Kevin Ward, "Business Improvement Districts: Policy Origins, Mobile Policies and Urban Liveability," *Geography Compass* 1, no. 3 (2007): 657–72, https://doi.org/10.1111/j.1749-8198.2007.00022.x.

18. Joe Soss, Richard C Fording, and Sanford Schram, *Disciplining the Poor* (Chicago: University of Chicago Press, 2011), www.press.uchicago.edu/ucp/books/book/chicago/D/bo12120768.html.

19. Anna Gawlewicz and Oren Yiftachel, "'Throwntogetherness' in Hostile Environments," *City* 26, no. 2–3 (April 20, 2022): 1–13, https://doi.org/10.1080/13604813.2022.2056350; James Holston, *Cities and Citizenship* (Durham, NC: Duke University Press, 1999).

20. Monica W. Varsanyi, "Interrogating 'Urban Citizenship' Vis-à-Vis Undocumented Migration," *Citizenship Studies*, August 22, 2006, https://doi.org/10.1080/13621020600633168.

21. Teresa P. R. Caldeira, *City of Walls: Crime, Segregation, and Citizenship in São Paulo* (Berkeley: University of California Press, 2001).

22. Gilberto Rosas, "The Thickening Borderlands: Diffused Exceptionality and 'Immigrant' Social Struggles during the 'War on Terror,'" *Cultural Dynamics* 18, no. 3 (November 1, 2006): 335–49, https://doi.org/10.1177/0921374006071618; Alison Mountz et al., "Conceptualizing Detention Mobility, Containment, Bordering, and Exclusion," *Progress in Human Geography* 37, no. 4 (August 1, 2013): 522–41, https://doi.org/10.1177/0309132512460903; Daniel Gonzalez, "Logistical Borderlands: Latinx Migrant Labor in the Information Age," *Society & Space*, April 12, 2019, www.societyandspace.org/articles/logistical-borderlands-latinx-migrant-labor-in-the-information-age.

23. Varsanyi, "Interrogating 'Urban Citizenship' Vis-à-Vis Undocumented Migration."

24. Neil Brenner, "Open Questions on State Rescaling," *Cambridge Journal of Regions, Economy and Society* 2, no. 1 (March 1, 2009): 123–39, https://doi.org/10.1093/cjres/rsp002.

25. Robert W. Lake and Kathe Newman, "Differential Citizenship in the Shadow State," *GeoJournal* 58, no. 2 (2002): 109–20, https://doi.org/10.1023/B:GEJO.0000010830.94036.6c; Faranak Miraftab, "Public-Private Partnerships: The Trojan Horse of Neoliberal Development?," *Journal of Planning Education and Research* 24, no. 1 (September 1, 2004): 89–101, https://doi.org/10.1177/0739456X04267173.

26. Brian A. Reaves, "Campus Law Enforcement, 2011–2012" (Washington, DC: Bureau of Justice Statistics, January 2015), www.bjs.gov/content/pub/pdf/cle1112.pdf.

27. Elisabet Van Wymeersch, Stijn Oosterlynck, and Thomas Vanoutrive, "The Political Ambivalences of Participatory Planning Initiatives," *Planning Theory*, November 30, 2018, https://doi.org/10.1177/1473095218812514.

28. Hallie Lieberman, "The Trigger Effect," *Atavist Magazine*, August 29, 2018, https://magazine.atavist.com/the-trigger-effect-scout-schultz-georgia-tech.

29. Brian N. Williams et al., "The Co-Production of Campus Safety and Security: A Case Study at the University of Georgia," *International Review of Administrative Sciences* 82, no. 1 (March 1, 2016): 110–30, https://doi.org/10.1177/0020852315573157.

30. "2018 CoC Junior Design Capstone Expo—Team Icarus," accessed May 5, 2022, www.facebook.com/watch/?v=10156358799249579.

31. "Browse Living Learning Labs Projects | Administration and Finance," accessed May 5, 2022, https://af.gatech.edu/browse-living-learning-labs-projects.

32. Varsanyi, "Interrogating 'Urban Citizenship' Vis-à-Vis Undocumented Migration."

33. Abigail Boggs, "On Borders and Academic Freedom: Noncitizen Students and the Limits of Rights," *Journal of Academic Freedom* 11 (2020), www.aaup.org/JAF11/borders-and-academic-freedom-noncitizen-students-and-limits-rights.

34. In the interest of not "snitching" on my subjects, plus IRB concerns about privacy and sharing information that could identify a subject, I refrain from sharing an image of this map.

35. See Gideon Lewis-Kraus, "Have Chinese Spies Infiltrated American Campuses?," *New Yorker*, March 14, 2022, www.newyorker.com/magazine/2022/03/21/have-chinese-spies-infiltrated-american-campuses.

36. Trevor Williams, "Pompeo Warns of Chinese Influence on U.S. Campuses in Georgia Tech Speech," December 11, 2020, www.globalatlanta.com/pompeo-warns-of-chinese-influence-on-u-s-campuses-in-georgia-tech-speech/.

37. See Nathan Crabbe, "Two Years after Being Shot, UF Grad Student Still Undergoing Treatment," *Gainesville Sun*, March 1, 2012, www.gainesville.com/story/news/local/2012/03/01/two-years-after-being-shot/31831791007/.

38. Boggs, "On Borders and Academic Freedom."

39. Irene Bloemraad, "Theorising the Power of Citizenship as Claims-Making," *Journal of Ethnic and Migration Studies* 44, no. 1 (January 2, 2018): 4–26, https://doi.org/10.1080/1369183X.2018.1396108; Bloemraad, "Theorizing and Analyzing Citizenship in Multicultural Societies," Sociological Quarterly 44, no. 4 (Fall 2015): 591–606, https://doi.org/10.1111/tsq.12095.

40. For an excellent summary of the aftermath of Scout's death, see Lieberman, "The Trigger Effect."

41. On property and the expectation of benefits, see Cheryl I. Harris, "Whiteness as Property," *Harvard Law Review* 106, no. 8 (1993): 1707–91, https://doi.org/10.2307/1341787.

42. I very strongly recommend Lieberman's "The Trigger Effect" for a lengthy retelling of the tragic aftermath of Scout's murder.

43. Bloemraad, "Theorising the Power of Citizenship as Claims-Making."

10

UNCOVERING THE RACIAL POWER OF CAMPUS POLICE

JUDE PAUL MATIAS DIZON

Following the murder of George Floyd by a Minneapolis police officer, Jael Kerandi, a Black college undergraduate woman, was among the first to respond. Kerandi's widely circulated open letter—first posted on Twitter—addressed the leadership of the University of Minnesota, where she was enrolled and serving as student body president. Kerandi demanded that the university end its partnership with the Minneapolis Police Department. The letter called for the university to align its actions with its purported values: "As a land-grant institution, statements professing appreciation of diversity and inclusion are empty and worthless if they are not backed up by action." President Joan Gabel conceded to the demands a day later. Kerandi's letter and the university's actions reinforced the urgency of confronting problematic police department.[1] At the same time, the response, which gained national prominence, placed a spotlight on the role of higher education in perpetuating racist policing.

Prior to 2020, Black and racially minoritized college students had begun analyzing how campus police shape the racial climate of college and university campuses. For example, in the fall of 2015, Black student demands from eighty-six postsecondary institutions included several reforms intended to address hostile campus environments resulting from repeated experiences of racial profiling and oversurveillance by campus police.[2] Since George Floyd's murder, college students and faculty members have responded to racist police violence on dual fronts by mobilizing to abolish municipal law enforcement *and* campus police departments. At the University of California, Los Angeles (UCLA), students and faculty demanded that the university end its partnership with the Los Angeles Police Department, defund the University of California Police Department (UCPD), and be fully transparent regarding UCPD staffing, funding, and activities.

A faculty letter specified that UCPD funds be directed toward justice-oriented curriculum, community engagement, and material support for Black students, faculty, and staff.[3] Similar efforts from across the United States resulted in the creation of the Cops Off Campus Coalition, which is committed to campus police abolition, decolonization, and community-centered well-being.[4]

Postsecondary administrators and state/federal policymakers have been ill-equipped to respond to these demands for change. Further, activist student and faculty analysis of the racialized aspects of campus policing has far outpaced similar analysis by scholars in criminology/criminal justice and higher education. Additionally, unlike their municipal counterparts, campus police have largely evaded public scrutiny and critical scholarly attention. Due to the educational setting in which they work, coupled with legal mandates relating to campus safety such as the federal Jeanne Clery Act and student/parental fear of on-campus victimization, campus police are thought to be friendlier and more student-oriented compared to municipal police.[5] Since the initial development of modern campus police departments in the 1960s, over 90 percent of four-year postsecondary institutions enrolling at least 2,500 students now employ campus police officers.[6] The institutionalization of campus police has subjected both historically victimized students and communities to even higher levels of policing.

The purpose of this chapter is to interrupt discourse that constructs campus police as an objective and necessary presence in increasingly diverse higher education communities. Framing campus police as a unique entity tends to set it apart from the systemic racism found in the general policing apparatus.[7] In what follows, I provide a brief overview of the racist character of policing in the United States. Next, I argue that campus police are *not* distinct from their municipal counterparts, as they replicate many of the same practices and generate the same kinds of issues that lead racially minoritized communities to experience harm and injustice at the hands of police officers. Here, I discuss findings from an original three-year study of the campus police at "Adamson University," a historically white, research-intensive institution on the West Coast, along with emerging research that demonstrates how campus police operate as a racialized system of social control.

POLICING THE US RACIAL ORDER

Policing is prevalent at all levels of government in US society. Recent data indicate there are sixty-five federal law enforcement agencies and more than fifteen thousand general purpose law enforcement agencies at the state, county, and municipal levels of government that employ more than seven hundred thousand full-time sworn officers.[8] What accounts for all this policing? From a liberal perspective, policing developed as a bureaucratic professionalized service provided by the state to address crime and disorder in the interests of society.[9] Critical scholars and activists argue that the idea that policing promotes safety and security is severely flawed because it ignores the possibility that policing serves to uphold white supremacy and unequal racial relations through state-sanctioned violence.[10] The significance of race is evident when examining policing's origins and its role in helping maintain the existing social order.

Policing's racist origins are largely obscured by a narrative of liberal progress that asserts the importance of policing to uphold individual liberty and maintain order.[11] Critical scholars suggest an alternative that envisions the police as instruments used to maintain slavery and white supremacy.[12] In brief, slave codes in the colonial period empowered whites to control enslaved Africans and regulate Black life through surveillance and violence. Individual and organized patrols of whites had the discretion to use force against slaves who resisted authority and attempted escape.[13] The slave patrol origins of policing extend to the issues faced by Black communities' postslavery. Writing in 1966 about Black life in Harlem, James Baldwin asserted, "The police are simply the hired enemies of this population. They are present to keep the Negro in his place and to protect white business interests, and they have no other function." Baldwin's insights illustrate the racial terror enacted by the police and its role in reinforcing obstacles that limited Black economic and social mobility. His observations could easily describe the policing of Black and racially minoritized communities today.[14]

Persistent racism in the general policing apparatus is evident through the documentation of statistical disparities in police interactions with members of racially minoritized groups. For example, a large body of empirical evidence shows that Black drivers are stopped, searched, and arrested at much higher rates compared to white drivers.[15] Researchers have also found that Black and Latinx individuals are disproportionately targeted by stop-and-frisk tactics.[16] Relatedly, a meta-analysis of twenty-seven independent datasets indicated nonwhite individuals are more likely to be arrested than whites.[17] Racial inequalities exist at every possible stage in a police encounter including potential life-threatening outcomes. For example, Black and Latinx men have been found to face higher mortality risks during police encounters compared to whites.[18] Postarrest, over 60 percent of inmates in US prisons are members of racially minoritized communities, with Black and Latinx men incarcerated at the highest rates compared to members of all other groups.[19]

The general policing apparatus in the United States does not result in equal experiences and outcomes for racially minoritized communities. The physical and psychological harm that results from the exercise of police power attests to how policing reinforces a racial hierarchy. When police stop and search someone because they appear "out of place" or when police presence is justified because high levels of crime are expected in, and inherent to, lower-income, nonwhite neighborhoods, policing operates as a race-making institution.[20] In turning to a discussion of campus policing next, the racist character of the general police apparatus in the United States must be considered despite the dominant discourse that homogenizes the notion of campus safety.

CAMPUS POLICE AS A RACIALIZED SYSTEM OF SOCIAL CONTROL

Similar to the establishment narrative of police officers as "crime fighters who serve and protect our communities," campus police in the higher education context benefit from a positive, exalted status as defenders of student safety and overall campus well-being.[21] In light of violent crime broadly and mass shootings in particular occurring on college campuses, the presence of campus police provides the default response from administrators and policymakers when assuaging stakeholder concerns about campus safety.[22] For example, in response to a campus shooter at Northern Illinois University in 2008, the state passed the Campus Security Enhancement Act, which reinforced the role of campus police as the primary responders to hazards and violent incidents at all Illinois public higher education institutions.[23] While concerns about physical safety and potential harm are real and must be given serious consideration, the narrow view of campus police as solely law enforcement and safety providers neglects how racial inequalities abound in campus police enforcement of property borders, institutional rules, and ensuring the comfort of university stakeholders. Moreover, one argument offered by administrators to activist demands for abolition asserts that campus police officers are a better alternative for students in comparison to municipal law enforcement.[24] Abolishing campus police would therefore lead to more harm for racially minoritized students due to an increased presence of municipal police. This claim thus attempts to distinguish *campus* policing from the general policing apparatus with which it is closely intertwined.

In what follows, I share insights from a three-year study of campus police with a focus on the experiences of racially minoritized students and faculty, alongside how campus police officers perceive racial dynamics in their line of work. I argue that campus policing operates as a racialized system of social control, mirroring the systemic racism that characterizes the broader general policing apparatus in the United States.

STUDY OVERVIEW

Adamson University (AU; a pseudonym) is a historically white, research-intensive institution located on the West Coast. AU employs more than two hundred sworn and nonsworn campus police officers who enforce campus rules and partner with the municipal police department to patrol nearby off-campus neighborhoods. In the last ten years, AU has increased security measures on campus, including installing gates and a closed-circuit camera surveillance system, contracting with a private security firm for additional on-campus patrolling, and developing policies designed to restrict access to the campus and its facilities. AU was an ideal case study not only because of its extensive campus police and security infrastructure but because of its student demographics and location. At AU, Black students make up about 5 percent and Latinx students about 15 percent of the student body. Among AU students, the median family income is $161,400. In contrast, the local community surrounding AU is predominantly Black (7 percent) and Latinx (47.7 percent), and the median household income approximates $18,533. My interest was with chronicling the experiences of students, staff, and faculty who attend or work at a highly policed campus situated in a racially and socioeconomically stratified context.

The campus police at AU are advertised to incoming students and their parents as a "service." Although the university is broadly considered as a prestigious institution, the local community has long suffered from racist and classist stereotypes that depict it as crime-ridden and a threat to members of the AU community. A representative from the campus police department speaks at every new student orientation to address safety concerns and assure parents that officers work hard to protect students. AU—like other universities—presents the campus police as a "good" that equally benefits *all* students, staff, faculty, and guests. Over a three-year period (2018–21), I explored how this narrative resonated with students, staff, and faculty in interviews and focus groups I conducted. I also interviewed AU campus police officers to learn about their experiences and perceptions of the role of race in policing. The 135 people that I interviewed were racially diverse (25 percent Black; 21 percent Latinx; 23 percent Asian; 24 percent white; 6 percent multiracial) and, along with university data, afforded me insights into how racialized meanings were produced and enforced by campus police.

RACIAL DISPARITIES IN CAMPUS POLICE CONTACT

One data source I used included data on AU campus police stops that was collected by a university-appointed community advisory board (CAB). Results of the analysis revealed an overpolicing of Black individuals by campus police. During academic year 2019–20, almost one-third of all campus police stops—on and off campus—were of Black individuals (31.7 percent), far above the 7 percent Black representation of the university's immediate neighborhood. The CAB suggested this was a conservative figure that may be much higher as the AU campus police do not make all police stop data publicly available. Among the two main reasons listed by campus police for stopping Black individuals were "suspicious activity" (56 percent) and "suspicious person" (35 percent). The data reflect long-standing racist assumptions of Blackness as criminal and Black bodies as out of place and not belonging, particularly in historically white and affluent spaces such as a university.[25] Campus police officers are legally empowered to subjectively evaluate someone as "suspicious" and therefore a target to be stopped and questioned. The data also mirror research on public police departments and racial disparities in police contact.[26]

CONSTRUCTING BELONGING AND THREAT

In addition to the numbers, which only tell part of the story of racialized campus police practices, qualitative data provided me a way to understand how campus stakeholders both experienced and understood the role of campus police. Individual and focus group interviews with students, staff, and faculty revealed that campus police constructed clear boundaries of who belonged on campus, who was a threat, and who was deserving of protection. The constant presence of campus police and observations of officers detaining individuals conveyed to AU stakeholders that Black and Latinx local residents were a criminalized class. For example, one white faculty member commented on the reported suspect descriptions appearing in campus crime alerts: "It's almost all Black and Brown or heavily Black and Brown when it's noted. It doesn't feel like it's students who are perpetrating the crimes." An undergraduate who worked in the campus library added, "We had so many local community members coming into our library just to hang out. [Officers] knew they were not students and treated them like, 'why are you trying to come in here.' Just very aggressive."

Black students and faculty were uniquely affected by the dynamic that resulted from the perception that campus police targeted Black and Latinx individuals. Participants I spoke to reported being aware that they could be stopped at any time by a campus police officer for presumably fitting the description of a crime suspect. A Black undergraduate male student critiqued the use of race in campus police practices: "If every day you get a text saying a Black person committed a crime, naturally you're going to believe that *all* Black people are criminals." As a survival tactic, Black undergraduate men at AU specifically shared they were mindful of how they dressed and behaved when they were near a campus police officer. Wearing AU apparel and attempting to look friendly were among the behaviors students presented to police to avoid negative interactions with them.

Finally, participants reported that campus police seemed to be in place to protect AU's reputation and capacity to attract wealth in the form of tuition. A white female faculty member expressed this sentiment: "I feel AU is more invested in liability issues and its security theater than in the actual lived experiences of the students. Those [crime] alerts serve liability and PR concerns." The faculty member's comment reinforces how the AU campus police department is presented as a service to student and employees and as a talking point to parents and the public when issues of campus safety arise. The daily protection offered by AU campus police is to "make parents' money safe," according to one undergraduate I interviewed. Moreover, AU's wealth comes primarily from white and affluent families who send their students and donate as alumni. White students and faculty I spoke to indicated that they had minimal experiences with campus police and were aware that the Black population of AU consistently reported negative experiences of harassment and profiling. The racialized perceptions of whom campus police were meant to protect and whom they targeted as threats constituted a psychological and material reality in which racially minoritized communities were vulnerable to harm.

DEMARCATING RACIALIZED "SAFE" SPACE

The context in which racialized campus policing occurs is important to consider. Historical studies of university expansion and urban development highlight how institutions often stigmatize local neighborhoods in the process and thereby justify the need for campus police.²⁷ Similarly, at AU, police activity and crime alerts instilled a sense that the local community was dangerous and crime-ridden. The local community was pejoratively referred to as a "ghetto" and "the 'hood" by students, which was indicative of long-standing racist and classist stereotypes associated with the area. One journalism school faculty member reported that when students are required to leave campus for news or photography assignments, they prefer affluent neighborhoods in Los Angeles. She remarked, "I've had students who, in the middle of the day, don't want to go out and do street photography around the perimeter [of the campus]. . . . There's an innate fear that inhibits their ability to explore." A comment from an undergraduate student echoed this perspective: "Whenever I think about campus police here on campus, I'm thinking about the police versus the criminals outside."²⁸ Although participants did not always use explicit racial and class descriptions, low-income racially minoritized communities have historically been criminalized and blamed for their poverty without regard to the effects of segregation, housing discrimination, lack of employment opportunities, and the defunding of education and social services commonly experienced by these areas.²⁹

In contrast, AU was understood to be a safe space, protected by the campus police who actively sought to eliminate crime and criminals. The racist stereotypes of the local community prompted students to consider that they "should stay on campus, in this little bubble, and not go out . . . and be kept safe," as one undergraduate shared. Students and faculty commented that the crime alerts often reported crimes off campus, suggesting that little crime occurred on campus property. However, whereas some AU stakeholders endorsed the notion of the campus as safe and the local community as dangerous, others recognized that this was an intended effect of the campus police and resisted. Participants referenced incidents of sexual assault and violence, news of which was circulated within the campus but never in campus crime alerts. Faculty described being fearful of threatening behavior by students, and there was a shared sentiment that fraternity row was a dangerous space for women. In other words, students and faculty expressed fears of being victimized by other members of the AU community rather than local residents. The perceived neglect of such concerns by campus police was described by interviewees as a form of gaslighting by AU, to draw attention away from the "underlying violence that occurs every day" on campus.

The experiences of Black undergraduates at AU revealed how higher education's legacy of racial exclusion persists to shape an anti-Black campus climate that privileges whiteness. Black men I spoke to shared how they negotiated coming to campus when they were aware of campus police activity or of a recent crime that had taken place. Students sometimes decided to avoid campus altogether, as one student shared: "I'd be very scared. I'd just stay in my room because if I'm an alleged criminal versus an AU student, I'd be treated very differently. So I just try and stay in my room until the next day."[30] The comment illustrates how higher education institutions reinforce "whiteness as property," a concept developed by legal scholar Cheryl Harris to describe how whiteness is the basis for property rights. In higher education, colleges and universities were historically the exclusive domain of white men from wealthy, landowning families.[31] Despite greater admission of racially diverse students, higher education continues to privilege white and upper-class students. At AU, the marginalization of the 5 percent of Black students was compounded by a campus police presence that resulted in their harassment, eroding the image of the campus as a safe space.

The experiences of campus stakeholders, particularly racially minoritized students and faculty, provide insight into how campus police shape the racial climate of the AU campus on a daily basis. The psychological and emotional impact of the presence of campus police has been given little attention in research on racism in higher education. Yet, racialized experiences, such as microaggressions, can negatively shape educational experiences, which is counter to the purported justification of campus police as a necessary support to an institution's academic mission. Problematically, campus police scholarship has tended to describe organizational structure and practices without regard for social context and social identity.[32] In doing this, no effort is made to link larger contexts and social identities with police practices and eventual outcomes, thus omitting how such linkages lead to racialized policing of college campuses. I now turn to examining how racialized campus police practices expose racially minoritized populations to harm.

BROKEN WINDOWS POLICING AS COMMUNITY ENGAGEMENT

AU campus police officers whom I interviewed consistently described the policing approach they adopted as one of "community engagement." The AU campus police department institutionalized community engagement as a specialized unit and as a department-wide practice. Over the last ten years, community engagement grew from a single officer's responsibility to the responsibility of an entire bureau. All the officers I spoke with discussed the importance of getting out of their patrol cars and walking the campus property and local neighborhood to facilitate conversation with members of both communities. One officer shared, "We want them [the community] to get to know us and especially on that personal level. It makes it better when they see you and say, 'hi,' and know who you are." In servicing a large campus population and the local community, officers gave examples of departmental outreach programs (e.g., "Coffee with a Cop") and regular points of contact with campus stakeholders, such as liaisons to the cultural centers and Greek life. The purported purpose of community engagement was to facilitate the ability of the AU campus police department to address crime as well as prevent threats to public safety. Officers described their role as being about more than strict law enforcement. Rather, their task was to ensure that campus and community stakeholders have their needs met, even if those needs fell outside the scope of law enforcement. One officer who had served at AU for more than twenty years—well above the average tenure of a campus police officer—described the task of the department this way: "The whole idea of community policing is solving community problems, which aren't necessarily crime problems, but quality of life."

Despite community policing being lauded by police scholars and practitioners as a much-needed major effort to reform the policing enterprise, a critical reading of community engagement (also termed community policing, community-oriented policing, and problem-oriented policing) frames this practice as one that upholds police power, racial inequality, and white supremacy. For the AU campus police department, monitoring the campus and community's quality of life is essentially akin to engaging in so-called broken windows policing. According to Justin Hansford: "Community policing integrates broken windows and stop-and-frisk tactics through its emphasis on 'proactively' promoting public order, involving 'hot spot policing,' often a code phrase for targeting lower-income areas where people of color reside, and 'zero tolerance,' which results in the criminalization of minor violations and nuisances."[33] Many observers have identified broken windows policing as the dominant model of policing since its emergence in the early 1980s. According to this model, crime and social problems are inherent to low-income, racially minoritized communities, which must then be proactively monitored and regulated. The broken windows perspective disregards structural explanations for poverty and violence. It is under broken windows policing that Black and racially minoritized communities experience disproportionately negative and violent treatment in major cities, such as New York and

Los Angeles, and in suburban areas like Ferguson, Missouri.[34] Considering how campus stakeholders perceive unequal racial treatment and the criminalization of the local community as a result of AU campus police practices, the strategy of community engagement can be seen as a form of broken windows policing that helps support a racist strategy of social control.

RACE-EVASIVE CAMPUS POLICING

How campus police officers view issues of race is important because attitudes and beliefs—whether implicit or explicit—are linked to behavior. Studies of municipal police have identified a moderate to strong relationship between implicit bias and the many racial inequities found in police-citizen contacts.[35] Research also documents how officers explain away racialized policing through race-evasive narratives such as "criminal profiling."[36] Far fewer studies have examined how campus police officers view their line of work, including their views of students and the campus community they police.[37] Some of this work is dated and does not include an analysis of race, thereby homogenizing campus police officers and students. In other words, little information exists to discern whether officers of differing racial identities bring similar or dissimilar perspectives when on patrol and exercising discretion. Studies of campus police officer decision-making present officer discretion as a mix of objective and contextual factors, except for the role of race.[38] Research such as this helps to reinforce the potentially incorrect belief that campus police departments operate according to objective, legal standards.

In my interviews with thirty-two AU campus police officers, I asked about their perceptions of race in campus policing. Officers almost always refuted accusations of racism when sharing anecdotes from patrols and when presented with data. For instance, officers were asked to respond to student data from an AU campus climate survey. Among Black student respondents ($n = 312$), approximately 49 percent reported they had had a personal experience of racism with AU campus police. Officers questioned the results by claiming to have "never actually seen examples of what they're talking about" to "I wouldn't be able to discredit any of those people that felt they were being treated some type of way, but I don't feel that's the makeup of our department." While officers did not explicitly invalidate students' reported experiences, by claiming to not see or know what students were reporting, officers indirectly challenged student reports of racist encounters. Officers also avoided commenting on whether the student responses were indicative of systemic issues in the department. Some officers did directly remark on the accuracy of student reports of racist campus policing, thus diminishing the credence of the survey data, as in this comment: "I'd be very surprised to hear that would be 50 percent. I'm not being defensive but a question I would have is what are they defining as racist.... Sometimes an officer might stop somebody who's Black and maybe they asked for their ID. Let's say it's totally appropriate. There are times when that happens." Campus police officers described many of their interactions with campus community members as routine "appropriate" uses of police authority that should *not* be considered racist in the event that the officer has stopped and questioned a Black individual. Officers also suggested that campus stakeholders misunderstood the nature of the work of campus policing. For example, an officer shared, "In [a] situation where they think we're stereotyping, or we're just targeting this race, no. There is training that the department gives our officers and I think it helps so that we don't get trapped in that situation."

The responses from AU campus police officers reflect what I will refer to as "race-evasive policing."[39] Race-evasive policing involves claims that policing is fair and predicated on equality of treatment. In privileging the campus police officer viewpoint, the current and historical experiences and perspectives of racially minoritized groups within the university and the surrounding neighborhood are disregarded. Negating racism because officers "have never seen" it occurs while promoting practices as "fair" without investigating how racial stereotypes may subtly inform the performance of their job. The implementation of popular reforms, such as implicit bias training, do not account for why AU stakeholders perceive race as a significant element in campus policing. Furthermore, training and other common reforms have not been shown to be effective despite their continued prominence in national discourse on policing.[40] The denial of the role of race in campus policing helps to account for the disconnect between campus police officers and the experiences of racially minoritized constituents on and off campus.

AS ARTICULATED through the experiences of racially minoritized students and faculty at AU, campus policing was perceived to operate as a system of social control that reinforced a racial- and class-based hierarchy, positioning Black, Brown, and poor bodies on the lower rungs while elevating whiteness and affluence to much higher rungs. Although campus police officers claimed to engage in "community engagement" and treat all constituents "equally," their denial of racism in campus policing and the lack of attention to the racist history of the larger policing apparatus contribute to the perception by many of the campus police department as a racist institution. While senior leaders at AU have promoted the campus police department as student-centered and distinct from the local police department, the racialized experiences and practices at AU mirror research on racism on the general policing apparatus. At AU, and in the higher education sector more broadly, campus police can no longer be thought of as neutral entities. Rather, campus leaders must take seriously how campus police departments are tied to the general policing apparatus. The recruitment of campus police officers from traditional academies and municipal police departments ensures that the issues in policing more broadly will spill over to the campus environment. Mimicking general police practices and modeling campus police departments after public agencies also merits critical investigation. As campuses diversify, higher education leaders should consider how investments in policing are commensurate with racial equity and student success goals.

NOTES

1. Abigail Johnson Hess, "Meet Jael Kerandi, the Student Leader Pushing University of Minnesota to Change Its Relationship with Police," June 30, 2020, www.cnbc.com/2020/06/30/jael-kerandi-helped-the-university-of-minnesota-reimagine-policing.html.

2. "The Demands," December 18, 2015, https://web.archive.org/web/20160126204438/http://www.thedemands.org/.

3. Divest/Invest UCLA Faculty Collective, "Divestment Now Demands from UCLA Faculty," June 11, 2020, https://ucla.app.box.com/s/sdt4rqz92i0a8115y53er8jkaegtd9t9.

4. Cops Off Campus Coalition, "Demands," May 1, 2021, https://copsoffcampuscoalition.com/demands/.

5. The Jeanne Clery Disclosure of Campus Security Policy and Campus Crime Statistics Act (20 U.S.C. § 1092) requires all Title IV–eligible colleges and universities to publicly report annual campus crime data, create programs designed to support campus victims of violence, and publicly outline institutional policies and procedures implemented to improve campus safety. Andrea N. Allen and Scott Jacques, "'He Did That Because I Was Black': Black College Students Perceive Municipal Police, Not Campus Police, as Discriminating," *Deviant Behavior* 41, no. 1 (2020): 29–40.

6. John J. Sloan, "The Modern Campus Police: An Analysis of Their Evolution, Structure, and Function," *American Journal of Police* 11, no. 2 (1992): 85–104; Brian A.

Reaves, *Campus Law Enforcement, 2011–2012*, NCJ 248028. (Washington, DC: Bureau of Justice Statistics, 2016).

7. For example, see Reed T. DeAngelis, "Systemic Racism in Police Killings: New Evidence from the Mapping Police Violence Database, 2013–2021," *Race and Justice*, online first October 19, 2021.

8. USA Facts, "Police Departments in the US: Explained," August 13, 2020, https://usafacts.org/articles/police-departments-explained/; Bureau of Justice Statistics, *Local Police Departments 2016: Personnel*, January 26, 2021, www.bjs.gov/content/pub/pdf/lpd16p_sum.pdf.

9. See Roger Hopkins Burke, *Criminal Justice Theory* (New York: Routledge, 2012), 266; and Charles Reith, *A New Study of Police History* (London: Oliver and Boyd, 1956), 294.

10. See Dylan Rodríguez, "Beyond 'Police Brutality': Racist State Violence and the University of California," *American Quarterly* 64, no. 2 (2012): 301–13; Nikhil Pal Singh, "The Whiteness of Police," *American Quarterly* 66, no. 4 (2014): 1091–99; and David Correia and Tyler Wall, *Violent Order: Essays on the Nature of Police* (Chicago: Haymarket, 2021), 335.

11. David Thacher, "Order Maintenance Policing," in *The Oxford Handbook of Police and Policing*, ed. Michael Dean Reisig and Robert J. Kane (New York: Oxford University Press, 2014).

12. Ben Brucato, "Fabricating the Color Line in a White Democracy: From Slave Catchers to Petty Sovereigns," *Theoria* 61, no. 141 (2014): 30–54.

13. Ben Brucato, "Policing Race and Racing Police: The Origin of US Police in Slave Patrols," *Social Justice* 47, no. 3/4 (2020): 115–36.

14. James Baldwin, "A Report from Occupied Territory," *Nation*, July 11, 1966, www.thenation.com/article/archive/report-occupied-territory/.

15. See Robin Shepard Engel and Jennifer M. Calnon, "Examining the Influence of Drivers' Characteristics during Traffic Stops with Police: Results from a National Survey," *Justice Quarterly* 21, no. 1 (2004): 49–90; and Charles R. Epp, Steven Maynard-Moody, and Donald P. Haider-Markel, *Pulled Over: How Police Stops Define Race and Citizenship* (Chicago: University of Chicago Press, 2014), 272.

16. Andrew Gelman, Jeffrey Fagan, and Alex Kiss, "An Analysis of the New York City Police Department's 'Stop-and- Frisk' Policy in the Context of Claims of Racial Bias," *Journal of the American Statistical Association* 102, no. 479 (2007): 813–23; Sharad Goel, Justin M. Rao, and Ravi Shroff, "Precinct or Prejudice? Understanding Racial Disparities in New York City's Stop-and-Frisk Policy," *Annals of Applied Statistics* 10, no. 1 (2016): 365–94.

17. Tammy Rinehart Kochel, David B. Wilson, and Stephen D. Mastrofski, "Effect of Suspect Race on Officers' Arrest Decisions" *Criminology* 49 no. 2 (2011): 473–512.

18. Frank Edwards, Hedwig Lee, and Michael Esposito, "Risk of Being Killed by

Police Use of Force in the United States by Age, Race-Ethnicity, and Sex," *Proceedings of the National Academy of Sciences of the United States of America* 116, no. 34 (2019): 16793–98.

19. The Sentencing Project, "Trends in U.S. Corrections," January 2023, www.sentencingproject.org/publications/trends-in-u-s-corrections/.

20. Rory Kramer and Brianna Remster, "The Slow Violence of Contemporary Policing," Annual Review of *Criminology* 5 (2022): 43–66. Additionally, consider how underpolicing is a racialized phenomenon alongside aggressive overpolicing (see Rod K. Brunson, "Protests Focus on Over-Policing: But Under-Policing Is Also Deadly," *Washington Post*, June 12, 2020).

21. Correia and Wall, *Violent Order*, 1.

22. Kelly J. Asmussen and John W. Creswell, "Campus Response to a Student Gunman," *Journal of Higher Education* 66, no. 5 (1995): 575–91; Bonnie S. Fisher and John J. Sloan, *Campus Crime: Legal, Social, and Policy Perspectives* (Springfield, IL: Charles C. Thomas, 2013): 416.

23. Joseph A. Schafer, Charern Lee, George W. Burruss, and Matthew J. Giblin, "College Student Perceptions of Campus Safety Initiatives," *Criminal Justice Policy Review* 29, no. 4 (2018): 319–40.

24. For instance, at the University of Southern California (USC), the president and senior leadership team confirmed that USC cannot ban law enforcement from its premises. Although USC conducted a review of its Department of Public Safety, "abolishing DPS would only usher LAPD onto our campuses, an outcome that, given LAPD's checkered history, might worsen rather than improve the safety of all people in and around our campuses" as written in the USC Community Advisory Board report *One USC: A Vision of Community Safety for All* (2021), 17.

25. Jennifer L. Eberhardt, Valerie J. Purdie, Phillip Atiba Goff, and Paul G. Davies, "Seeing Black: Race, Crime, and Visual Processing," *Journal of Personality and Social Psychology* 87, no. 6. (2004): 876–93; William A. Smith, Walter R. Allen, and Lynette L. Danley, "'Assume the Position . . . You Fit the Description': Psychosocial Experiences and Racial Battle Fatigue among African American Male College Students," *American Behavioral Scientist* 51, no. 4 (2007): 551–78.

26. Margaret Bull Kovera, "Racial Disparities in the Criminal Justice System: Prevalence, Causes, and a Search for Solutions," *Journal of Social Issues* 75, no. 4 (2019): 1139–64.

27. Davarian L. Baldwin, *In the Shadow of the Ivory Tower: How Universities Are Plundering Our Cities* (New York: Bold Type Books, 2021), 272; Steven J. Diner, *Universities and Their Cities: Urban Higher Education in America* (Baltimore, MD: Johns Hopkins University Press, 2017), 192.

28. Jude Paul Matias Dizon, "Protecting the University, Policing Race: A Case Study of Campus Policing," *Journal of Diversity in Higher Education* (2021): 8.

29. Douglas Massey and Nancy A. Denton, *American Apartheid: Segregation and the Making of the Underclass* (Cambridge, MA: Harvard University Press, 1993), 312.

30. Dizon, "Protecting the Campus, Policing Race," 9.

31. Cheryl I. Harris, "Whiteness as Property," *Harvard Law Review* 106, no. 8 (1993): 1707–91.

32. See Eugene A. Paoline and John J. Sloan, "Variability in the Organizational Structure of Contemporary Campus Law Enforcement Agencies: A National-Level Analysis," *Policing: An International Journal of Police Strategies and Management* 26, no. 4 (2003): 612–39; and Nicholas Michael Perez and Max Bromley, "Comparing Campus and City Police Human Resource and Select Community Outreach Policies and Practices: An Update," *Policing: An International Journal of Police Strategies and Management* 38, no. 4 (2015): 664–74.

33. Justin Hansford, "Community Policing Reconsidered: From Ferguson to Baltimore," in *Policing the Planet: Why the Policing Crisis Led to Black Lives Matter*, ed. Jordan T. Camp and Christina C. Heatherton (Brooklyn, NY: Verso, 2016), 221.

34. Jonathan Oberman and Kendea Johnson, "Broken Windows: Restoring Social Order or Damaging and Depleting New York's Poor Communities of Color," *Cardozo Law Review* 37, no. 3 (February 2016): 931–54.

35. See Florie Fridell and Hyeyoung Lim, "Assessing the Racial Aspects of Police Force Using the Implicit- and Counter-Bias Perspectives," *Journal of Criminal Justice* 44 (2016): 36–48.

36. Megan Welsh, Joshua Chanin, and Stuart Henry, "Complex Colorblindness in Police Processes and Practices," *Social Problems* 68, no. 2 (2021): 374–92.

37. Andrea N. Allen, "Campus Officers' Explanations of Traffic Stop Sanctions," *Police Quarterly* 17, no. 3 (2014): 276–301; Andrea N. Allen, "Campus Police-Citizen Encounters: Influences on Sanctioning Outcomes," *American Journal of Criminal Justice* 40, no. 4 (2015): 722–36.

38. Allen, "Campus Officers' Explanations of Traffic Stop Sanctions"; Allen, "Campus Police-Citizen Encounters: Influences on Sanctioning Outcomes."

39. See also Welsh, Chanin, and Henry, "Complex Colorblindness in Police Processes and Practices."

40. Robin S. Engel, Hannah D. McManus, and Gabrielle T. Isaza, "Moving beyond 'Best Practice': Experiences in Police Reform and a Call for Evidence to Reduce Officer-Involved Shootings," *Annals of the American Academy of Political and Social Science* 687, no. 1 (2020): 146–65.

11

CAMPUS POLICE AND RACIALIZED BARRIERS TO REPORTING SEXUAL ASSAULT FOR BLACK WOMEN

KAMARIA B. PORTER

Sexual assault, intimate partner violence, and harassment remain pervasive problems on college campuses. In its 2020 climate survey, the American Association of Universities (AAU) found over a quarter of women undergraduates (25.9 percent) and 22.8 percent of Trans/GenderQueer, and Nonbinary students (TGQN) experienced sexual assault by force or without the ability to consent since beginning college.[1] For intimate partner violence (IPV), incident rates were 14 percent for women and 21.5 percent for TGQN students. Research suggests Black women in higher education experience all forms of sexual misconduct at greater rates than their white counterparts.[2] Black women, as multiply marginalized by gender and race, consistently describe sexual harm as racialized.[3] In other words, Black women's description of harassment and exposure to assault includes comments and behavioral motivations from abusers that invoke gendered racist stereotypes about Black women's bodies, sexual mores, and their very humanity.[4] These stereotypes of Black women, coined "controlling images" by Patricia Hill Collins, are highly adaptable, persistent, and hegemonic, meaning they are "seen as natural, normal, and inevitable."[5]

Survivors of campus sexual assault rarely report to legal authorities. Federal surveys suggest student survivors are significantly less likely to report sexual assault compared to similarly aged peers outside of higher education.[6] National surveys of campus survivors show that only between 2 to 11 percent ever make a report to police.[7] AAU found 11.2 percent of survivors contacted campus police and 9.4 percent contacted municipal police.[8] Campus sexual assault literature in general and studies of reporting patterns mainly rely on samples of majority white, cis-gender, heterosexual women.[9] These studies rarely examine institutional factors, policy contexts, or the "sociohistorical contexts" of US universities.[10] Without situating sexual assault within university contexts and examining how survivors evaluate reporting options, researchers and leaders are left with microlevel explanations of low reporting rates of sexual assault that leave institutional structures and policies undisturbed.[11] This chapter focuses on the narratives of Black women and nonbinary survivors to understand how they evaluated postsecondary institutional reporting options through the lens of race *and* gender. By way of context, I examine how campus police confirmed Black women and nonbinary students' perceptions of the law, resulting in their reluctance to report campus sexual assaults to relevant authorities.

REPORTING OPTIONS FOR CAMPUS SEXUAL ASSAULT

In higher education, students have two reporting options after sexual assault exposure. Under the criminal legal system—represented by police departments of various jurisdictions, prosecutors, and courts—reporting involves claiming injury under legal definitions of sexual assault and rape. The criminal legal system is currently intertwined with medical services for survivors, meaning a person seeking medical attention and treatment after sexual harm can have that treatment coincide with the collection of evidence. Trained medical staff perform forensic medical exams, documenting injury and traces of the assailant on and in the survivor's body and clothes. Police are dispatched to emergency rooms to get statements from survivors. In this setting, a person may have already described the incident to multiple doctors, nurses, sexual assault nurse examiners, and hospital staff in addition to police, all documenting the story on different forms and records. Survivors may be waiting for hours with a rotating set of professionals coming in and out, asking questions, conducting exams, and providing treatments for sexually transmitted infections and preventing pregnancy. Legal proceedings resituate the survivor from the harmed party to a witness asked to provide evidence of crimes committed by the assailant.

The second option for students is the university Title IX procedure. This route defines sexual harm as a violation of a student's civil rights, as sexual harassment and assault are understood as sex discrimination that can deny one's right to an education.[12] The process may start with a student contacting university administrators tasked with investigating cases of sexual or gender misconduct. Students may accidentally disclose to a university official with mandatory reporting obligations and thereby prompt the official to initiate a complaint process.[13] Title IX officials may refuse to pursue an investigation, telling students their injury does not rise to the level of a policy violation. Universities rely on students to bring complaints, identify the assailant(s), give multiple statements, identify witnesses, and respond to questions in a hearing.[14] Survivors may have an advocate or support person, but the process demands mental and emotional energy from survivors who are already dealing with trauma from the assault.[15] The decision of whether the assailant committed a policy violation resides with a hearing panel or university official.

Campus police are listed as one of many possible resources that students can contact to report an incident of sexual assault. However, campus police do not take a prominent role during a criminal legal or campus complaint process. Crimes of rape are prosecuted at the state level, so campus police will likely refer reports to municipal police. Campus police officers typically do not provide forensic rape exams and may not be able to successfully refer a student to a place on or near campus to access a rape kit.[16] If a complaint of sexual assault is handled through the Title IX office, personnel in that office will investigate and prepare evidence prior to a hearing. Campus police officers may provide notes or commentary in that report for hearing board members to consider. Under these organizational arrangements, campus police have minimal involvement with active sexual assault complaints. However, the actions of campus police, as representatives of both the carceral state and universities, may influence how survivors view official reporting options. For students, the distinctions mentioned here may not be relevant, as they may see campus police as representing "the law" and "the university."

CONCEPTUAL FRAMEWORK

Black Feminist Thought

Black feminist thought emerges from a multiply subjugated social position within (but not exclusive to) systems of race, gender, and class.[17] From the position of multiple marginalization, Black women develop a distinctive and collective understanding of systems of domination.[18] Black feminism aims to recover Black women's experiences by combatting gendered racism and exposing the intersectional failures of legal structures, political movements, and institutional policies and practice. To conceptualize the linkages between Black women's experiences of sexual assault and their perceptions of reporting options, I use the theory of legal cynicism.

Legal Cynicism

Legal cynicism is a "cultural frame" held by marginalized groups who view the law and legal authorities—especially law enforcement—as "illegitimate, unresponsive, and ill equipped to ensure public safety."[19] Legal cynicism is a consequence of the approaches to policing undertaken in economically disenfranchised communities of color, where the police are both absent when residents need protection from crime and oppressively present otherwise through police brutality, hypersurveillance, and lethal force.[20] Defined as "anomie about the law," legal cynicism captures the "sense of social estrangement, meaninglessness, and powerlessness" that is produced by extreme social disenfranchisement, exclusion, and violence.[21] Legal cynicism has been used to understand why people from marginalized groups rarely call or cooperate with police.[22] Black women students from underprotected and overpoliced neighborhoods may already hold cynical or estranged attitudes about the law that then shape their view of campus reporting options, particularly reporting to the campus police.

In the context of gender-based and sexual violence, Black women's legal cynicism involves a "dual frustration" of having no protection from the violence they experience in their households and communities and not turning to the police for fear of instigating state-sanctioned violence against Black men and/or the entire Black community.[23] Black women experience crime—in the form of public violence and sexual victimization—and criminalization by police through the "presupposition [that Black women] are deviant."[24] In other words, Black women experience a double bind of silence when considering reporting sexual assault. They cannot depend on law enforcement to believe them because of gendered racist assumptions about rape combined with controlling images of Black women's sexuality.[25] Because both sex and sexual assault are primarily intraracial, Black women fear that reporting sexual assault to law enforcement will only produce violent outcomes for Black men.[26] Additionally, Black women fear violence, sexual harassment, and assault from law enforcement officers during reporting an incident.[27]

Using this framework, the chapter presents my analysis of how forty-six Black women and nonbinary students who experienced sexual assault during college or graduate school evaluated reporting options through an intersectional lens, attending to how racism and sexism, referred to here as *gendered racism*, influenced their decision-making. The analysis reveals how Black women students' legal estrangement from reporting their victimization arises from growing up in underprotected and overpoliced neighborhoods. Additionally, I demonstrate how the everyday actions of campus police confirmed Black women's legal estrangement while on campus. The chapter explores these issues using results of interviews conducted during 2020–22 of forty-six Black women and nonbinary students attending HBCUs and predominantly white institutions.

DATA AND METHODS

Data for the study were collected from thirty-two participants who attended Predominantly White Institutions (PWI) and from fourteen who attended Historically Black Colleges and Universities (HBCU). I recruited participants through responses to social media ads and posts on Twitter, Instagram, and Facebook. I conducted semi-structured, narrative-based interviews via video conferencing. As a former rape crisis counselor/survivor advocate and to mitigate retraumatization, I infused narrative inquiry methods with trauma-informed practices.[28] Together, these activities and considerations form what I call *trauma-informed narrative inquiry*—a methodological approach that foregrounds theoretical and empirical affordances of stories and storytelling and compassionate research designed to promote catharsis and healing.

Trauma-Informed Narrative Inquiry

In practice, trauma-informed narrative inquiry necessitates transparency about the topics for discussion, ongoing informed consent (reminding participants they could opt out of questions or the study throughout the interview), check-ins to track participant's well-being, and an open, uninterrupted, narrative opportunity for participants to describe in their own words any experiences of sexual trauma. For researchers examining experiences of sexual assault, substantial preparation and training about sexual trauma is required.[29] My preparation comes from receiving sixty hours of training on sexual violence and domestic violence through Rape Victim Advocates and accompanying survivors post-assault through medico-legal decisions in Chicago emergency rooms for two years. Additionally, I have researched, worked, written, and taught for over a decade in the areas of sexual violence, Title IX, and the adjudication of campus sexual violence. That preparation allows for what Jeong Hee Kim described as the emergence of *phronesis* in the trainee, "the moral, ethical judgment to act wisely and prudently, which is more than the possession of epitome (general content knowledge) or techno (skills or techniques)."[30] In trauma-informed narrative inquiry, phronesis represents the ability to actualize content knowledge on sexual violence and skills from advocacy work into sensitive and responsive interactions with participants and critical reflection on narrative data and its analysis.

FINDINGS

Black women and nonbinary survivors drew on previous experiences with police, both direct and collective, to evaluate reporting options to on-campus sexual assault. Many held attitudes associated with legal cynicism, meaning they distrusted all law enforcement, including campus police. As students, Black women also observed campus police engage in racial profiling, abuse, and use of lethal force against Black people. These behaviors by campus police confirmed Black women's legal cynicism regarding campus reporting options.

Bringing Legal Cynicism to Campus

Participants articulated distrust and alienation from law enforcement based on the mistreatment of Black communities by police more broadly. As one participant, Tessa, described it: "In the Black community, we can't count on systems to do what they're supposed to do, and we can't count on law enforcement to do what they're supposed to do. If anything, they're doing the wrong thing, and so if we want justice, we have to do it ourselves. That's always been the message I think that I received growing up." Black women students experienced the "dual frustration" of law enforcement failing to protect their communities from crime (especially sexual violence), while also witnessing oversurveillance and police violence against Black people.[31] Oliva, an Afro-Latina from the Southwest, described her neighborhood as a place where police did not "patrol" or respond to resident calls but only came when "they're trying to find crime." Growing up mixed-race, Taylor witnessed systemic racism in the differential treatment of her parents. After the 2016 murder of Philando Castile in her home state of

Minnesota, Taylor noticed the different ways police behaved, depending on which parent was driving. When her Black stepdad drove her and was pulled over, she witnessed how "police hyper-criminalize Black men." This differed from how police interacted with her white mother in the driver's seat. Sucre, an Afro-Indigenous graduate student, discussed family members being abused by police while in custody. Witnessing or hearing about mistreatment cultivated a distrust of police among participants, thereby deeply influencing their reporting decisions after an assault. Monica Bell described this form of legal estrangement as "vicarious marginalization."[32] That is, Black women shared "a cumulative, collective experience of procedural and substantive injustice" that fueled their cynicism of law enforcement, including campus police.[33]

Many participants shared how their distrust of police influenced their decision to not report campus sexual assault. Martha, for example, was sexually assaulted while attending an HBCU and did not report the incident to any law enforcement. She explained, "I think for myself and just Black women, in general, even though Black men hurt us, often, we still want to protect them from being incarcerated because we just know how bad that system is." Harriet was assaulted several times by an intimate partner during graduate school. She saw reporting to law enforcement as a betrayal of the education she received at an HBCU, an education that often centered on combatting institutionalized racism. Harriet elaborated on this sense of betrayal, "I saw it as, well, you're contradicting those four years of work that you put in at [the HBCU]. You're hurting your own community." Black women students viewed reporting to law enforcement after a sexual assault as dangerous, leading to overly punitive consequences for the Black men who caused them harm.

Black women participants discussed feeling "responsible" for protecting Black men who assaulted them. Lorraine did not report or tell many people about her sexual assault exposure during her first month of college. When asked about her reasoning, she responded: "Yeah, I think one of the major issues for me, besides the fact that it was someone I knew and the roommate of somebody that I liked, was the fact that it was a Black guy, so I didn't want to say who it was, and I didn't want to press charges or seek anything like that because I also knew it would be different for him because he is Black." The distinctions Lorraine makes in drilling down to why she did not report—or even informally disclose the incident—represent a unique barrier to reporting sexual assaults to campus police. For Black women, the implications of reporting carried more identity-based weight. For Jade, the responsibility to protect Black men was not theoretical. During her childhood, she lived briefly in Pulaski, Tennessee, the birthplace of the Ku Klux Klan.[34] Growing up listening to her grandmother's stories of racial terrorism gave Jade a "strong semblance of deep-seated, rooted racial prejudice" of the past and present. Attending a PWI within a majority-white area amplified Jade's sense of needing to protect the assaulter from law enforcement.

After sexual assault exposure from a Black male student, Taylor read multiple articles and reflected on her experiences of seeing Black men harassed and brutalized by police. As a Black woman who understood the "historical and current implications of accusing a Black man of sexual violence," Taylor decided not to report to campus police or other university officials. Taylor also worried her mixed-race identity might amplify any possible punishment. Taylor grew up seeing how, based on her skin color, she was "racialized differently" from her Black friends. Taylor described her enactment of a mixed-race identity as "self-effacing," explaining, "There's ways in which I try to make myself smaller and not take up space because I understand that there are ways in which me being of a lighter skin tone, me having connections to my white family and how that privileges me in certain ways." Taylor "subconsciously" knew her identity and presentation would intensify the already racist law enforcement project of overly punishing Black men for sexual violence. Black women were active allies and protectors of Black men. However, that allyship was not reciprocated.[35]

LEGAL CYNICISM FROM POLICE ENCOUNTERS

Black women cited previous experiences with law enforcement as factors for why they did not report sexual assault exposure while in school. Sucre purposefully avoided reporting to any form of law enforcement saying, "I don't trust police. I don't trust that they have my best interests at hand." Sucre described several incidents where police of different jurisdictions violated her sense of safety. When Sucre was around eleven years old, she was playing football with some friends and "someone called the cops on us." The police arrived and "scold[ed]" Sucre and her friends. Experiencing criminalization as a child contributed to Sucre's distrust of police. As a young adult, Sucre observed how the New York Police Department (NYPD) used excessive force against peaceful protesters. Sucre also experienced abuse by Border Patrol agents. She explained, "I have not had good experiences with police. I was abused at the border last year on my birthday, and that's not the first time I've had issues like that." Black and Brown women more frequently experience physical and sexualized violence in interactions with police, compared to white women in similar contexts of lower-income/high-crime neighborhoods.[36] Sucre articulated both personal and structural injustices in her interactions with police. She viewed all these forms of law enforcement as "stemming from colonial structures that are not meant for Black and Brown people." Together, these experiences of criminalization and abuse made it clear to Sucre that she could not rely on campus police after sexual assault.

Well before setting foot on a university campus, Black women have already learned that law enforcement cannot be trusted to handle issues of family and relationship violence. Mae discussed the failure of the legal system to protect her from domestic violence as one of the primary reasons she did not report. Mae saw her mother being physically abused by her father and go through a contentious divorce. During a "court-mandated" visit with her father, he strangled Mae, making her pass out. It took two years for her mother to gain full custody to protect Mae and her siblings from his abuse. Entanglement with the law through domestic violence and child custody arrangements only increased the abuse. Mae viewed the legal system as part of the problem in domestic violence situations, and her experiences left her with a serious sense of distrust of law enforcement and how they handle sexual assault.

Serena spent her childhood on military bases, where hers would often be one of only a few Black families on base. Growing up, she noticed her father minimized how racism shaped his experiences, in order to conform and succeed within the military. When she was five years old, she and her sibling witnessed a domestic violence episode between her parents. Some law enforcement personnel arrived and escorted Serena, her mother, and younger brother to a shelter. During the encounter, Serena remembered the cops asking her mother if she wanted to file a report of domestic violence. Serena described her mother's reaction: "My mother said, 'No, because I don't want to ruin his career.' That's what she said. So I think that experience just stuck with me, like hey, we can leave a situation to help ourselves, but we can't do too much because we don't want to ruin this man's career." This moment from her childhood informed how Serena viewed the police through a racialized and gendered lens. Her mother demonstrated how engaging the legal system through a report would create more harm for the family. Black women often feel responsible for protecting abusive partners from law enforcement because of police brutality, overly punitive consequences, and lack of protection for Black women in society.[37] Serena learned at an early age that involving police would only cause more harm to her family. Black women shoulder the responsibility of not adding to a system they know to be punitive and racist, while also experiencing harm, trauma, and broken trust in their relationships with Black men.

LEGAL CYNICISM IN PRECOLLEGE SEXUAL ASSAULT

Victim-blaming behavior from medical professionals also shaped how Black women viewed reporting options, including the option to report to law enforcement. Mae explained her perceptions of reporting originated with an insulting interaction with a healthcare provider after sexual assault exposure in high school. The high school student who assaulted Mae did so without a condom, prompting Mae to find a health clinic for testing and possible treatment. The first nurse she talked to about the assault asked Mae whether she abused alcohol before the assault. Mae did not drink and was insulted by the nurse's assumption that Mae was at fault. Mae described feeling hurt "that a healthcare professional and adult would say this to me. At the time, I was 17 and so it really made me realize how people treat survivors, and that is often awfully victim blaming, and so the idea of having to relive such a humiliating and degrading moment to police officers, to lawyers in a court of law, with the first assault, I couldn't imagine anything worse." Having a medical professional try to blame Mae for the assault gave her insight into how legal authorities might treat her if she reported it. What Mae experienced aligns with secondary victimization, or "second rape."[38] The nurse deployed "victim blaming attitudes" by insinuating Mae was drunk. It is important to note Mae was seventeen at the time, so the nurse additionally criminalized (assumed deviant behavior based on gendered racism) Mae with the assumption of underage drinking. Alternatively, the nurse may have engaged in another gendered racist practice of adultification with Mae.[39] The adultification of Black girls stems from controlling images, as tropes of Black women rooted in white supremacist–patriarchal drives to normalize the sexual victimization beginning with enslavement.[40] Adultification denies Black girls their youth and need for protection, making it a particular form of victim blaming produced by interlocking forms of oppression.[41] The harm Mae experienced trying to seek help after assault translated to cynicism and estrangement toward the law when she was assaulted in college.

Campus Police Confirm Black Women's Legal Cynicism

Several Black women and nonbinary students referenced misconduct by campus police as a factor for not reporting campus sexual assault. During Josephine's junior year, a campus police officer at her PWI, a white man, murdered a Black high school student. Josephine expressed disappointment in her institution for delaying sanctions against the officer (who was later acquitted for the murder). Seeing campus police engage in the racist murder of a Black boy and her university's lack of appropriate response showed Josephine "that the institution is there to protect the institution, and if you're not with that, then tough shit, essentially." Jade attended a public PWI in the Midwest and began her narrative by saying, "The cops there and the people, like some of them were just really, really racist." Jade witnessed Black students, faculty, and administrators targeted with racist harassment, counting police treatment as part of the structural exclusion of Black people on and around campus. Serena, who attended and worked at an HBCU, distrusted campus police because of reports of sexual abuse by officers. She stated, "And I also think our campus police need to be vetted better because some are the leading predators. And I know this from experience from some of my students." Hitchens and colleagues found young Latina and Black women experienced or witnessed police engage in "gender-based mistreatment" during interactions more often than white women.[42] They term the practice of male police officers using their power to sexually coerce, abuse, and threaten women as "punitive chauvinism."[43] Research shows Black trans and cis-women and girls are at higher risk for punitive chauvinism in police interactions, including physical and sexual assault.[44] Knowing campus police used lethal force and punitive chauvinism against Black people convinced Black women survivors to not report sexual assault.

Black women and nonbinary students experienced and witnessed racial profiling by campus police, leading them to avoid interactions with law enforcement post-assault. Giselle, a nonbinary student at a prestigious PWI, observed several ways campus police unfairly targeted Black students and staff with racist harassment. Giselle explained campus police regularly stopped Black people, demanding to see their identification. Giselle explained that campus police "will go up to random students with go-karts for them to present their student identification—especially the workers on campus, like Black workers and those who come on campus at later hours of the day. Just trying to get to their shift, a lot of times they get profiled as people that are robbing or doing theft or whatever." Giselle regarded this behavior as one of many ways Black students and staff were excluded as equal community members. Giselle also saw this in the way Black social gatherings were overpoliced. Parties hosted by Black student groups "consistently get shut down before midnight," even though students are permitted to have parties until 2:00 a.m. Giselle observed that while Black student parties are interrupted before the allowed time, white students are "partying until 3:00 a.m. and nothing happens. Nobody gets called." Black students struggle to find and occupy spaces to be together socially on PWI campuses because prime living and partying spaces are allotted for elite white students and their organizations.[45] Having those few Black social spaces patrolled and unfairly sanctioned by campus police deepens Black students' sense of exclusion. For Giselle, a nonbinary sexual assault survivor, these behaviors deterred them from turning to campus police for help.

The institutional context of campus policing matters when analyzing Black women's legal cynicism on campus. Black women who attended Spelman College—a historically Black college for women—spoke with a sense of pride and belief the institution cared about them, which was rare in the sample. Angie, who attended Spelman, talked about two incidents where men followed her at night. In the first incident, Angie noticed a man taking the same shortcuts as she was toward the Spelman campus. Once she knew campus safety could see her, she confronted the guy and scared him off. Another time, Angie and other Spelman women were followed by Black male students who cat-called them. Angie again pushed back, declaring, "Stop following us!" She also reported the men to public safety, who stopped them from following her and her friends. Angie felt safe at Spelman, knowing the public safety staff wanted to protect students. That knowledge seemed to empower Angie to rebuke street harassers. She explained, "I've been more aggressive and, I think, protective of myself in that way. Even in other situations that's not that, I'm more willing to speak my mind and say stuff and be more bold." For Angie, campus police were there to protect the Black women students at Spelman, not surveil or criminalize them. Angie's appreciation of campus security officers was rare across the entire sample of Black women and nonbinary students. For participants in my sample from Spelman College, who were all cis-gendered women, they connected their sense of safety and educational success to being on a campus "designed for Black women." Black women at other HBCUs enjoyed much of their institutional experiences;

however, their gender and sexuality remained areas of subordination. Angie still did not report sexual assault exposure, fearing that she, as a Black woman, would not be believed.

Campus Policing and Carceral Responses to Campus Sexual Assault

Black women remained suspicious of campus police and Title IX responses based on university policies mirroring racist criminal legal processes and outcomes.[46] Pauli, a nonbinary student at an elite Catholic university, felt all available options of reporting were gendered and racist. Pauli explained, "And we don't want to be around the police, either. It doesn't work. And even then, I think it was interesting because a lot of Black people take African-American Studies, at least a couple classes. . . . We learn a lot about patriarchy, and race, and the carceral system, and how punishment isn't necessarily always the right way to go, or more so, like the type of punishment that people are trying to use isn't always the best." Pauli viewed reporting options on campus as reinforcing gendered racism, carceral in nature, and ultimately producing unhelpful outcomes for survivors. Like Harriet, Pauli took courses to understand systems of oppression and applied that knowledge to reporting options. Black women conflated campus reporting options with the criminal legal system, seeing both as gendered and racist. Sometimes that conflation emerged from institutional connections between campus police and municipal police. Lorraine discovered sexual assault resources on her elite PWI campus were directly working with a municipal police department. She explained, "I haven't personally been in contact with Public Safety about my assault. . . . But I know that there's a huge relationship with the sexual assault hotline and Public Safety. And there's a relationship with Public Safety and NYPD." By connecting the institutional dots, Lorraine saw this collaboration as proof that campus police would likely mirror the gendered racist responses of the NYPD. Lorraine wanted a system that prioritized "keeping the survivor safe." For Lorraine and other Black women participants, campus police and Title IX did not provide an alternative to the criminal legal system. Lorraine felt there was a "dichotomy" in her available choices, of either "potentially re-liv[ing] your trauma, and go[ing] through the legal system" or being "quiet" about the assault with no middle ground. By mirroring and collaborating with criminal legal institutions, universities reproduce the harm Black women want to avoid and silence them from telling their stories of assault.

PROTECT BLACK WOMEN

Black women's experiences with gendered racism at the hands of police before and during college have profoundly informed their suspicions and distrust of campus police. The participants' attitudes toward law enforcement were informed by racist policing practices in their neighborhoods, personal and vicarious marginalization by police, and the direct harm they felt when legal and medical professionals blamed them when they tried to report precollege assaults. Informed by these previous experiences, campus police subsequently confirmed Black women's legal cynicism when they witnessed campus police harass Black people on campus and overpolice Black student party spaces. The use of campus police to respond to sexual assault only perpetuates Black women's cynicism and estrangement from the university, silencing them from seeking help. As an antidiscrimination law, Title IX responses should be focused on restoring Black women survivors' sense of safety after assault and ensuring they stay in school. Universities should invest in trauma recovery resources that address the sexual and racial trauma of intracultural sexual victimization.[47] By moving away from carceral responses, such as campus police, universities can innovate alternatives that actually serve Black women survivors, creating more space for healing and student success for all sexual assault survivors.

NOTES

1. David Cantor et al., *Report on the AAU Campus Climate Survey on Sexual Assault and Misconduct* (Rockville, MD: Association of American Universities, 2020), ix.

2. Brittany C. Slatton and April L. Richard, "Black Women's Experiences of Sexual Assault and Disclosure: Insights from the Margins," *Sociology Compass* 14, no. 6 (2020), https://doi.org/10.1111/soc4.12792.

3. Nicole T. Buchanan and Alayne J. Ormerod, "Racialized Sexual Harassment in the Lives of African American Women," *Women & Therapy* 25, no. 3–4 (October 29, 2002): 107–24, https://doi.org/10.1300/J015v25n03_08; Jennifer M. Gómez and Robyn L. Gobin, "Black Women and Girls & #MeToo: Rape, Cultural Betrayal, & Healing," *Sex Roles* 82, no. 1 (January 1, 2020): 1–12, https://doi.org/10.1007/s11199-019-01040-0; Krystle C. Woods, Nicole T. Buchanan, and Isis H. Settles, "Sexual Harassment across the Color Line: Experiences and Outcomes of Cross-versus Intraracial Sexual Harassment among Black Women," *Cultural Diversity and Ethnic Minority Psychology* 15, no. 1 (January 2009): 67–76, https://doi.org/10.1037/a0013541.

4. Patricia Hill Collins, "The Tie That Binds: Race, Gender and US Violence," *Ethnic and Racial Studies* 21, no. 5 (January 1, 1998): 917–38, https://doi.org/10.1080/014198798329720; Patricia Hill Collins, *Black Feminist Thought: Knowledge, Consciousness, and the Politics of Empowerment*, 2nd ed. (New York: Routledge, 2000).

5. Collins, *Black Feminist Thought*, 7.

6. Sarah Jane Brubaker et al., "Measuring and Reporting Campus Sexual Assault: Privilege and Exclusion in What We Know and What We Do," *Sociology Compass* 11, no. 12 (2017): 1–19, https://doi.org/10.1111/soc4.12543.

7. Kathryn J. Holland and Lilia M. Cortina, "'It Happens to Girls All the Time': Examining Sexual Assault Survivors' Reasons for Not Using Campus Supports," *American Journal of Community Psychology* 59 (March 1, 2017): 50–64, https://doi.org/10.1002/ajcp.12126.

8. Cantor et al., *Report on the AAU Campus Climate Survey on Sexual Assault and Misconduct*, xv.

9. Jessica C. Harris, Krystle P. Cobian, and Nadeeka Karunaratne, "Reimagining the Study of Campus Sexual Assault," in *Higher Education: Handbook of Theory and Research*, ed. Laura W. Perna, vol. 35 (Cham, Switzerland: Springer International, 2020), 1–47, https://doi.org/10.1007/978-3-030-11743-6_12-1; Chiara Sabina and Lavina Y. Ho, "Campus and College Victim Responses to Sexual Assault and Dating Violence: Disclosure, Service Utilization, and Service Provision," *Trauma, Violence, & Abuse* 15, no. 3 (July 1, 2014): 201–26, https://doi.org/10.1177/1524838014521322; Brubaker et al., "Measuring and Reporting Campus Sexual Assault."

10. Harris, Cobian, and Karunaratne, "Reimagining the Study of Campus Sexual Assault," 30.

11. Harris, Cobian, and Karunaratne, "Reimagining the Study of Campus Sexual Assault."

12. Kamaria B. Porter, Sandra R. Levitsky, and Elizabeth A. Armstrong, "Gender Equity and Due Process in Campus Sexual Assault Adjudication Procedures," *Journal of Higher Education*, June 15, 2022, 1–27, https://doi.org/10.1080/00221546.2022.2082784.

13. Kathryn J. Holland, Lilia M. Cortina, and Jennifer J. Freyd, "Compelled Disclosure of College Sexual Assault," *American Psychologist* 73, no. 3 (2018): 256–68, https://doi.org/10.1037/amp0000186.

14. Porter, Levitsky, and Armstrong, "Gender Equity and Due Process in Campus Sexual Assault Adjudication Procedures."

15. Shamus Khan et al., "'I Didn't Want to Be 'That Girl': The Social Risks of Labeling, Telling, and Reporting Sexual Assault," *Sociological Science* 5, no. 19 (2018): 432–60, https://doi.org/10.15195/v5.a19.

16. Anuj Shrestha, "After a Sexual Assault, Where Can You Get a Medical and Fo-

rensic Exam?," NBC News, December 28, 2020, www.nbcnews.com/health/sexual-health/after-sexual-assault-where-can-you-get-medical-forensic-exam-n1240035.

17. Collins, *Black Feminist Thought*.

18. Collins, *Black Feminist Thought*.

19. David S. Kirk and Mauri Matsuda, "Legal Cynicism, Collective Efficacy, and the Ecology of Arrest," *Criminology* 49, no. 2 (2011): 447, https://doi.org/10.1111/j.1745-9125.2011.00226.x.

20. Monica C. Bell, "Police Reform and the Dismantling of Legal Estrangement," *Yale Law Journal* 126, no. 7 (2017): 2054–150; Brooklynn K. Hitchens, Patrick J. Carr, and Susan Clampet-Lundquist, "The Context for Legal Cynicism: Urban Young Women's Experiences with Policing in Low-Income, High-Crime Neighborhoods," *Race and Justice* 8, no. 1 (January 1, 2018): 27–50, https://doi.org/10.1177/2153368717724506.

21. Bell, "Police Reform and the Dismantling of Legal Estrangement," 2084.

22. Patrick J. Carr, Laura Napolitano, and Jessica Keating, "We Never Call the Cops and Here Is Why: A Qualitative Examination of Legal Cynicism in Three Philadelphia Neighborhoods," *Criminology* 45, no. 2 (2007): 445–80, https://doi.org/10.1111/j.1745-9125.2007.00084.x; Bell, "Police Reform and the Dismantling of Legal Estrangement."

23. Amber Joy Powell and Michelle S. Phelps, "Gendered Racial Vulnerability: How Women Confront Crime and Criminalization," *Law & Society Review* 55, no. 3 (2021): 429–51, https://doi.org/10.1111/lasr.12561; Beth E. Richie, *Arrested Justice: Black Women, Violence, and America's Prison Nation* (New York: NYU Press, 2012).

24. Powell and Phelps, "Gendered Racial Vulnerability," 432.

25. Crenshaw, "Mapping the Margins"; C. Shawn McGuffey, "Rape and Racial Appraisals: Culture, Intersectionality, and Black Women's Accounts of Sexual Assault," *Du Bois Review* 10, no. 1 (2013): 109–30, https://doi.org/10.1017/S1742058X12000355; Patricia Washington, "Disclosure Patterns of Black Female Sexual Assault Survivors," *Violence Against Women* 7, no. 11 (2001): 1254–83, https://doi.org/10.1177/10778010122183856.

26. Gómez and Gobin, "Black Women and Girls & #MeToo"; Lily D. McNair and Helen Neville, "African American Women Survivors of Sexual Assault: The Intersection of Race and Class," *Women & Therapy* 18, no. 3–4 (1996): 107–18; Slatton and Richard, "Black Women's Experiences of Sexual Assault and Disclosure."

27. Powell and Phelps, "Gendered Racial Vulnerability"; Richie, *Arrested Justice*; Angela Y. Davis et al., *Abolition. Feminism. Now.* (Chicago: Haymarket, 2022).

28. Rebecca Campbell et al., "'What Has It Been Like for You to Talk with Me Today?' The Impact of Participating in Interview Research on Rape Survivors," *Violence Against Women* 16, no. 1 (2010): 60–83, https://doi.org/10.1177/1077801209353576; Lisa Aronson Fontes, "Ethics in Violence against Women Research: The Sensitive, the

Dangerous, and the Overlooked," *Ethics & Behavior* 14, no. 2 (2004): 141–74, https://doi.org/10.1207/s15327019eb1402_4; Michael G. Griffin et al., "Participation in Trauma Research: Is There Evidence of Harm?," *Journal of Traumatic Stress* 16, no. 3 (2003): 221–27.

29. Rebecca Campbell, *Emotionally Involved: The Impact of Researching Rape* (London: Taylor & Francis Group, 2001), http://ebookcentral.proquest.com/lib/umichigan/detail.action?docID=1222755; Fontes, "Ethics in Violence against Women Research: The Sensitive, the Dangerous, and the Overlooked."

30. Jeong Hee Kim, *Understanding Narrative Inquiry: The Crafting and Analysis of Stories as Research* (Los Angeles: Sage, 2016), 105.

31. Powell and Phelps, "Gendered Racial Vulnerability."

32. Bell, "Police Reform and the Dismantling of Legal Estrangement," 2133.

33. Bell, "Police Reform and the Dismantling of Legal Estrangemnt," 2105.

34. Elaine Frantz Parsons, "The Roots of the Ku-Klux Klan in Pulaski, Tennessee," in *Ku-Klux* (Chapel Hill: University of North Carolina Press, 2016), https://doi.org/10.5149/northcarolina/9781469625423.003.0001.

35. Gómez and Gobin, "Black Women and Girls & #MeToo."

36. Hitchens, Carr, and Clampet-Lundquist, "The Context for Legal Cynicism"; Powell and Phelps, "Gendered Racial Vulnerability."

37. Bell, "Police Reform and the Dismantling of Legal Estrangement"; Collins, *Black Feminist Thought*; Crenshaw, "Mapping the Margins"; McGuffey, "Rape and Racial Appraisals."

38. Rebecca Campbell et al., "Preventing the 'Second Rape': Rape Survivors' Experiences with Community Service Providers," *Journal of Interpersonal Violence* 16, no. 12 (December 1, 2001): 1239–59, https://doi.org/10.1177/088626001016012002.

39. Michael G. Curtis, Annika S. Karlsen, and Leslie A. Anderson, "Transmuting Girls into Women: Examining the Adultification of Black Female Sexual Assault Survivors through Twitter Feedback," *Violence Against Women*, April 19, 2022, https://doi.org/10.1177/10778012221083334.

40. Collins, *Black Feminist Thought*.

41. Curtis, Karlsen, and Anderson, "Transmuting Girls into Women."

42. Hitchens, Carr, and Clampet-Lundquist, "The Context for Legal Cynicism," 38.

43. Hitchens, Carr, and Clampet-Lundquist, "The Context for Legal Cynicism," 38.

44. Davis et al., *Abolition. Feminism. Now.*

45. Antar A. Tichavakunda, "Studying Black Student Life on Campus: Toward a Theory of Black Placemaking in Higher Education," *Urban Education*, November 11, 2020, https://doi.org/10.1177/0042085920971354; Elizabeth A. Armstrong and Laura T. Hamilton, *Paying for the Party: How College Maintains Inequality*, *Paying for the Party* (Cambridge, MA: Harvard University Press, 2013), https://doi.org/10.4159/harvard

.9780674073517; Jennifer S. Hirsch and Shamus Khan, *Sexual Citizens: A Landmark Study of Sex, Power, and Assault on Campus* (New York: Norton, 2020).

46. Erin Collins, "The Criminalization of Title IX Symposium: Rape Law Revisited," *Ohio State Journal of Criminal Law* 13 (2015): 365–96.

47. Gómez and Gobin, "Black Women and Girls & #MeToo."

12

ED TECH IS SURVEILLANCE TECH

Pedagogies of Surveillance in Physical and Digital Campuses

VINEETA SINGH

On November 8, 2019, students enrolled at Virginia Commonwealth University's (VCU) first-year writing classes received an email informing them that they were part of a new pilot program called Ram Attend, which would track their connection to the campus Wi-Fi as a proxy for their course attendance.[1] The $96,000 pilot program, run by the ed tech start-up Degree Analytics, would monitor every time their phone, tablet, or laptop connected to the college's Wi-Fi and compare the times and locations of those connections to class times and locations to record their class attendance.[2] VCU's wireless network covers university-owned buildings including residential spaces and recreational spaces. Richmond Police and VCU Police have concurrent jurisdiction over the area and share records and equipment.[3] This seemingly benign use of technology raised profound questions about the extension of police power and surveillance into the classroom.

Education technology has become a legal battleground, not just for students' privacy rights but also for conversations about campus policing.[4] This is not news to many teachers across the country. As our institutions developed contracts with ed tech companies like Blackboard, Proctorio, and Top Hat, teachers have increasingly been asked to create, log, and sort data ranging from attendance logs to databases of state-issued IDs to protect academic integrity. Academic surveillance tools like lockdown browsers, proctoring software, and plagiarism checking software, for example, create and maintain records of students' photo

IDs, video, audio, location data, keystroke patterns, speech patterns, mouse clicks, eye movements, and "other behavioral cues."[5] The explanations behind such data gathering have been unsatisfactory at best and insidious at worst. This data is shared in ways we do not always understand, with companies we do not necessarily trust, and ultimately used to increase the power of policing on and off campus. Despite teachers' best intentions, every use of ed tech generates data about students that can be used to track their behaviors and target them for state-sanctioned violence. From this vantage point, ed tech's increasing penetration into campus spaces is fortifying a web of surveillance relations that extends through physical and digital spaces patrolled by campus officials. Further, teachers are increasingly deputized to take punitive actions against students to protect the institutional brand.

Many teachers know or at the very least sense that education technology is "cop shit."[6] Jeffrey Moro coined the phrase in 2020 to articulate the carceral logics and political economy of education technology that surveils students and assumes they are always-already in violation of, or seeking ways to be in violation of, school policies. This essay builds on Moro's call to name and reject "cop shit" in our classrooms. I argue that our classrooms and our campuses are being used as laboratories for untested and untest*able* surveillance technologies that expand the reach of campus police. In cities like Richmond, where campus police share "records, materials, and equipment" with city police, this data collection also expands the reach of city police to monitor students and faculty on campus and in their homes. They empower police to mark "at-risk" students (i.e., students most vulnerable to state violence) for increased interactions with police, actually increasing their risk of being targeted for state or state-sanctioned violence. In some ways, ed tech simultaneously displaces the physical figure of the campus police officer but amplifies the officer's reach by disaggregating and distributing the functions of campus police (surveillance, "forensic" data gathering, predicting and modifying behavior) into invisible algorithms and compliant instructors.

ACADEMIC SURVEILLANCE

When the Ram Attend pilot at VCU was initially announced, student and local journalists reported that students' names would not be sent to Degree Analytics, "only their personal school identification number." Conflicting reports later stated that student names would only be purged if students opted *out* of the pilot program; however, that would not prevent their connection data from being shared with the vendor. VCU did not issue any further clarification on what exactly students were opting out of when they selected to opt out. Students reported being confused about why the institution needed another layer of attendance tracking when faculty were already empowered to track student attendance. Students also wondered why the program was launched midsemester in November, why the university was being "so secretive about this program," why they "hid" the opt-out Google form in "just another email" instead of "in a more fashionable way catered to students such as an Instagram or Twitter post," and why students had to opt *out* instead of opting *in*.[7]

In response, students created and shared informative posts across social media platforms. They shared the opt-out link so rampantly and effectively that within two weeks, 2,414 students of the original 4,000-student sample had opted out of the program.[8] The following January, the university quietly announced the failed "conclusion" of the pilot program. Between a smaller-than-expected sample size, students not using the VCU SafeNet Wi-Fi network, and faculty holding classes outside of assigned classrooms, Ram Attend was not able to offer reliable information about whether students were in class, and "as a result of the pilot, VCU has concluded that automated Wi-Fi connectivity-based attendance recording is not the best tool for VCU at this time."[9] The pilot had effectively failed to gather enough data to prove its own utility.

Colleges and universities that employ attendance tracking programs such as Ram Attend fundamentally misunderstand the correlation between attendance, student retention, and graduation rates. VCU professed that it wished to track attendance because it is "one of the most important indicators of student success."[10] In the most generous reading of VCU's intentions, we might think that automating attendance would relieve faculty of a bureaucratic function and free up their time to focus on teaching. But this is not actually a problem in classes with reasonable student-instructor ratios, like the fifteen-person first-year writing seminars in which Ram Attend was deployed. Any time spent taking attendance in such courses is also time spent learning students' names, becoming aware of who they are, which students they've connected with in class, and whether they are being incorporated into a larger community of students in the classroom. Yes, attendance is an "issue" in three-hundred-person lecture halls, but the "issue" is not that students are not coming to class. The issue is that we have created classes whose value students rightly do not see. When we turn to enforcing attendance, we have failed to diagnose what is wrong with the classrooms our institutions have built. Tracking attendance with technology that logs students' physical presence anywhere the campus Wi-Fi extends is a clear violation of students' privacy and creates a reservoir of information about them that could be weaponized against them by campus and city police in the future.

Although there is a chance the university's failure to clearly communicate about the pilot program was a sign of incompetence, understanding the common logics that inform rampant surveillance remains critical. In a study of platform capitalism through the lens of racial capitalism, sociologist Tressie McMillan Cottom cautions that "sometimes, a firm or organization performs secrecy just for the sake of secrecy. This reinforces its ability to do so and its right to do so. . . . [I]t expands obfuscation as a logic, even in organizations or institutions that have a public mandate."[11] That is, neglecting to clearly explain how their surveillance technology works creates a precedent for the institution to continue not explaining how future surveillance technologies and techniques will work, and it accustoms students, instructors, and campus workers to not knowing when or why they are being monitored. This pedagogy of surveillance normalizes surveillance in campus spaces and stacks the odds in favor of expanding the campus and city police's access to student data.

It is also possible that institutions like VCU are asking students to generate mountains of data on the off chance that these mountains will contribute to amorphous ideas about academic integrity and prestige. Still, this does not change the reality that generating these piles of data and licensing them to private companies creates databases about student behavior that can be used against student interests. Extracting location data under the guise of student success is unfair and deceptive. As the Electronic Privacy Information Center states in its unfair business practices lawsuit against major academic surveillance tech companies (Respondus, ProctorU, Proctorio, Examity, and Honorlock), the data collected by such tech is far in excess of what would be needed for the programs' stated aims. And to top it off, students cannot reasonably avoid the collection of their personal information. Further, the suit alleges that "the use of opaque and secret AI systems and algorithms prevent[s] students from understanding how their information is analyzed, making it impossible for students to consent to such uses."[12] Apart from the purported value generated for student success, there are also immediate financial motives for ed tech companies to gather data for their own sake.

These behavioral databases have become valuable assets for tech start-ups like Degree Analytics, not only for institutional use but also because behavioral data in the aggregate remains a lucrative proposition. For example, the $2 billion sale of Instructure, the publicly traded company that developed the Canvas learning management system, is backed by the Big Data the company has extracted from students. Market actors speculating in artificial intelligence and predictive modeling are especially enthusiastic about longitudinal datasets that follow groups of users over a period of years. No coincidence, then, that Instructure has been working to extend its products from the K-12 market, through college, and most recently to include Portfolium, a $43 million ePortfolio platform for college students transitioning to the workforce, and Bridge, its software for employee training and professional development programs. The more data such companies can gather per person per year, the more valuable they become for continuing experiments with AI and predictive technologies.[13] The value comes not from the data themselves but "from their predictive power and inducing behavior in others."[14] That is, as in predictive policing, what is valuable is not that the algorithm can discover a knowable truth about the user/subject but that it can induce the user/subject to act in ways that produce true predictions.

Aware of these interests, ed tech companies themselves are attempting to use these datasets to create algorithms that predict and correct students' behavior. In the summer of 2021, Blackboard CEO Bill Ballhaus set out a long-term vision for Blackboard's personalized learning in which he compared ed tech to online shopping, healthcare, and entertainment, arguing that "a critical mass of data powers proactive nudges" in these arenas and that education would do well to "[keep] pace with the shift to customized experiences that other industries [have] achieved."[15] A nudge refers to the notifications students would get when their data is flagged as being "off-track" for success. An analogue would be a FitBit buzzing to notify the wearer that they have been stationary for an hour. Blackboard has 25 *billion* interactions with students every week, and it wants to use this data to create predictive models.

Much excitement surrounds the idea of early warning systems to identify students at risk of failing a course, for example, through excessive absences. Yet scholars have challenged the strong causal inference boosters draw between systems like Course Signals and actual student retention as the initial research has not proven reproducible in other contexts.[16] Perhaps even more troublingly, further research also shows that the "learning analytics" ed tech generates are not meaningful motivators for students. Student-facing dashboards have been negatively associated with intrinsic motivation.[17] When it comes to the display of GPAs, even high-achieving students are "unable to make accurate interpretations of statistics shown in dashboards," which in turn only offer diagnostic assessments, not guidance on how to change the learning analytics outcomes.[18]

A big part of why Ram Attend failed at VCU was because the data it gathered was so obviously redundant. It is not a lack of data that troubles ed tech. We are swimming in data that is generated and collected without intention or deliberation. It is gathered for its own sake (that is, for aggregation) and for its utility to train and "perfect" the predictive algorithms being developed by surveillance capitalists—that is, it treats the college campus as a training ground for artificial intelligence, predictive modeling, and behavioral nudges—the leading edge of predictive policing.

Universities are sold on location data gathering by companies like Degree Analytics promising to sort students and assign them "'risk scores' based on factors like the frequency of visits to the library . . . [and] by tracking visits to the cafeteria or gym, determine 'signs of personal anguish' such as student isolation or eating disorders."[19] That is to say, surveilling students and algorithmically interpreting their behavioral patterns will allow institutions to target specific students for various interventions. Blackboard CEO Bill Ballhaus uses the seemingly innocuous examples of tracking students' movements to the cafeteria and the gym, but of course this technology could just as easily be used to track which students frequent the Black Student Resource Center or the LGBTQ Resource Center. It could track patterns of students gathering in the lead-up to, or during, student protests.[20] The fear that universities might use ed tech to track student activists' location has already proven to be justified. In December 2019, NBC reported that UNC Police and the North Carolina Statue Bureau of Investigation used "geofencing," to identify students who protested the campus's "Silent Sam" statue commemorating Confederate soldiers. Geofencing locates any cell phones that cross into a specific area by locking onto their geolocation systems, then recording social media posts and sometimes other data from those phones. UNC had been paying Social Sentinel $73,500 a year to use this software from 2016 to 2019. Capturing this information, especially in the absence of a warrant, creates Fourth Amendment concerns.

ACADEMIC SURVEILLANCE AND THE DEPUTIZATION OF TEACHING FACULTY

The physical web of surveillance developed in the physical spaces of campus through tracking programs like Ram Attend has expanded drastically during the pandemic and the emergency shift to online education. Ed tech lends a veneer of objectivity to the policing of ideal student bodies and behaviors in the classroom. The US college classroom has historically been a fraught place for Black students, queer students, and neurodivergent students, who have had their bodies and behaviors marked as deviations from the ideal student. Ed tech not only gives cover to instructors' suspicions that students of color and historically underrepresented students are sullying their university's brand but also assumes an antagonistic relation between student and instructor. Algorithmic automation removes the proximal eyes and hands involved in extracting, collating, and acting on surveillance data. As argued above, this creates troves of poorly understood data that can be weaponized against students. It also deputizes college instructors to become enforcers of the racial surveillance state's work of sorting and marking (in the American and English senses of the word) students based on their perceived productivity for the racial capitalist state.

In January 2021, a faculty member at the Geisel School of Medicine at Dartmouth University reported to administrators that they were concerned that students *could have* cheated during remotely administered exams.[21] To accommodate remote teaching during the pandemic, Geisel had required students to download ExamSoft, a lockdown browser that promises "to protect the integrity of your exams and assessment data."[22] Students using ExamSoft are made to download an encrypted exam file onto their device. At the time of the exam, students are given a password that allows them to access the encrypted exam file and begin answering questions. During the exam, ExamSoft blocks their computer from Wi-Fi internet connections and prevents them from accessing anything else on their computer while they are using the exam. Once students have completed their exams, ExamSoft uploads their exam responses to the Web, and returns control of their device to the student.[23] Geisel also required students to have a second device connected to the internet on hand. The *New York Times* later reported that "the faculty member's report made administrators concerned that some students may have used their backup device to look at course material on Canvas [their electronic learning management system] while taking tests on their primary [locked-down] device."[24]

In mid-March, the Committee on Student Performance and Conduct emailed seventeen students, accusing them of violating the student honor code. They were given less than forty-eight hours to "respond to the charges, were not provided complete data logs for the exams, and were advised to plead guilty though they denied cheating or were given just two minutes to make their cases in online hearings."[25] Most students appealed, citing that the investigation had mistaken automated Canvas activity for human behavior. By April, ten students had been either expelled or suspended.

Students protested. Alumni protested. Faculty at Geisel and other medical schools spoke out. The *New York Times* reported on the outcry. In June, the dean of the Medical School, Duane A. Compton, announced that he was dismissing all the honor code charges and expunging students' academic records; he apologized to the students "for what they have been through."[26] The incident became an occasion for skeptics of proctoring software to find a common voice and share resources for how to convince institutions to disinvest from this software. While Dartmouth continues their contract with Examsoft, many faculty members in and outside Dartmouth are turning away from it. Meanwhile, the Electronic Privacy Information Center (EPIC) has begun legal proceedings against five online test-proctoring services, accusing them of unfair and deceptive collection of excessive personal data; unfair use of opaque, unproven AI systems; deceptive uses of facial recognition; and deceptive claims about the reliability of their products.[27] Ed tech is expanding the web of campus surveillance into students' homes. Teachers who are untrained in how to gather or interpret data from these softwares but are nonetheless deputized to protect the college's brand can easily ascribe nefarious motives to student behaviors.

The media coverage and public academic discussion of the failures at Dartmouth tended to center two poles of academic surveillance discourse: misrecognition and privacy. Misrecognition is students being unrecognizable to the facial recognition technology (a particular difficulty for dark-skinned students as most facial recognition algorithms are trained on databases containing few dark faces) or as was the case at Dartmouth, students are misidentified as engaged in cheating. Misrecognition indexes the implausibility of Black, Brown, queer, neurodivergent innocence.

Reporting on Geisel's failures repeatedly mentioned that Canvas, the learning management system the students were logged into during their exams, is not designed as a "forensic" tool, meaning that it could not be relied on to give an accurate account of students' activities. The implication, of course, is that it is possible and desirable to perfect a system that monitors students' every digital and physical move during an exam or during any kind of instruction.

As education scholar Roxana Marachi and political scientist Lawrence Quill write, "With no federal privacy laws governing student data brokers, student data can be collected, sold, and bought without any apparent legal protections from widespread exploitation."[28] The collection of all this data leads to worries about data breaches exposing students' private data. And rightly so. Education writer Audrey Watters calculated that between 2005 and 2017, US universities had their confidential data breached 550 times, exposing nearly thirteen million records. But there is a larger privacy concern we must keep at the fore of ed tech discussions: the *existence* of these records is itself a breach of student privacy.

Academic surveillance companies typically claim they do not sell user data to third parties, but often they *are* third parties (that is, ExamSoft *is* TurnItIn), and generally state that they can share data with law enforcement whenever the company deems necessary. Even without sharing, data gathering is profitable in itself. This data is what trains and "improves" the reliability of the proprietary algorithms and software surveillance tech companies sell.[29]

The Dartmouth incident is a reminder that the presence of data is not, in itself, a meaningful measure of teaching and learning. Students and instructors are essentially being made to create value for ed tech companies. In doing so, we are interpellated into a web of surveillance that treats our classrooms as sites of experimentation. To the extent that teachers generate data for "early warning stems" for students who miss classes and fail assignments, we might be creating data that can be weaponized against the students most at risk of state-sanctioned violence.

ABOLITIONIST PRAXIS

The COVID-19 pandemic and the emergency shift to online education have provided a pretext for a drastic expansion of surveillance in physical and digital spaces students and staff have to occupy to work at universities. During the pandemic, the Electronic Frontier Foundation (EFF) and the Reynolds School of Journalism at the University of Nevada, Reno, started a database to document law enforcement agencies' use of surveillance technologies across the country. In doing so, they "documented more than 250 technology purchases . . . adopted by more than 200 universities in 37 states." They found 152 campus police departments using body-worn cameras; 10 campus police departments that use drones; 49 universities and colleges that use automated license plate readers—"cameras attached to fixed locations or to security or parking patrol cars that capture every license plate that passes"—then upload the data captures to a searchable database with the time, date, and GPS coordinate of each license plate recorded.[30]

At least four police departments at universities in Florida use biometric identification through their access to a statewide facial recognition network called Face Analysis Comparison and Examination System (FACES), operated by the Pinellas County Sheriff's Office. In San Diego alone, at least five universities and college campuses participate in a facial recognition program using mobile devices. San Diego State University, part of the California State University system, conducted 180 facial recognition searches in 2018 alone, before California enacted a three-year statewide moratorium on facial recognition technology (FRT) in 2019. Even as FRT has been in the headlines, schools have been experimenting with other biometrics, for instance installing iris scanning stations at the University of Georgia's dining halls in 2017.[31]

At least eight university police departments are on record as using gunshot detection software such as ShotSpotter, a notoriously unreliable technology that adds to privacy concerns by capturing conversations, which prosecutors have (so far unsuccessfully) attempted to use as evidence in court proceedings.[32]

Finally, some universities and colleges have enhanced their video surveillance through the use of video analytics or "computer vision," algorithms for round-the-clock monitoring without the manpower required to monitor video cameras 24–7. These systems can "track objects and people from camera to camera, identify patterns and anomalies, and potentially conduct face recognition" (EFF). Some schools, including three campuses of the University of Maryland, also maintain lists of local residents and businesses who own security cameras and can be called upon to "volunteer" footage when asked.

But this is also not new for the settler colonial academy. The colonial power and propensity to "sort, categorize, and order human activity" by creating "human natural resources" who are objects to be acted upon by "technologically superior" subjects who can know them but not be known by them is at the heart of US higher education's historical promise AND the pedagogical logic embraced by many of us as teachers. It does the racial surveillance state's work of sorting and marking students based on their perceived productivity for the racial capitalist state. Indeed, as I and many others have argued in the scholarship of teaching and learning, if higher education understands academic integrity to mean academic surveillance, it is time for all stakeholders to revisit what it is we hope to get out of the college classroom.[33]

Recognizing that data collection is a reification of vulnerability into risk, perhaps it is time for every syllabus statement to include a data collection policy, making transparent to students what data is being gathered through their learning management systems and their online tools, even when we are not actively using this data. Instructors and students must also clearly communicate about what data we have the power to delete and when we will do so.

I have argued here that ed tech simultaneously displaces the physical figure of the campus police officer but amplifies the officer's reach by disaggregating and distributing the functions of campus police (surveillance, "forensic" data gathering, predicting and modifying behavior) into invisible algorithms and compliant instructors. In researching this dissemination of policing powers, I have found myself surrounded by a kind of technological nihilism. Even the most trenchant critiques of academic surveillance technology sometimes betray a belief in the inevitability of an irresistible and unceasing expansion of the ed tech industry, of the datafication and commodification of every teacher, student, worker behavior. I structured my own contribution to this volume around three instances where ed tech has failed students, instructors, and workers *and*—due to their resistance—failed to spread and grow itself. Not every ed tech story has ended this way (yet), but the illusion of its ineluctable growth is part of what we must combat if we are to contain the web of surveillance and create our own ways of being in relations of study. We have the tools to make the expansion of police powers visible and containable.

NOTES

1. Daniel Payne, "VCU Rolls Out Program to Track Student Class Attendance Using WiFi Connections," *College Fix*, November 22, 2019, www.thecollegefix.com/vcu-rolls-out-program-to-track-student-class-attendance-via-wifi-connections/.

2. Katie Hollowell, "VCU Pilots New WiFi Tracking Program for Class Attendance," *Commonwealth Times*, November 14, 2019; Katie Hollowell, "VCU Pilots New WiFi Tracking Program 2," November 19, 2019.

3. Megan Schiffres, "Richmond City Council Accepts Police Data Sharing Proposal Despite Community Outrage," *Dogwood*, February 10, 2021.

4. See, for instance, Electronic Privacy Information Center (EPIC), "Complaint and Request for Investigation, Injunction and Other Relief" submitted to the Office of the Attorney General of the District of Columbia, December 9, 2020, https://epic.org/wp-content/uploads/privacy/dccppa/online-test-proctoring/EPIC-complaint-in-re-online-test-proctoring-companies-12-09-20.pdf.

5. EPIC, "Complaint and Request for Investigation."

6. Jeffrey Moro, "Against Cop Shit," *Jeffrey Moro* (blog), February 13, 2020, https://jeffreymoro.com/blog/2020-02-13-against-cop-shit/. Moro articulates the carceral log-

ics and political economy of education technology that surveils students and assumes they are already in violation of, or seeking ways to be in violation of, school policies.

7. Hollowell, "VCU Pilots New WiFi Tracking Program 2"; Tagwa Shammet, "Tea Time with Tagwa: They're Watching You," *Commonwealth Times,* November 19, 2019.

8. Katie Hollowell, "VCU Will Not Move Forward with WiFi Program for Attendance Tracking," *Commonwealth Times,* February 2, 2020.

9. Strategic Enrollment Management and Student Success, VCU, "Ram Attend," accessed May 18, 2022, https://semss.vcu.edu/ram-attend/.

10. Hollowell, "VCU Pilots New WiFi Tracking Program for Class Attendance."

11. Tressie McMillan Cottom, "Where Platform Capitalism and Racial Capitalism Meet: The Sociology of Race and Racism in the Digital Society," *Sociology of Race and Ethnicity* 6, no. 4 (2020): 443.

12. Electronic Privacy Information Center (EPIC), "Complaint and Request for Investigation."

13. Roxana Marachi and Lawrence Quill, "The Case of Canvas: Longitudinal Datafication through Learning Management Systems," *Teaching in Higher Education* 25, no. 4 (2020): 418–20.

14. Janja Komljenovic, "The Rise of Education Rentiers: Digital Platforms, Digital Data and Rents," *Learning, Media, and Technology* 46, no. 3 (2021).

15. Bill Ballhaus, "Bringing Personalized Experiences to Education with You," *Blackboard Blog,* June 8, 2021, https://blog.blackboard.com/bringing-personalized-experiences-to-education-with-you/.

16. Kimberly Arnold and M. Pistilli, "Course Signals at Purdue: Using Learning Analytics to Increase Student Success," *Proceedings of the 2nd International Conference on Learning Analytics and Knowledge* (2012): 267–70.

17. For instance, Lisa Lim, Srećko Joksimović, Shane Dawson, and Dragan Gašević have shown that learning analytic dashboards peg students' self-evaluation to the performances of their peers, either discouraging them or motivating them to compete with other students. In neither case are students oriented toward learning content and skills (Lisa Lim, Srećko Joksimović, Shane Dawson, and Dragan Gašević, "Exploring Students' Sensemaking of Learning Analytics Dashboards: Does Frame of Reference Make a Difference?" *Proceedings of the 9th International Conference on Learning Analytics* [2019]: 250–59).

18. Neil Selwyn and Dragan Gasevic, "The Datafication of Higher Education: Discussing the Promises and Problems," *Teaching in Higher Education* 25, no. 4 (2020): 533–34.

19. Michael Kwet and Paul Prinsloo, "The 'Smart' Classroom: A New Frontier in the Age of the Smart University," *Teaching in Higher Education* 25, no. 4 (2020): 518. These specific examples come from Aaron Benz, the founder of Degree Analytics, and were

cited in Drew Harwell's 2019 report for the *Washington Post,* "Colleges Are Turning Students' Phones into Surveillance Machines." The report includes general descriptions of how universities like VCU, Purdue, Syracuse, and UNC have been using the SpotterEDU service, along with testimonials from campus staff about the benefits of the service, but schools are reluctant to share the specific features they employ or whether/which labels they might be using for students. See, for instance, Temple University's refusal to disclose its uses of SpotterEDU in response to journalist Jason Koebler's request for their release under the Pennsylvania Right to Know Act (Drew Harwell, "Colleges Are Turning Students' Phones into Surveillance Machines," *Washington Post*, December 24, 2019.

20. Ari Sen, "UNC Campus Police Used Geofencing Tech to Monitor Antiracism Protestors," NBC News, December 21, 2019, www.nbcnews.com/news/education/unc-campus-police-used-geofencing-tech-monitor-antiracism-protestors-n1105746.

21. Natasha Singer, "Dartmouth Medical School Drops Case against Students," *New York Times*, June 10, 2021.

22. "Assessment Data That Transforms Education," Examsoft, accessed May 28 2022, https://examsoft.com/why-examsoft/.

23. "Assessment Data That Transforms Education."

24. Natasha Singer and Aaron Krolik, "Online Cheating Charges Upend Dartmouth Medical School," *New York Times*, June 10, 2021.

25. Singer, "Dartmouth Medical School Drops Case."

26. Singer, "Dartmouth Medical School Drops Case."

27. Electronic Privacy Information Center (EPIC), "Complaint and Request for Investigation"

28. Marachi and Quill, "The Case of Canvas," 424.

29. Further, students' intellectual property generate value for ed tech companies like TurnItIn that are meant to keep students from using others' work without credit, but themselves rely on taking students' work without compensation to build their own databases and the value of their own intellectual property as they use student work to teach their AI and algorithms.

30. Dave Maass, "Scholars under Surveillance: How Campus Police Use High Tech to Spy on Students," Electronic Frontier Foundation, March 9, 2021, www.eff.org/deeplinks/2021/03/scholars-under-surveillance-how-campus-police-use-high-tech-spy-students/.

31. Maass, "Scholars under Surveillance."

32. Maass, "Scholars under Surveillance." Gunshot detection involves setting up a series of 'acoustic sensors' (recorders) that alert law enforcement whenever they detect a loud noise (gunshot, firework, etc.) Despite claims that this recording equipment is only used to detect gunshots, in at least one case (*People v. Johnson,* a 2013 California

course) police have successfully entered into record audio recordings of people's speech that was captured on the same technology (see Electronic Frontier Foundation, "Street-Level Surveillance," www.eff.org/pages/gunshot-detection; and Hannah Gold, "ShotSpotter: Gunshot Detection System Raises Privacy Concerns on Campuses," *Guardian* July 17, 2015).

33. See, for instance, Moro, "Cop Shit"; Brenna Clarke Gray, Maha Bali, Benjamin Doxtdator, Sava Saheli Singh, Chris Gilliard, Jesse Stommel, Audrey Watters, and Cory Doctorow, "Teach-In Against Surveillance," December 1 2020, www.youtube.com/watch?v=RzzddjbplJQ; Marianne Madoré, Anna Zeemont, Joaly Burgos, Jake Guskin, Hailey Lam, and Andréa Stella, "Resisting Surveillance, Practicing/Imagining the End of Grading" *Journal of Interactive Technology & Pedagogy* 20 (2021), https://jitp.commons.gc.cuny.edu/resisting-surveillance-practicing-imagining-the-end-of-grading/; Sandy Grande, "Refusing the University," in *Toward What Justice?: Describing Diverse Dreams of Justice in Education*, ed. Eve Tuck and K. Wayne Yang (New York: Routledge: 2018), 47–65.

PART IV
TRANSFORMING CAMPUS SAFETY

13

CAMPUS POLICING AND THE EXPERIENCES OF FORMERLY INCARCERATED STUDENTS

An Interview with Ryan Flaco Rising

RYAN FLACO RISING, GRACE WATKINS, JOHN SLOAN,
YALILE SURIEL, AND JUDE PAUL MATIAS DIZON

BACKGROUND Ryan Flaco Rising is a member of the Underground Scholars Initiative (USI), which supports formerly incarcerated and system-impacted students within the University of California system. In this interview, he discusses his own experiences and observations of the effect that pervasive campus policing has on formerly incarcerated students. Students with direct experience of the criminal legal system have specific and often-unaddressed needs within higher education and are targeted by campus police, which presents particular challenges for students on probation or parole. He also reflects on the aims, objectives, and challenges facing the statewide movement to support system-impacted students and the Cops Off Campus Movement. The interview has been edited for length and clarity.

QUESTION *Can you tell us a bit about yourself and your early experiences?*

RYAN FLACO RISING I'm a formerly incarcerated student, part of the Gaucho Underground Scholars program here at the University of California, Santa Barbara (UCSB). I'm finishing up my bachelor's degree in sociology with a minor in education, and I was accepted as a PhD candidate into UC Irvine within the Criminology, Law, and Society department.

My background is that I went through the school-to-prison pipeline starting at the age of six. Like many other kids coming from marginalized communities, school officials and health professionals mistreated me. By the age of twelve, I was incarcerated as a juvenile. This was the start of a very dark path where my spirit was broken. I was totally dehumanized by the humiliation that I experienced in juvenile hall at the hands of the staff members. Then sent back out to my community broken internally and dealing with an institutionalized mindset where I didn't respect my community any longer because of the way I was being treated as a little kid. I had a very poor education due to this. I didn't know how to write with periods or commas. I didn't know my times tables. I didn't know how to really be a student. I wasn't trained on it. I was pretty much used and pushed through education.

After being incarcerated as a youth, I found myself incarcerated as an adult in the county jail. I did seven years in the California Department of Corruption. I was a part of the 2011–13 prisoner hunger strikes to demand rehabilitative services. One major success of these strikes was that the prison ended the use of indeterminate segregated housing units, where they were housing many of our elders. Another was that the prison began offering college courses. I began to study at Lassen Community College and I felt amazing. It was the biggest accomplishment of my life thus far to get A+ grades, so I kept studying. Then I got released on August 12, 2015.

Like most people, I didn't have any family connections, because I had been isolated from my family for so long, so I was transient and houseless. I was released to the streets and slept my first night out of prison on a bench in front of San Diego City College. When I woke up the next morning, I looked at the college sign and said to myself, "I'm going to go to college here." With support from my parole officer and reconnecting with my mom, I got signed up for college.

QUESTION *What were your experiences like with campus police once you got to college?*

RYAN FLACO RISING In my view, any school that has a police department attached to it is invested in the school-to-prison pipeline. At San Diego City College, it was disgusting how much the police control that campus. They were ticketing everyone for the smallest parking violations and harassing folks that were living on the street even though they really respected the campus.

I'm tatted up so it was hard walking around the streets. The police would pull me over and sit me on the curb. They'd ask me, "What gang you from?" Then they would search me and humiliate me in front of my community. This happened on numerous occasions. I'll never forget this one time I got stopped. The officer was like, "We've never seen you here before." And we're in a tourist city, so I was looking around and thinking, "Have you seen any of these people?"

There was another incident that really sticks out to me that took place right before I graduated. On campus, I saw a Black man sitting there on his computer, minding his own business when two officers jumped out. When they grabbed the guy he passed out. The way they picked him up caused his head to start hitting the concrete. I began filming and telling the officers to leave him alone. They told me that they were arresting him for trespassing because he was a transient. My feeling was, even if he was a transient, it doesn't matter—there are houseless students too. Maybe he was trying to use the Wi-Fi to sign up for classes. How can San Diego City College promote social justice but have police officers patrolling through campus and slamming a man's head on the concrete? For me, it is a public community college. He had every right to sit there, and he wasn't bothering anybody.

After I graduated, I came up to UC Santa Barbara, where there are five different police agencies policing this little twelve-mile radius. And the UCPD [University of California Police Department] has had seven lawsuits filed against its officers in the past couple of years, including a very serious sexual harassment case filed by a student, but they continue to police the neighborhood. It's another example of the lack of accountability that exists within these police agencies that are hyperpolicing students.

The university administration responded to my complaint about police harassment by saying that they wanted to introduce all of the formerly incarcerated students on campus to the UCPD so that they would know to not harass us. But they shouldn't be harassing us period. I told the administration that we've worked so damn hard to do the right thing and then are treated like this. I'm studying, I'm writing papers, I'm holding down a 3.94 grade average. And in response my family and I get surveilled and intimidated by campus police on a regular basis. For me, it's been one of the most humiliating experiences. The UC system gives millions of dollars to its police department that are continuing to cost them even more through lawsuits for misconduct, and yet there's no funding for formerly incarcerated students and system-impacted students.

That says to me, what are you really invested in? You're invested in people that work for UCPD to sexually harass and degrade women and make them feel unsafe in this community. But you won't invest in helping formerly incarcerated students and their families uplift themselves and develop upward mobility and create careers for themselves. You won't invest in us, but you'll allow the UCPD to exist. It's an example of the lack of accountability and the lack of moral compass. There's no morality in allowing this police division to exist here anymore. Let it go, shut it down, bring that money back to the students. That way we can build our own connections with one another and develop our own ways to uplift each other instead of having this police station tear us down. They use us as a revenue scheme through aggressive ticketing while continuously pumping students into the school-to-prison pipeline. They pull up and harass people and humiliate them in front of their colleagues.

QUESTION *What is the Underground Scholars Initiative?*

RYAN FLACO RISING We're a student-led organization creating a pathway for formerly incarcerated and system-impacted individuals to enter into higher education. We're reversing the notorious school-to-prison pipeline by developing the prison-to-university pipeline through recruitment, retention, and advocacy. We work with college students inside and outside of prison, building a pathway that makes possible a safe transition from prison to the university.

We work with students one-on-one to make sure all their basic needs are met, so that they can just focus on their studies and be a student. That's why I fight so hard and that's why I show up and I call these police out. The Underground Scholars program has allowed me to take back my own narrative. It's allowed me to do more than just feel bad about my past. It's helped me take a step back and shift a lot of this burden of responsibility to the systems that got us there in the first place. We are all plenty more than a collection of redemption stories. We're researchers. We are developing knowledge and producing knowledge that's creating solutions to the pressing issues in our communities. It's about us. We really are invested. Those that are closest to the problem are closest to the solution. We're all tired of being used as pawns where people are stepping on us and using us to build their careers. We're tired of these careerist police officers, judges, and district attorneys building their careers off of oppressing us. We're fighting back, and we're unwriting all the stuff that they've written up against us.

At Underground Scholars, we're all about political education and leadership skills. We're all about abolition. It's raised my consciousness, and I've got radical professors like William Robinson who've uplifted my spirit and helped me understand what's taking place here, what's happening in our communities, and why I went through the school-to-prison pipeline in the first place. I would have never been able to do that without the Underground Scholars and the warm hand-off system that they've created. They've warmly handed me off to mentors, to guidance, to folks shining the light so I can see the road ahead of me and then shining a light behind me as well, so I can look at the road behind me and see all the obstacle courses that were put in front of me. The prison industrial complex extracts $15.7 billion away from our communities here in California all under the pretense of serving and protecting them. But really it's driving our communities deep into poverty.

QUESTION *What work does the Underground Scholars Initiative do on campus police specifically?*

RYAN FLACO RISING We offer an Abolish the Police Fellowship to students, and we're also a part of the Cops Off Campus Coalition. One of the cofounders of the USI, Gilbert Murillo, is doing amazing work at UCSB to build a rainbow coalition of multiple student organizations to oppose the police by collecting data and exposing their tactics. A lot of students—especially marginalized students—come to campus with a clean record but leave UCSB with a conviction history due to the hyperpolicing of the UCPD.

QUESTION *Do the different chapters of the USI regularly interact?*

RYAN FLACO RISING Every UC school has an Underground Scholars program, and we have statewide leadership. We meet on a weekly basis to talk about everything that's going on at our campuses for two hours. We're also connected to Project Rebound [the program for formerly incarcerated and system-impacted students in the California State University system] and the Rising Scholars Network [the program for formerly incarcerated and system-impacted students in the California Community Colleges system]. We have to be constantly in communication in order to not lose the power and the strength of the unity that exists today. At the end of the day, universities are more financially invested in the prison industrial complex than they are in prevention programs, so organizations like USI, Project Rebound, and Rising Scholars must work together.

QUESTION *How is the UC student experience shaped by the constant campus police presence?*

RYAN FLACO RISING It's ruining people's lives and destroying the student experience. You're constantly seeing police drive up and down the housing units, looking to generate some sort of activity. When the UCPD is parked in the middle of campus, it makes you feel uncomfortable like there's some sort of threat. Whenever I see the police, the first thing I think is, "Is there something going on? Is there a shooting?" I'm constantly dealing with anxiety when I see a cop. If there's a cop parked in front of my student housing, the first thing I think is, "Do I need to keep my kids inside? What's going on out there?"

Also, no one's ever been arrested or lost their jobs for the sexual harassment case against the UCPD, which sends a message to the frat houses that rape culture is accepted here. I get so many different Clery Alerts of all these rapes that are happening, but with UCPD taking no responsibility and experiencing no repercussions for sexual harassment themselves, it sends a message to students that there is no accountability for sexual violence. I am disgusted to be in an institution that has this rape culture so heavily instituted into its culture.

QUESTION *What has the response of the university administration been when the Underground Scholars Initiative has raised these concerns?*

RYAN FLACO RISING: They try to tell us what they think we want to hear and then do nothing about it. We're tired of lip service. We're tired of being treated the way we get treated around here. They use their bureaucratic game to try to tire us out and make us burn out. The administrators' response is always to try to get us to meet with the campus police and take PR photos with them. It's just a photo op game for them, and they don't care about the risks or repercussions that could result from us taking photos with the police. Administrators don't ask any other organization to meet with the police on a quarterly basis. Why do formerly incarcerated students need to meet with them?

QUESTION *How would your life change if cops were removed from campus?*

RYAN FLACO RISING We would see programs like Underground Scholars fully funded. We would see scholarships for formerly incarcerated, system-impacted students, and marginalized students. We would all feel comfortable being here in school. We wouldn't feel like we're constantly being monitored and surveilled with the police waiting for us to make one little mistake. We could focus on our studies.

As a formerly incarcerated student, I have to set out time in my day to account for frequently being pulled over by the police. If I'm walking on the street, I have to be ready to get pulled over by the police and get questioned. That's going to take an hour and a half out of my day. So I have to forecast that into my day if I'm going to walk to school. If cops were removed from campus, I wouldn't have to plan for being stopped by the police and being asked who I am, if I fit a custody description, if I am a gang member. I wouldn't have to deal with any of that. I would just be able to be myself. Formerly incarcerated students are not here to assimilate whatsoever. We're here to prove a point: we are not the monsters that the police make us out to be. If we receive support and opportunities, we shine bright. The Underground Scholars have a 3.56 average GPA and a 100 percent completion rate. We're creating groundbreaking new research and policies like the Rising-Murrillo Freedom Act, which would automatically expunge people's records as soon as they receive their bachelor's degree.

There's so much that could happen for us as a community if we abolish the police on school campuses. We can be students and not feel like we're criminals. That's the way they make us feel with all of this police presence. Everybody walking around this community is treated like a potential suspected criminal, when all I see is a bunch of students.

QUESTION *What are ways that we can all support the Underground Scholars Initiative and formerly incarcerated students on campuses across the country?*

RYAN FLACO RISING Join the movement, get involved, advocate for formerly incarcerated students, and help reverse policies that have historically oppressed and criminalized our communities. Donate to programs like the USI because as it stands, we get little to no funding. Let's start paying people that are coming out of prison who are doing the right things and allow them to flourish and sustain themselves.

Another way to be involved is to get the word out about the Underground Scholars Initiative and let people know we exist. Formerly incarcerated people need to know that they belong in college. Just because you've made a mistake doesn't mean that you can't uplift yourself out of that situation and advocate for something better in the future. You're not alone. We're fighting for each other.

We need student organizations to unite and fight to end this incarceration epidemic that has destroyed our communities and ransacked marginalized groups and destroyed their lives. Build a committee to dismantle the hyperincarcerating policies that exist in your community. Dismantle and abolish the police system that's attached to your school. Most of all, challenge the stereotypes of formerly incarcerated people. We're not monsters; we're human beings. We're not gang members; we are human beings. We are not criminals; we are human beings. We're not what they said. We are your neighbors.

14

HOW STUDENT ACTIVISTS ARE WORKING TO DEFUND, DISARM, AND ABOLISH THE CAMPUS POLICE

An Interview with Jael Kerandi

BACKGROUND   Jael Kerandi was the University of Minnesota's (UMN) first undergraduate Black woman student body president. She made national headlines when, on May 26, 2020, she demanded the university police department immediately cease any and all partnerships with the City of Minneapolis Police Department (MPD) in a letter written on behalf of student leaders to UMN president Joan Gabel, UMN Board of Regents leadership, and senior administration. The letter was signed and supported by more than 2,800 members of the UMN community and outsiders. The next day, President Gabel publicly announced the school would "limit collaboration" with the Minneapolis Police Department and would no longer use its officers and K-9 unit for support during large campus events. Ms. Kerandi sat down for an interview with the coeditors of this book to talk about her advocacy, influences on it, and her views on campus police. The views expressed in this interview are Jael Kerandi's and do not represent those of her employer. The interview has been edited for length and clarity.

QUESTION   *To begin, can you tell us a little about yourself and your early experiences?*

JAEL KERANDI   I was born in Kenya and moved to the US when I was eighteen months old. My family eventually settled in Minnesota, where I was raised in the suburbs of Minneapolis. I am the youngest among my siblings but was raised in a household full of humble servants. We all learned from our parents how to be leaders. Our parents encouraged us to develop a strong work ethic, but we also learned the importance of community and giving back. We were taught to recognize people for their humanity and think collectively about how we live in our world.

In the earliest parts of my adolescent years, I began looking at the world with a lot of curiosity, continuously asking the question "why?" It didn't matter if it was a minor issue or the systemic issues at a larger scale, I took few things at face value and refused to accept things as they were. I always wanted to know more. While my questioning probably gave my patient parents a bit of a headache, my curiosity grew and ultimately fueled my leadership and often my success—it was part of who I became.

QUESTION *What influences helped shape your student leadership at UMN?*

JAEL KERANDI I started in student government as a first-year student in the Minnesota Student Association (MSA) intern program. During my first year I worked closely with our student body president, Trish, on initiatives within athletics and with the leader of our D&I [Diversity & Inclusion] Committee, Chloe, on our Rename & Reclaim initiative. In my second year, I served as the ranking representative to the Board of Regents serving our entire system of campuses. I was shaped by the experiences I had on the campus, and the initiatives that student leaders were working on inspired me. I watched student leaders fight tirelessly for infrastructure changes to add accessibility to our citywide transit. I saw student leaders fight to have the names changed on our buildings that commemorated discriminatory past leaders. I saw student leaders fight for a fair student wage comparable to the city. I was influenced and inspired by the student leaders that fought every day and by the students we advocated for—not only the current Gophers but the baby Gophers to come. I was energized by the many changes that needed to take place on our campus.

The first large project I worked on was the Rename & Reclaim initiative that asked our university to take a hard look into its past. Each year I was at the university we made incremental steps toward receiving a decision, but ultimately the decision was made not to explicitly rename those buildings but institute policy that would allow us to make such actions in the future. Our community held differing opinions on the topic but the job of our student advocates was to do just that—advocate for students. It is unusual for an issue to be black-and-white; the answers usually lay in the nuance. There were so many perspectives to consider and to register, but we were clear on our goal, and that is what we worked toward. The impact these issues had on students today was too important not to fight for. Students are *the* most important stakeholders of any higher education institution. The diversity statements that were shown on our website and in marketing could not just be statements of acknowledgment; we wanted clear action—otherwise the meaning of those diversity statements would be diminished. As student leaders, our advocacy was to extend to every student and ensure that their university experience was a return on their investment. The same held true when it came to policing and its impact on students.

When Trayvon Martin was murdered and local authorities failed to convict his assailant, I distinctly remember the feelings that I had. I remember how we all felt as we heard the verdict on the radio; we were in disbelief. I was not permitted to protest, and I remember feeling extremely hopeless. It could have been me, my brother, my cousin, my father, a friend, anyone. This could have been anybody close to me, and I held little to no power to make impactful change. In 2020, when George Floyd was brutally murdered minutes from our campus—the action required was not only clear, but *demanded*. There was nothing else *to do* but protest. There was no way we could be in agreement with the actions of the MPD. It's funny that people always ask me about fear. Fear is not your primary thought when what you are fighting against is death. Our lives hang in the balance, and the police decided that they get to hold the strings—that is what causes fear. Not our protest against it. Every day our mothers fear a similar outcome, individuals fear running in their neighborhoods, going to the grocery store, or going to church. We've [collectively] become numb to these acts of violence; we've become numb to the loss of Black life. And that is simply not okay.

QUESTION *Can you describe the relationship between the UMN police and City of Minneapolis Police Department when you were at the university?*

JAEL KERANDI On paper, I'm sure there are multiple differences, but they work closely together. The UMPD has jurisdiction over the University of Minnesota, and the MPD has jurisdiction over Minneapolis. Many of our students live in Minneapolis and have had interactions with the Minneapolis police. They partner on events and on different procedures; and to the students' general eye, it is difficult to tell the difference between the two. Our university is integrated and ingrained in the fabric of Minneapolis; it is likely you will encounter one or both in a typical day.

In 2019, the Somali Student Association held an event that resulted in blatant police disrespect toward students and their families. As students, we asked the administration, How could the situation be remedied? What steps could be taken to prevent this from happening again? The administration's response often felt quite dismissive; I remember feeling extremely frustrated. We all knew what happened despite the [best] intentions of the [UMN] police department. The impact of the UMPD on students was stark, and I just don't think they were hearing us. While their impact may have differed from their intent, the impact was what remained with students.

QUESTION *How would you say the student experience has been impacted by campus policing?*

JAEL KERANDI It is different for everybody. Policing takes on many forms outside of law enforcement. It is not the issue of one "bad apple" [police officer]. Rather [the issue is] what the uniform itself represents, a system that is so grossly disrespectful, harmful, and literally lethal to our communities. That is what we can't ignore.

The impact of policing in education begins in K-12, and specifically K-5. Black students are disproportionately reprimanded for mirroring infractions compared to their peers.[1] This form of policing students shapes how students see law enforcement throughout their life. But we now know that the police are not an institution that was truly built to serve and protect everyone. They originated [in part] as slave catchers.[2] We cannot [collectively] ignore these roots. They impact how Black people interact with law enforcement today. We teach our young boys police etiquette by the time they are ten. Life itself is such a precious thing, but we lose sight of that. We become desensitized to the killings of Black people by law enforcement; it becomes just another part of the news cycle, another story, another thing. But it isn't; it is a part of our livelihoods, a part of the anxiety we face, and the impressions it leaves on our minds creates generational trauma. It alters our worlds starkly—we see life differently and question its purpose. Our livelihoods become interlinked. To literally survive, we must protest.

QUESTION *Why is it important for people to pay attention to these issues?*

JAEL KERANDI Senior leaders and boards of trustees [at colleges and universities] need to pay attention to the impact of policing on their students because students are human beings. They are not simply the largest liquid investment into an institution, but the very reason an institution exists. Before I am a student, I am a Black woman. It is a salient identity that cannot be ignored. You must treat students as wholistic persons before you focus on their learning capabilities. My understanding and learning in the classroom is threatened by the lack of safety and security I may feel. We deserve to be safe in our learning environments. How can we teach medicine and the story of Henrietta Lacks goes untold? How do you want me to be present in my finance classes when we don't even talk about the destruction of Black Wall Street? Why do you want me to sit here and talk about urban planning when you won't even talk about the destruction our neighborhoods through gentrification and redlining?

Our society needs to understand that law enforcement is but one facet of the prism of policing. People often ask, "What does safety look like in practice?"—and to be honest, we don't know. We are starting to reimagine those bounds and to redefine what a true safe place looks like. People look at the Abolitionist Movement and condemn it based on political ideology, but if you were to look at it pragmatically– anything that doesn't work, that *intentionally* kills its people, why would we want to *maintain* it? If we noticed that there was a trend of doctors administering a certain drug resulting in death, would we keep administering that drug? Of course not. Because on a macro-scale life is highly valued. That's what going on with the police—we are being poisoned, we are being hurt, we are being hunted, we are being murdered—and we keep allowing it to happen. This is a human issue. It has nothing to do with divisive politics that are often used to gaslight the matter at hand. Lives are being lost, and we aren't doing anything to stop it.

QUESTION *Can you reflect on the role of university committees in addressing campus policing?*

KERANDI Respectability politics and internal politics can often become a barrier to advancement. When it came to matters of safety and campus policing at UMN, it was no different. There always seemed to be a committee, a special committee, formed to forward ideas or recommendations to the general committee, then to the president, and finally to the Board of Regents. Appointing a committee to address an issue doesn't always address the issue—at times it prolongs a process that has direct stakeholders. But we get lost in the bureaucracy and forget the purpose and the matter at hand. While these methods can bear fruit, we often lose community, state, and student engagement due to the extended timing to see true action occur. Decisions often take their own course, and when it comes time to make the decision, the student leaders fighting for it have often graduated and due to its frequency, it feels methodical. Our university's leadership should have the students' best interest at heart—therefore it is paramount that all student leaders have strong relationships with the president and the executive cabinet. When issues are brought forth, a more efficient way to address these issues must also arise.

QUESTION *What do you want future generations of UMN students to understand or remember about the efforts to push for change that took place during your tenure?*

JAEL KERANDI I hope that student leaders understand that their single most important stakeholder is, and will always be, students and that their role and duty is to serve them to the highest level possible. Our advocacy must expand across the institution and delve into each of its sectors to support student needs. I hope student leaders see the weight of the responsibility they have been blessed with and they don't take it lightly; but I also hope that they take time to rest and restore. Every day was not easy, but knowing that students trusted me, our entire administration and organization was the biggest honor I had throughout my tenure. I hope that if students ever look back at UMN history and wonder who I was, then I hope they know my fight was for students. I hope they know that while we weren't perfect, the work that we did everything was for them and for the future Gophers who are in elementary school right now [and] who will one day be in our institution. Our role was to create lasting generational change that was truly student centered. Finally, I hope they know we didn't do it alone. That there was a team of individuals who cared deeply, who went out on faith, and on a limb, to make change each and every day. I truly thank God for the opportunity and chance to lead and stand alongside courageous leaders.

NOTES

1. Renee Ryberg, Sarah Her, Deborah Temkin, and Kristen Harper, "Despite Reductions since 2011–12, Black Students and Students with Disabilities Remain More Likely to Experiences Suspension," Child Trends, August 9, 2021, www.childtrends.org.

2. NAACP, "The Origins of Modern Day Policing," n.d., https://naacp.org/find-resources/history-explained/origins-modern-day-policing.

15

RETHINKING THE ARCHIVES ON CAMPUS POLICING

An Interview with Kacie Lucchini Butcher

BACKGROUND Kacie Lucchini Butcher is a public historian. She currently serves as the director of the University of Wisconsin (UW)–Madison Public History Project (as of 2023 renamed the Rebecca M. Blank Center for Campus History), which is a multiyear effort to uncover and give voice to histories of racism and discrimination on campus as well as resistance. She has curated several award-winning exhibits. She has a master's degree in heritage studies and public history from the University of Minnesota. The interview has been edited for length and clarity.

QUESTION *How did you get interested in the topic of campus policing?*

KACIE LUCCHINI BUTCHER [The year] 2020 was tumultuous. At the time, I was living in Madison, Wisconsin, even though my husband and I had lived in Minneapolis for most of our adult lives. When the pandemic started, I went back to Minneapolis because I didn't want to be in Madison alone, and I knew that we were going to be working digitally, for what we originally thought was going to be three weeks—joke's on me, joke's on all of us. So I went there thinking I'd be there for three weeks and it ended up being six months.

This put me right in the epicenter of the George Floyd uprising. It was a really wild experience. I took off work for two weeks, and we were out in the streets. There was tear gas wafting into our apartment, and I got shot with a rubber bullet and tear-gassed multiple times. And that's when I realized, nothing will radicalize you like meeting the state, the power, and the violence of the state face-to-face. And I think particularly being in a protest crowd with a lot of white people, it was really interesting to see the way that older white people were like, "This violence is not supposed to be directed towards me," but now it was. It was even surprising for me, you know.

But being met with state violence face-to-face really radicalized me to a degree that I hadn't been before, like I think it did to many other people as well. I had definitely been doing a lot of reading and soul searching on what is the role of police in our society and is this a useful thing? I had been reading a lot of Mariame Kaba, Angela Davis, and a lot of those real introductory texts. I was already really realigning my opinions on the police, and then George Floyd happened, and it was like a switch had flipped.

So through that lens and then additionally having this job as the director of this public history project where our goal and our mandate was to look at these areas of discrimination, all of this was how I zeroed in on campus policing. When I got to UW, we had this very long list of research topics that people wanted us to look into, but we also do a lot of crowdsourcing. We go across the campus community and ask, "What do you want us to research? What are areas where you see discrimination playing out?" It was clear from the beginning that people wanted us to look into campus policing.

In my case, it was very much the coalescing of all of these things that were happening that led us to research campus police. Our campus police research actually started in January of 2020 (pre–George Floyd). We had new students who started, and they really looked at the list of topics and said, "Oh, I think I want to take that one on." And so it was really through that.

Then once we started researching, we realized that there were multiple students who kind of had an interest in this, so they formed a little team and I was supporting them. I would say that after George Floyd our conversations as a team and our dedication and passion for it really increased. Just because, how could it not? I think this is going to be the story of this generation, of activists. This was the moment, right? This was one of the big turning points. There was a before and there was an after.

QUESTION *What are the issues you're working on with regard to campus law enforcement, and why is it important for people to pay attention to these types of issues?*

KACIE LUCCHINI BUTCHER Because of the mandate of this Public History Project, but also because of the skill set that I have, I'm really looking historically at campus policing. What does campus policing look like on our campus? And when we find it on other campuses, how does UW–Madison shape up in relation to those spaces? I've really focused on how the *history* of campus law enforcement can help us have better conversations about campus policing *today*.

We could probably talk for hours about the importance of history, but I think that there's just really no way to have a conversation about policing without talking about the *history* of policing. The history of policing as an institution being linked to slave patrols is something that really shocked people as they learned about it post–George Floyd. I also think that for our campus community, when we started talking about where campus police came from, it was really surprising for people, that they started out largely as people who were facilities planning and management folks—people who are making sure doors were locked and who were responding to minor vandalism—but are now suddenly this armed violent powerful organization is on campus. And so really, I think history is the root, not only for showing how we got here, but also where we kind of went wrong. . . .

I also think one of the biggest things for our campus community has been getting people to see that there has *always* been resistance to the police. There's this cultural narrative that hating the police or being against the police is a new concept. That somehow, it's only post–George Floyd that people have had problems with the police or only post-Ferguson. But when you study the history of policing, you realize that students have always been asking questions about the role of police on campus. And that, particularly in the 1960s and at UW–Madison, it was a very, very common part of the conversation to ask, "Do we need campus police?" Not only from students but also from campus leaders and the Board of Regents. And so we found that uncovering this history serves as a kind of keyhole to having some of the more difficult conversations but also to really informing those conversations about fixing this institution or dismantling this institution.

QUESTION *In doing all this work, what have you learned from your activism on campus law enforcement?*

KACIE LUCCHINI BUTCHER Oh, God, what haven't I learned? Again, I'll reiterate campus policing is just one of our projects. We also research discrimination and resistance at UW more broadly, and so this was one tiny part of that but one that, I think, took a lot of like mental and physical energy from myself and our team. Because I think what it showed me is that there are some topics that people just do *not* want you to talk about, and campus policing was definitely one of them.

We fought tooth and nail at every turn to just keep doing the research and to release the research. I think that shows you that it's probably something you *should* research if people are really that concerned and are trying to stop you. Maybe it's just the rebel in me, but I'm like, "We should keep going, we're clearly doing something right because some people don't like what we're doing." And so one of the big things I learned was that people were going to have resistance to certain topics but that there are certain topics where people will really FLEX that power to have you not talk about these issues, and campus policing was one of them.

One of the bigger things that I learned in the whole process was just the way that people see campus policing as inherently different than regular policing. No matter how much you talk to them about how *not* different they are, some continue to think they're totally different. So it was really hard to have conversations, not only with my students who are looking at the materials but also with the campus community. So that's still a conversation that's happening on campus—Are they different? How so? And if they're not, what does that mean for us?

One of the other things I learned is that systemically, it is one of the harder things I've had to research. It's *really* hard. Especially when you hit these archival gaps, and we have to think about whether those are intentional and who those gaps serve and don't serve. For example, we have a really clear understanding of a very small piece of campus policing history at UW–Madison. We have very good documentation of the 1940s and 1950s up until the early 1960s; after that everything dries up, it becomes like a desert—an archival desert. Why is that? And who's that serving? Overall, I've learned so much, just like anybody who does anything that is kind of in the realm of questioning the police or questioning the institution of policing. It has changed the way I see everything. There's not a part of my life that hasn't been altered by looking at these fundamental questions, and so, everything that I've done, whether it was campus policing or reading on policing broadly, has changed the way that I generally see the world.

QUESTION *Can you talk a little more about the flexing of power when it comes to releasing the history of campus police?*

KACIE LUCCHINI BUTCHER Generally speaking, I think when you talk about racism in *any* way, people are *deeply* uncomfortable. I don't think that's a new phenomenon. I think it's getting worse because of what's going on culturally with the CRT [critical race theory] panic and all these other things. But I think people have always been deeply uncomfortable when you point out discrimination of any kind, and I don't know where it stems from. For some people, it's the bootstraps narrative that "everybody's equal in America," and they don't want that narrative disrupted. For other people, I think it's the belief that we've progressed so much, so why are you focused on this bad thing that happened in the past?

I think for a lot of people when you focus on the past and when it's not a positive past—and particularly at a place like UW where the brand is really strong—this upsets people. People have an idea of what this place is, and when you start talking about these things, they don't match with that brand, and it's uncomfortable. And it goes against this impulse that we want to have, to believe that we're really progressive or that the world is better than it was fifty years ago.

So there's like these weird, interesting limits where people are willing to talk about things, and I joke with people that there's the "fifty-year rule," which is that if something's passed by fifty years, everybody's okay to talk about it. For example, in 1969, Black students protested and now the university loves it, they're like, "Oh, my God, this is so great. Look what our Black students did. We love them, this is incredible." Conveniently overlooked is the fact that none of those students have their degrees because the university wouldn't allow it, and they were also not allowed to complete their degrees at other institutions. And when we tried to get them honorary degrees, the university said "no." The narrative that they sell is very uplifting—except the reality is not.

We'll tell certain stories after fifty years, and they're okay to tell *if* you tell them in a certain way. So we get challenged on almost everything we put out, I'm not going to lie. There's stories we put out where I'm like, "There could not possibly be an issue with this, we've told this in such a fair way," and yet people will *still* raise something to me about it.

But there are some things where the pushback has been worse than others. The campus policing history project was by far the worst one. We got pushback from all across campus, from university leaders who just didn't want us to talk about it and, particularly, they were saying, "It's not the right time because we're still living in the fallout from George Floyd." And my response was, "When is the right time?" Do you know what I mean? Like, I can guarantee you that the police are going to continue to murder people; it might not be in Minneapolis but somewhere police will murder someone, so when is it a good time to talk about it?

QUESTION *Where are you seeing hope in this work?*

KACIE LUCCHINI BUTCHER Some of the ways I think I see hope in this work is in talking with students about the research that we've done. Even just seeing a new generation that has a different understanding of policing or is at least willing to question and critically think about this institution, unlike our parents' generation. They don't question these things. When I try and bring up these questions or concerns, they do not see the problems. And so I think that's hopeful, right? That there is a new generation that's willing to think critically about these issues, that is willing to question and open to changing their opinion.

The work that I've done with my students, maybe it's not going to dismantle the UWPD, but when somebody googles UWPD history, they will find our article and maybe they read it, and then they learn something new. And maybe they will question something or have a conversation about how that is definitely not how the police should behave. I think it's important to keep in mind the scale of impact. There are ways that you can have this really individual small impact and big impact at the same time.

QUESTION *What are some of the biggest challenges that you face, particularly from the archival perspective?*

KACIE LUCCHINI BUTCHER Our project generally has faced so many archival challenges because we're documenting history at the university from the perspective of people who aren't often talked about, whose stories aren't often told or aren't often central to the narrative. And with the police, you know, I think we had some of the basic problems of when you go to the catalogue and you search police, you get a couple boxes with annual reports. We have pretty much every annual report from the last twenty to twenty-five years. You also get newspaper clippings, which, I kid you not, are pieces of copy paper—individual pieces of printer paper. Each folder has about four hundred pieces haphazardly jammed together, and there are two of them, so you have about eight hundred pieces of copy paper. And it was any article where UWPD was mentioned, some is "mentioned in passing," but some of it involves central stories.

For example, articles about UWPD wrongfully arresting somebody for scalping tickets to a football game. Some of it is about their crowd control tactics, and then some of it is coverage of small things like when the UWPD commented on a vandalism case. Some of it is pure advertisement or propaganda, for example, that UWPD has this new initiative, and you know it's always light and sparse on the details, which is how we would also characterize their annual reports as well. As annual reports usually do, you put forward what you think are the most notable things that you did in the past year from your perspective, and they're largely positive. And they are light on the details, very light. And so that was kind of our starting point, and we realized this is not enough to do anything with. It is virtually nothing, to be honest.

We thought about doing some financial analysis, because the annual reports do have budget information, but we were like, what would we really learn? We would learn what we already knew, which is that the police were getting more and more money, they're getting more and more staffing, they're getting more and more "professionalized." That was something we could have told you anyways. So we kind of had this moment with our archivists at the UW Archives and with our students where we were like "somebody is in charge of these people. Who is in charge of them?" Because that's maybe where their records are going to be.

What we figured out—and this was weird—but we went through this whole process of asking ourselves, "Who would they have been reporting to?" We knew that they were considered facilities people at first, and then they changed, and so we found a lot of their early records in facilities boxes. When we pulled the facilities boxes, they were organized in alphabetical order by subject, and we realized that they weren't called "police" at the time, they were called "Protection and Security" or "Security" or "Campus Security" or "Campus Protection." And so we started getting more creative with our search terms and looking at the boxes in new ways, so we've done a lot of stuff that way.

Then we realized that there was this organizational change where they got moved out of facilities and they moved under where they currently sit, which is [under] the "Vice Chancellor of Business and Finance." I'm not sure why they sit there. But they got moved, in part, in response to student demands aggressively coming out against the UWPD in the 1940s and 1950s because of one officer in particular, Officer Joseph Hammersley, who was, to be quite honest, a menace to the campus community; that is the nicest term I could use for it. But we found all these records because the buck stopped with the "Vice Chancellor of Business and Finance" boxes, so anytime there was an issue, anytime you needed to change something, it all went to him for approval. And so with these records we got this really good snapshot of silly stuff and more consequential stuff. Silly stuff like people writing letters because they got a parking ticket. Consequential stuff like UWPD decided that to become more professional they need marked vehicles, and so we want to buy marked vehicles and put campus police on them, or we believe that our campus police officers should have to be in uniform and so we want to buy uniforms, and here are the three uniform options we have.

These files gave us such rich detail about the way that they were professionalizing and the way that they were structured. This was where we found some inkling of disciplinary action against Hammersley and at least that there were conversations going on about his behavior. So it not only gave us this kind of loose structure, but obviously the more names that we got, the more issues that we found, the better newspaper searching we could do, so it was really one tiny little find opened up a hundred more things that we could dig into. But it was only through that creative archival searching.

When records dry up, which for us is around the 1960s beyond those annual reports and really bad newspaper clippings from the 1980s and 1990s, being more creative is necessary. For us there's nothing from the late 1960s, which was a really tumultuous time at UW and there's nothing from the 1970s, when there was that kind of backlash to the tumultuous 1960s. And we largely believe it was because there was a change in the thinking about records management. Police records became something that was private and something that you'd have them manage themselves. And something that they still manage themselves.

So the only records that we have today from UWPD are the records that they send themselves to the UW archives, which they're not very good about. Additionally, we can request through open records laws in Wisconsin—which hold that pretty much anything created by a state employee is considered property of the state—so anybody could open records request by emails, which I think about when I send emails. And so they do that too; they think about what they put in an email versus what they say over a phone call that is not open records. We know that there were some controversial cases because they made the newspaper, but it really becomes about the newspaper and about this outward image, instead of all those internal rich documents, which do not exist in our archives past 1962 so we have just this huge gap that obviously affects the way that we can see the past. That was a really long answer, but it was complicated.

QUESTION *What can university archivists do to help preserve and make publicly available records about campus policing?*

KACIE LUCCHINI BUTCHER I think one of the great things about the Public History Project (that was maybe an unintended benefit) was we learned a lot about what our UW archives actually had. Our head archivist was pretty new. For a long time, we had archivists that were more aligned with resource librarians, meaning helping people find things, but the new archivists are like traditional archivists, they were like, "We have got to get these collections in order to figure out what we even have and we also have to get rid of stuff that we don't need" because nobody's been following a retention schedule. So one of our archivists, she's been overhauling, and one of the things that came out of the project was really knowing what we have and what we don't, and so now, when people say, "I want to research UWPD," they don't just get annual reports, because we know where all these collections are. And so we've been able to say, "If you actually want to know, here's where everything is that we found," so that's been helpful for them to know but also for future researchers to know.

The other kind of interesting thing that's come out of this work, and I wrote an article about this,[1] but we've faced a lot of archival restrictions—things that were restricted by the university for various reasons. I'm always questioning why they were restricted and whom do they protect? One of the things that's restricted is what we believe are papers that talk about disciplinary action against [Officer] Hammersley by the university. So we don't know what's in there. On the other side of that, I have argued in favor of restrictions when there are things that I have found that, I'm like, "You shouldn't be able to just pull this box and see this information; it's against people's privacy and I think it's really harmful."

One instance of this occurred when we pulled these UWPD boxes and we found a rape case that was in there with the victim's name. It has all of Hammersley's notes, where he degrades the victim and talks about how he doesn't believe her, he talks to the victim's boyfriend, and talks about how he believes the victim's boyfriend over her because he's a medical doctor at the university. You should not be able to just see her name; it's been bothering me the whole time, and so that's restricted now, and you would have to request it to access it. Does that affect our ability to talk about the way that UWPD has handled cases? Yes, but I think it's more important to protect the victim in this case, that would be my argument, but we had a lot of conversations about whether that was appropriate or not. The archives are doing their best to walk that line of, like, "let's make things accessible, but let's also protect people who have been harmed."

The way that archives work today and the way, I think, that our culture has almost warped people's minds is that, like, you know, UWPD is very aware about putting on a public face, and so is everybody else, like our chancellor is leaving right now. She is sending a bunch of records to the university archives. She's sending things to make herself look good. Of course, she is, right? She's thinking about her legacy; she's thinking about what she wants people to say about her in the future. You want it to be positive. Well, UWPD does too, so when they think about what they send to the archives, it's annual reports, it's things that make them look good, it's new initiatives. They're not sending the other things, and so I think that that is always going to affect what stories we are able to tell, if that is the framing of it.

QUESTION *What advice can you give to researchers on how to approach and navigate university archives?*

KACIE LUCCHINI BUTCHER   I hadn't done a lot of archival research before I got this job, which I always feel bad admitting. I'm a public historian, we do archival research, but it wasn't as intense until I got here, and so I did learn a lot on the job. Some advice I've already mentioned. For example, thinking creatively about approaching the archive and the search terms you are using. Thinking creatively about where to look. We also found good stuff in Student Affairs, basically anybody who interacts with this institution of policing, how might the records be hidden there.

So looking at chancellor's files, Student Affairs files, dean's files, department files, and individual departments who had interactions with the police, and on that last point, we haven't even done that kind of minuscule searching. We had hit the high notes, but there could be a huge file in the English Department files, for example, but we haven't pulled every single department file and looked at every single index to say, "Oh, is there a folder on security in here?" So thinking really creatively about where they would exist. Obviously, consulting with your archivists as well. It was an archivist who helped us find a lot of this. And every historian has to make choices; there were stories that I wanted to tell but that we just didn't have enough evidence for, and so we set those things aside and we didn't tell them publicly. That doesn't mean that they still aren't useful; we created a really intensive timeline of all of the history that we found. We ended up focusing our article on the 1950s because that was the meat of the archival research, particularly on Hammersley, whom they were still celebrating here until our work came out. And of course, when we released it, they were like, "We disavow this man."

We encourage people to do more research. We're not saying this is everything; in fact, there's a lot more that needs to be done. So if you want access to our research and you want to expand on it, please do. I think that's kind of where the public history approach has actually been really helpful. Public historians are really about collaboration, I want everybody to work with us. Because the reason that we're doing this is not about getting personal journal articles published; the reason that we're doing this is because this information is going to help us change our culture's association with policing. And maybe in some distant future, we won't have policing anymore. So, our goals, I guess, are different, and so when we weren't even doing the research, we hoped this is useful to activists, we hoped this is useful to organizers, we hoped it's useful to UWPD and that they think differently about their behavior. I would encourage people to think about what would be useful to activists, or be useful to community members.

QUESTION *What advice can you give to researchers on how to make these campus policing histories more broadly accessible, or is that even the right framework for thinking about it?*

KACIE LUCCHINI BUTCHER I think one of the things we should keep in mind is that of course research should be credited. We want our researchers to get credit; we want them to be cited and to be known for their work. But at the same time, we have to remember that they don't necessarily *own* that work. I'm really clear with my students that I want you to own your intellectual property, but at the same time this history is not just yours. You do not own this history individually—it's for the campus community, it's for all of us, this is *all* of our history. So I really urge transparency, and all of our research materials are publicly accessible. If people come to us and say, "Can I see the source that you have on citation 27?," I'll email that to them; it's not like some big secret thing.

I think there is a way to be accessible, not only with like the details and the sources but also thinking really creatively about different ways to get information out to people. For example, we have the blog posts, which is great because a lot of people read our blog online. Not long after the blog, an "Abolition at UW" account also got started, and they took pieces of our article and credited us. But going further, they took pieces of the article and made them Instagram graphics, which is great because that's a whole different audience that engages with it on Instagram. Then I was asked to write an article for a local magazine called Tone, which is kind of a radical online printing operation.[2] And I wrote from a different angle about what the process was like of researching and why I think it's important to research the history of policing, so that's a different audience.

A general rule of public historians is always try to think creatively about how you're going to get people to see your research and to work with you. So Instagram, blog posts, getting interviewed on a podcast about it, on the radio, etc. I will do anything that I think will be useful to people in any way that they can engage. This work is also going to go on our physical exhibit that we have opening; it's going to go on our digital exhibit website. All of our online content is available for a screen reader; it all has alt text. We've tried to be really careful, as a project that's focused on discrimination, that we don't perpetuate discrimination by not being thoughtful.

QUESTION *Can you speak more about the process of this collaborative approach to student research and excavating the history of the UWPD?*

KACIE LUCCHINI BUTCHER Almost all of it is done by student researchers. I've taken up a couple topics, for example, I'm a housing historian—that's one of my specialties—so I did all the research on housing. I also happened to do all the research on blackface, not because I like had an affinity for it but just because a lot of our graduate students were Black and they really didn't want to do that. We also had students who came to me and said, "I want to research the police. I think I can do this and I'd really like to do this." So we had me and three students who worked on the history of policing; one student was doing oral history and actually did do an oral history interview with our former chief of police, who left in 2016—she retired after a very high-profile controversial incident, and it was an interesting three-and-a-half-hour interview.

So they were doing oral history, which gave us one angle, and then we had another student who was just newspapers, because you would not believe the amount of hits you get with UWPD. Then we had another student who was doing archival research and we had a main kind of box folder where everybody put everything. We would have meetings every two weeks and talk about the big themes that we were finding, ask how can we make sure that the person who's reading the newspaper articles is also connecting it to what the archival research person is doing, and vice versa, and then the oral histories can come in and supplement.

It was a complicated process, which is why it took so long, so it took us over a year to research this enough to where we could put out a product that I felt confident in. We started in January 2020, and we put out our article in March 2021. We had started drafting in fall of 2020, but we weren't really ready to go until spring of 2021. And now we have this huge box of materials that we can just share with people. And we have this big timeline document that's a Google Doc that's open so anybody could see it as long as they have the link, which we share freely because, again, it's not ours; we do not own this history.

Importantly, our students are not cited by name as the authors of our articles and publications, and that is because *they* requested not to be. We had a lot of conversations about protecting our student researchers. And about two months before we went to print on our article, the UWPD tweeted at a student and named them on Twitter. It was a student body leader who is part of student government, and that was when all of my students were, like, "I don't want to be named if they're calling out students individually and tagging them on Twitter." So a couple of my students I know have it on their CV, and if anybody questions why their name isn't on the article, they can obviously email me and I'll confirm that was the student that did it. But it was really to protect them. Because they were, like, "I don't want to be targeted by the police," or a lot of them were worried about job prospects.

In the end this was a very, very collaborative process. Our students are really, really passionate about the project, and honestly, they were fine with not getting credit. I think because of the safety thing they were just so worried, which says so much, particularly because if you read our article, I would argue, we could have gone a lot farther. But we had this internal conversation about how do we want to frame this history as to not alienate a lot of people who would otherwise be open to listening to this perspective?

We did not write a piece with the framing of "I want to abolish UWPD and here's the history that supports that"; instead we were, like, "Let's ask some really critical questions about what is the history of this organization, and how is this organization still functioning today, and what are the connections between the two?" So that we could at least start the conversation and not alienate a bunch of people. We know that people are at different points in their understanding. We try and bring people along with us, and that's both the mission of the project, but also we really believe that the point of doing this work and it's not always to jump to the end. It's the process of reckoning. I didn't start out as an abolitionist when I picked up Kaba's book on day one; I had to get there. And so we were, like, "Let's be part of the getting people there."

QUESTION *Lastly, could you reflect on what it is like taking on this work in the state of Wisconsin?*

KACIE LUCCHINI BUTCHER   I think anywhere you go, policing is this hot-button issue. You are going to get pushback, and it's not a conversation that people want to have. The police really feel like a secret, untouchable institution, where you start to question it and people really don't like it. Madison, Wisconsin, is very liberal, and so when we talk about it here, there is more of a little bit of wiggle room about having the conversation, and there is a really big activist movement, a lot of abolitionists organizers who have given us a lot of support.

At the same time, outside of that bubble, this topic is a really controversial thing. Wisconsin is absolutely, politically, a very conservative state. We are gerrymandered through the roof in the state, and so our elected officials are not representative of the people's wishes, and so politically it's a very toxic place. There's a new study that shows that Wisconsin is one of the worst states for democracy at this point, so it's not a safe thing to talk about.

I would say the organizing networks in Wisconsin are just smaller, and that's not a critique, it's just the truth. But I will say the good thing about it being smaller is that you know more people, so when something comes up, I know who to contact for the most part or I contact somebody who knows who to contact. And we've gotten a lot of support. But working in such a conservative state has prompted questions such as, Am I going to publish this article, with my name on it and saying I'm an abolitionist? Am I going to get fired? What if I can't get another job in the future? I have had to think about how far I want to go, and what I've decided is that I just don't want to compromise, and so, if I lose my job, at least I did it for something that I felt was really important.

NOTES

1. Kacie Lucchini Butcher, "More Questions Than Answers: Interrogating Restricted Access in the Archives," *Journal of Historical Behavioral Science* 58, no. 2 (April 2022): 223–31, https://doi.org.10.1002/jhbs.22179, Epub 2022 Jan 18. PMID: 35040127.

2. Kacie Lucchini Butcher, "How the Gaps in UWPD's History Harm Our Community," March 16, 2021, https://tonemadison.com/articles/how-the-gaps-in-uwpds-history-harm-our-community/.

16

AN INTERVIEW WITH COPS OFF CAMPUS RESEARCH COLLECTIVE

ELI MEYERHOFF, NICK MITCHELL, BRENDAN HORNBOSTEL, ZACH SCHWARTZ-WEINSTEIN

EDITORS' NOTE The Cops Off Campus Research Collective is a group of abolitionist researchers who are developing collaborative projects to study and organize around the interrelations of policing and higher education institutions across the United States.[1] The interview has been edited for length and clarity.

QUESTION *How did you first come to the topic of campus police?*

ZACH SCHWARTZ-WEINSTEIN I started researching campus police kind of by accident. I knew that city police would factor into some of my research, but in the process of finishing my dissertation I was inadvertently granted access to some embargoed material from the university that I was studying in the Office of Labor Relations. And from there it became clear to me that the university police were kind of enmeshed in the university's labor relations practices in ways that I had not sufficiently understood prior to encountering this material.

For example, that university police were spying on workers, that they were compiling or helping the administration compile dossiers on members of the bargaining committee, and they were polling or questioning members of the bargaining committee about the union's tactics and then reporting what they learned back to Labor Relations officials. Finding all that material (and also encountering some testimonials of how university police responded to the strike that I was writing about) led me to become interested in figuring out how that institution and its relationship to management had come into bloom.

NICK MITCHELL I *want* to say that I've *always* been interested, but the reality is that the uprisings of 2020 was what made the urgency of campus police really obvious to me. As a scholar of the intersection of social movements and universities, I had a couple of folders of stuff that I encountered on things about university policing, but I really think that the summer of 2020 made it something that I really paid attention to. The uprisings in the streets made it so that as a scholar of higher education, and someone who certainly researched the FBI files and understood how the state has been organized to police university students, I finally saw campus policing as an actual category to focus my research. Posing the inquiry about the nature and the history of campus policing as a discrete entity really started two years ago for me, and it started because social movements actually made the urgency of doing so feel as though, in order to be a scholar in an ethical way, I need to focus my attention and have something to say about the history of the institutionalization of campus policing.

ELI MEYERHOFF I echo what Nick said about how the 2020 uprisings against policing inspired me to focus on researching campus police. I had been primed to be interested in campus police because of my previous organizing in a prisoner solidarity group in Durham, North Carolina, called "Inside-Outside Alliance" from 2013 to 2018. It was basically a group that supported the organizing of incarcerated people in the Durham county jail and their family members and friends by talking with people who were visiting the jail and by corresponding with people incarcerated in the jail through letter writing. We then compiled the incarcerated folks' letters into newsletters that we sent back into the jail, so that they could communicate with each other across their cell walls, using the newsletter as a kind of organizing tool. We then amplified their demands through protests in the streets outside the jail and at county government meetings.

So, I had become interested in how the carceral institutions of the jail and police were related with the university [Duke] that dominates the city. I thought about questions such as, Why does the knowledge of incarcerated folks tend to be treated as not valuable in comparison with the knowledge that academics produce? This norm is in tension with how, in our organizing, we found the prisoners' knowledge to be the most valuable, relevant kind of knowledge. This got me thinking about how the regime of knowledge production of higher education, and of the education system as a whole, is coconstituted with the carceral institutions of the jail and policing.[2] These sorts of questions primed my interest in campus police.

BRENDAN HORNBOSTEL   I would like to imagine that I was first interested in campus policing while running from the UCPD in undergrad, but that might be more of an auto-mythologizing. In reality, I had these parallel paths at the end of undergrad—on the one hand, I found a passion for radical study through groups like the Undercommons Freedom School at UCLA, while also starting to get more involved in police abolitionist movements off campus in Los Angeles. But I can't say I ever really connected those two projects of abolitionist community organizing and undercommons radical study until 2020.

Finding the "Abolitionist University Studies: An Invitation" that Nick, Eli, Zach, and Abbie [Boggs] wrote was a transformative moment where I started thinking about the university as not just a workplace that I inhabit but also a location that's deeply intertwined with all of these things that I study and organize against, whether it's statecraft or capitalism or imperialism. So, 2020 was definitely the moment where I found radical study and community organizing coming together and located it on campus as a way to really ground my thinking about what abolition means for me.

QUESTION   *How did your collective come to be?*

ELI MEYERHOFF   A few of us were continuing our work on abolitionist university studies in 2020, and the George Floyd uprisings popped off, which inspired an explosion of Cops Off Campus organizing across the US. We wanted to do some kind of collective project that could be useful for that organizing. The basic idea was that we wanted to create a kind of crowdsourced nationwide survey and database about the interrelations of universities and policing. Since the four of us didn't have much quantitative social science skill, we put out a call for people with abolitionist sensibilities who had those kinds of research skills.

After a few new folks joined us in response to that call, we used a program called Airtable to create a survey, which has lots of questions for people involved in Cops Off Campus organizing to answer about policing on their campuses, and we created tutorials and toolkits to give guidance on how to do research for collecting that data for the database.[3] In addition to the goal of collecting the contents of this research, we also had a more process-focused goal of thinking about how, through doing this research, people could strengthen and expand their relationships and networks, both on and across campuses.

We saw this as a way to help groups share knowledge, coordinate, and share tactics for how to do this research. Also, we envisioned this as a kind of abolitionist pedagogy, where groups and individuals could learn how to use these research methods (archival, qualitative, and quantitative social science) for abolitionists purposes. We saw this as a way that groups could build their capacities, strengthen their networks, and be able to more effectively analyze their institutions, ideally in ways that would be useful for their organizing. After we launched the survey, we were excited to see it circulate a lot on social media, but unfortunately not that many people were responding to the survey itself. So, our group decided to focus more on developing workshops that could help people learn how to do this research.

NICK MITCHELL   I could add a couple of context points. 2020 was quite a year, I think we can probably agree on that, and so one of the things that, in retrospect, the collective came out of, was just the convergence of a lot of different kinds of collectivity that were already in motion. So, a lot of the Cops Off Campus stuff, even the *cops off campus* phrase, I associated very directly with chants and demands issued at the picket line during the wildcat graduate worker strike at UC Santa Cruz that started with the withholding of student grades in December 2019 and then turned into a full labor stoppage in February 2020.

As one of many faculty who were trying to figure out how to organize in solidarity with that, I was part of a large intercampus UC solidarity group. The university responded to the full labor stoppage with the deployment of just a huge number of cops at the picket line. Graduate workers were striking because rent inflation was making their work environment overwhelmingly untenable, and their tactical escalation from grade strike to picket line was organized to express the urgency of the situation. In response, our university administration approached the picket as a threat to campus safety, throwing millions of dollars into what amounted to an intimidation campaign that sought to crush the picket as quickly as possible.

Ultimately it was the pandemic, rather than policing, that dealt the death blow to the picket. Over the course of the months that followed, the intercampus solidarity group essentially refashioned itself as a Cops Off Campus group once the George Floyd uprisings started. By summer's end it had renamed itself UCFTP, playing on the myriad uses of the FTP acronym. The decision to really zero in on university policing and its specificity was also partly strategic. We'd initially been told to expect that sheltering in place would allow things to reopen around May or June 2020. By midsummer, however, we had reason to be very confident that classes would be remote for most if not all of the 2020–21 academic year. We speculated that, viewed from an abolitionist perspective, a year of moving university operations fully online offered some meaningful leverage: it allowed us to negotiate around the conditions under which we would return to campus. We could, in theory, organize around the refusal to return to a campus with police.

We started organizing the Cops Off Campus Research Project (COCRP) around the strategic possibilities presented by pandemic life also.

We assumed that a strategic possibility that in the transition to online classes, educators were going to be open to new approaches and frame workers: After all, teaching online was going to force them to think of their classrooms differently, to reshape their pedagogy in new ways, and therefore to be open, at an unforeseeable scale, to new kinds of experimentation. The classroom, we speculated, might be newly up for grabs and newly available for abolitionist interventions.

When we developed our university policing database, we theorized that we could use the database project as a way of occupying one to two weeks in someone's fall class where they could use the classroom time because everything was kind of up for grabs. We could use that as an opportunity and occasion, both for bringing students into the production of knowledge about university policing but also to crowdsource it as much as possible. So, our organizing developed by attempting to test a theory of what the strategic possibilities of the pandemic shift in educational production might look like. That's part of why we settled on the database as a specific goal to try and develop so that we could use the kinds of capacity that were being made possible at that moment.

BRENDAN HORNBOSTEL I just want to second what Nick was saying, as it helps me frame how and why I came to this project. I was not someone who was previously involved with these folks on the abolitionist university studies project. Rather, I had been involved in grad worker unionizing in Washington, DC, at my university, and that was generally a multiyear failure. So, I was really struggling to find out how to do radical organizing on campus when the pandemic hit. Hearing Nick talk about UCFTP's connections to the wildcat strike makes me realize how important and perhaps how overlooked it is that Cops Off Campus was born out of other struggles.

For me, coming to this project has always been one of trying to better understand how to do this kind of work at a university that often feels inhospitable. I don't think I've necessarily solved this issue, but I've been organizing with all kinds of student comrades to create abolitionist spaces and mutual aid networks on campus, so understanding the need for bridging local struggles with broader organizing across campuses has been a major takeaway for me in doing this work.

QUESTION *How does research on campus police fit into the broader effort to abolish these departments and beyond the broader carceral regime as well?*

NICK MITCHELL This is really underlining one of the points that we are exploring theoretically through abolitionist university studies, which is trying to, in some ways, move away from a knowledge exceptionalism in the way that we relate to universities. We want to think of knowledge production as the *outcome* of various forms of organizing and as itself a *form* of organizing. And in imagining how research can exist in relation to a social movement. We could have called ourselves the Universities and Policing Research Collective. It probably would have made us eligible for grants or things like that and opened up some possibilities in one direction or another, but putting the abolitionist aims up front as part of how we organize the imperative of the research—I think that's part of how we're kind of imagining that it fits.

Additionally, in suggesting that university policing has a history, suggesting that it has a context—this is calling attention to one part of the university that the university *doesn't* always want to call attention to and that it doesn't want to necessarily see itself as convergent with policing. So, in putting those two things together, we are making it possible as a research category to ask questions, trying to actually make it legitimate to do abolitionist research and build that network, and also to give real historical foundation to the questions that activists are asking.

Having a database on university policing that people can go to and making that available to people with abolitionist content attached, all of it is about trying to build a relationship between the knowledge that's available, the organizing resources that exist, and the questions that people can ask as researchers, and to put them together so they fit as interconnected pieces of a much broader project. Theoretically, this was one of the ideas that we tried to build this project to test, and also to try to extend as well.

ELI MEYERHOFF In thinking about how this research can be useful for movements, putting that kind of political relevance question in the forefront of our approach is one of the goals that we had in making a survey/database project.

We were thinking about how this could help address the challenge that campus organizers have of overcoming the usual cycles of increased activity, followed by a lull of inactivity, which is especially a problem for undergraduate student-centered organizing. When the activated students cycle out every few years, the administration can pretend to engage with their demands, maybe even making some minimal, reformist reforms, while stalling indefinitely on any abolitionist reforms that would actually reduce policing.

As a partial way to address that problem, we see this database as a tool that could help groups on and across campuses have a better sense of historical memory and institutional memory—both for understanding their institutions and the history of organizing efforts at and against their institutions. So, the survey for the database asks questions both about the institutions and about organizing efforts. Organizers could find the results of this survey useful at particular campuses and also from learning about these histories *across* campuses.

Another kind of cross-campus benefit potentially would be that this database could help groups push for their own institutions to release data about policing—fostering a PR competition or "arms race" between institutions. For example, if the University of Chicago is more transparent in releasing this kind of information, that could help organizing at some other elitist institution to say "look at what our peer institution is doing with transparency, our administration should be this transparent, it's embarrassing that we are not this transparent."

BRENDAN HORNBOSTEL I'd just add that over the last few years there has been a lot more focused abolitionist analysis of state power that understands how policing diffuses beyond officers with a badge and a gun. One of the things that I have come to realize doing research on campus policing is how the logics of policing are wrapped up in all different kinds of university administration. Being able to name that helps folks see the convergence of campuses and cops instead of treating them as odd bedfellows. That also means analyzing the carceral creep or carceral logic of the university beyond whether the campus police are autonomous or disguised as a public safety department.

Beyond that, I'm realizing I made this generative mistake in hearing this question and wondering whether "departments" referred to police or university administration itself. It makes me think that this work is not just about historicizing cops on campus, but the campus as cops, or the university as a site of police power. Thinking about policing as a central tool of governance for the university opens up ways of rethinking what kind of university, if any, we are trying to build, as well as helping us better connect our own campus organizing with struggles across the city or region.

QUESTION *What projects are you currently working on?*

NICK MITCHELL   I think that the database did not have as much success as we wanted. There were a lot of challenges. We are people who started as a group without the kind of quantitative expertise and the tech expertise to figure out what it means to roll these things out and what our options were. That became tricky, and the timeline that we thought it would take to roll it out was not the timeline that we had imagined in terms of matching up with potential classes. Then there was a question of capacity, which you know is an artifact of labor life in a pandemic world and its ebbs and flows.

More recently, we have been thinking about what kind of collective project would be good for both us *doing* research, using the knowledge that we've amassed, and getting in contact with social movements, as well as potentially reaching broader audiences. After a lot of discussions, the project we've landed on is a podcast. We think this will blend the research we have done, the research we are interested in, develop the skills that we wanted to be able to possess ourselves, and reach a broader audience.

For the last few months we have been in development in terms of figuring out what aspects of university policing we want to focus on. How comprehensive? What should the actual format look like? Do we want to have an open-ended, ongoing podcast where we're interviewing people, or one that's more of a limited run and hyperfocused? What kind of focus? Should it be historically focused? Should we focus on one specific institution, or do we want to focus on a series of campuses? It's been useful for me to just figure out how to both balance the justified large range of interest and also the need to have specifics and developed stories. Storytelling is useful and also difficult because you want to have a beginning, middle, and an end.

We have a tendency to bite off more than we can chew. It's a vice and a virtue. We kind of have to figure out ways to counteract and manage those tendencies. I think it's been a really useful intellectual project and really, really exciting in terms of bringing us into conversations with people and figuring out who is part of these conversations and who knows this stuff better than we necessarily do as well.

BRENDAN HORNBOSTEL: I also want to shout out the workshops that we've done, including ones that I've been a part of with Cops Off Campus groups at the University of Chicago and the University of Michigan, because those have been really great moments. For folks at the University of Chicago, Audrey Beard (another member of the collective) and I, despite neither of us living in Chicago, took this basic research question about campus police jurisdiction and university land acquisition and ran with it. We knew that the university police jurisdiction at UChicago was expanded in 2014, and we wanted to understand how that relates to recent property purchases made by the university as gentrifiers, colonizers, and landlords of the South Side.

We basically drummed up a quick-and-dirty (what Audrey calls a cooking-show style) research demo to map out university land ownership and its relationship to police patrol jurisdiction, and then we brought that to folks at Care Not Cops as a research offering. Instead of approaching them like, "Let us tell you what you know or what you don't know but should know," we offered a basic research methodology as an offering that they could develop with their much more intimate, local knowledge of campus patrol practices and university land ownership. That was a model of collaborative research that I would love to see us do more in the future.

ELI MEYERHOFF Another workshop that we started developing but have put on hiatus temporarily is one we called "Abolition for Techies." With this workshop, we aimed to help organizers learn more technical research methods that might involve programming skills. For example, we could use a program to scrape a university's website to get budget information. Another possibility is to use Geographic Information System (GIS) mapping software to analyze and represent the policing jurisdiction for campus police on and beyond the campus to show how the area of campus police can affect a much larger part of the city, and these maps could then be related with the university's complicity with processes of gentrification and "student-ification."

We were developing a workshop that could help teach these kinds of techie research skills, and we decided to start by focusing on one of our campuses, and Brendan graciously volunteered their campus, George Washington University, as a case study for us to experiment with. One challenge that we found was in thinking about how to make these workshops and the research methods in them generalizable across different campuses. We found that different campuses have very different kinds of websites and databases, and they make available (or not available) vastly different kinds of data. Given this variety, we will likely have to develop each new workshop in collaboration with organizers at a particular campus, but that can have the silver lining of being able to build relationships through such focused collaborations.

BRENDAN HORNBOSTEL Thanks to the digging of one of our research comrades, Syd White, we found that campus policing in DC falls under a broad "special police" statute and that the consortium in the DC area includes a training program called the Campus Public Safety Institute. In other words, the question of campus policing in DC is not really one that can be understood campus by campus. It's a broader question that falls under the same university relationships that make it possible for students to take classes or borrow books from other universities in DC.

Finding this out raised an important question about what it means that the structures of campus policing make possible the university we labor under, or how the university actually necessitates policing as foundational to its very functioning. By understanding that this Consortium of Universities of the Washington Metropolitan Area is the same mechanism by which police are trained to manage these campuses, we were able to reframe the issue of campus policing not as separable from the functioning of the university, but perhaps its central operating logic. This underlines how much our organizing against policing on our campuses has to be in relationship with folks at the other universities in our cities and regions. And this also highlights the limitations of how focusing solely on cops at a single campus can often end up reifying the space of the campus as exceptional to policing rather than as constitutively connected.

Realizing that university policing is not separate from the overall university education project forces us to understand that all the organizing we do—whether it's radical study, mutual aid work, or organizing against campus police—has to take place across campus spaces and within local communities to avoid reifying the kinds of police violence that makes the campus appear exceptional in the first place.

ELI MEYERHOFF Learning about that consortium of universities that collaborate to train police in DC motivated us to look at other metropolitan areas to see if there are similar sorts of consortia. I looked at my area of the so-called Research Triangle in North Carolina to see if universities here collaborate for facilitating training of campus police across different universities. I found that they do collaborate, but it's a different sort of collaboration that doesn't happen through a consortium. Rather, police training happens at community colleges all across the state of North Carolina. So that gives us another reason to analyze the whole system of higher education rather than just focusing on individual campuses.

Learning about this motivated me to get in touch with other researcher-organizers at other colleges and universities in the Triangle area who are involved in Cops Off Campus efforts, in order to collaborate on research on these training programs at community colleges. This is an example of how research can help build relationships for organizing and studying across campuses. These kinds of cross-campus networks can also be helpful in addressing the challenge of the relatively short lives of organizing efforts. Having relationships across campuses can keep the project going after undergraduates cycle out at any particular campus. I also think that, compared to undergrads, staff (like myself) often have much longer and more grounded relationships with campuses and their surrounding communities. So, involving staff could be a way to give more stability and longevity to these organizing efforts.

QUESTION *Could you reflect more on the biggest challenges facing researchers of campus police? What have you encountered and what are things that you'd like to bring to people's attention?*

BRENDAN HORNBOSTEL I think the methodology question is so important. When I first joined this project, as someone who doesn't have a lot of computer or tech skills, I thought that the data on campus policing was out there somewhere and that we just needed to develop tools to collect it and study it. This project has taught me that there is no such thing as just "the data" out there somewhere. Instead, the methodology of data collection has become for me one of the key ways that this project links organizing and study. For instance, we can think creatively about generating our own data, and I think that's one thing that the survey can be so helpful for.

Collecting people's experiences with campus policing creates new kinds of data that the university could never provide. But also, I think it's crucial to recognize that so much of the data that we do have on campus policing is heavily tied to the activities of campus police or even produced as a form of policing itself. At one of our workshops in 2021, I led a working group on analyzing Clery Act data, because that was one of the kinds of data that is more accessible across campuses. Beyond mere statistics on arrest records and crime logs, though, this kind of data collection was actually crucial to justifying the recent expansion of campus policing, especially at smaller private schools.

So, what does it mean to read the data of a Clery Act crime log as an act of policing itself, or as a fundamental tool of campus policing, rather than merely a reflection of something called "crime at the university"? In other words, studying campus police involves a consistent, critical analysis of university data as a kind of archive of counterinsurgency that legitimizes policing through knowledge production.

ELI MEYERHOFF I think another big challenge facing this kind of organizing is the challenge of avoiding co-optation into reformist efforts. I think, often, Cops Off Campus groups can get seduced into joining university task forces or other forms of institutional governance that can serve as a means of moderating the demands of the groups, thereby absorbing the more militant abolitionist energies of a movement and seducing members of those groups into adopting reformist demands that don't actually reduce the amount of policing. When groups get co-opted into these task forces, the administration can wait out the broader movement. The time scale is often so drawn out that they can dismiss the movement. Administrations can wait until the broader movement dies down and also keep waiting until the students who have been most active and militant graduate out or are pushed out. They wait until the forces and relationships that give strength to the movement are depleted and then they can push students to settle for more reformist kinds of negotiated demands.

As an antidote, doing the kind of research we're hoping to facilitate with our project can help groups learn about how co-optation has happened on campuses and provide a better sense of whether joining a university task force would be useful or not for their goals and to learn about what kinds of pitfalls to look out for. Resisting co-optation can help keep the broader movement going, and enabling collaborations between groups on and across campuses can help them to sustain and renew their organizing energies for the long haul.

NOTES

1. For more information on the Cops Off Campus Research Collective's projects, see https://abolition.university/cops-off-campus-research-project/. For more on abolitionist university studies, see Abbie Boggs, Eli Meyerhoff, Nick Mitchell, and Zach Schwartz-Weinstein, "Abolitionist University Studies: An Invitation," *Abolition: A*

Journal of Insurgent Politics, August 28, 2019, https://abolitionjournal.org/abolitionist-university-studies-an-invitation/.

2. For more of Meyerhoff's reflections on this question of the coconstitution of educational and carceral institutions in racial-colonial capitalism, see his essay, "Prisons and Universities Are Two Sides of the Same Coin," *Abolition: A Journal of Insurgent Politics*, July 24, 2015, https://abolitionjournal.org/eli-meyerhoff-abolitionist-study-against-and-beyond-higher-education/. See also his book *Beyond Education: Radical Studying for Another World* (Minneapolis: University of Minnesota Press, 2019), as well as Boggs et al., "Abolitionist University Studies: An Invitation."

3. The collective invites responses to their ongoing survey. For the survey, tutorials, and toolkits, see https://abolition.university/cops-off-campus-research-project/.

17

"A MOMENT OF PROFOUND COUNTERINSURGENCY"

A Reflection on Faculty Abolitionist Praxis with Dylan Rodríguez

BACKGROUND Dylan Rodríguez is a professor in the Departments of Black Studies (as of 2023) and Media and Cultural Studies at the University of California, Riverside. Dr. Rodríguez is a founding member of the abolitionist organization Critical Resistance and has long critiqued campus police as a tool of racist, anti-Black, and colonial state violence. Dr. Rodríguez discussed how his work in prison abolition informed his involvement in the Cops Off Campus Movement at the University of California. In this interview, he shared his insights on how the intertwining of universities and campus police results in state-sanctioned violence perpetrated against historically subjugated and excluded populations in higher education. The interview has been edited for length and clarity.

QUESTION *Can you tell us a little bit about yourself and the origins of your thoughts on campus policing?*

DYLAN RODRÍGUEZ My day job is as a faculty member. My real vocation is engagement with radical forms of activity and creativity toward the converging and distinct possibilities of abolition, anticolonial and decolonial transformation, Black liberation, and other forms of possibility and impossibility. i've been devoted to those various forms of collective work and thought for essentially my entire adult life. i'm a professor at University of California, Riverside (UCR), where i'm finishing my twenty-first year.

i arrived at UCR having already been formed and taught by multiple overlapping communities of revolutionaries, abolitionists, and radicals throughout my graduate studies, which were based in the Bay Area. i did my PhD at UC Berkeley, but i'll say that my study extended so far beyond the university that i can't really credit UC Berkeley with my education. Many of my most important teachers were from communities of formerly incarcerated people, especially former political prisoners and social movement organizers, people who are survivors of direct state violence and repression. i got vital aspects of my political and intellectual formation through being in community with these folks.

My entrance into working to get cops off campus was entirely inevitable because i have long experienced university campuses–public, private, and otherwise–as institutions and sites that directly reproduce, extend, and distort relations of dominance and violence.

QUESTION *How does your perspective inform your involvement in the Cops Off Campus Movement?*

DYLAN RODRÍGUEZ The University of California is one of the largest research apparatuses on this planet. It has sustained structures, systems, and histories of domination and violence. When colleagues, friends, and loved ones began to convene Cops Off Campus, i felt it was long overdue. There was urgency around it, but it was probably overdue. What keeps me so deeply committed to the work of Cops Off Campus is the fact that the group, in addition to having explicit and militant objectives about eliminating police presence and state violence, has been a movement and collective that has never been anything other than 100 percent committed to the centrality of collective study and building mobilization, which i find vital and in many ways, refreshing. It's a direct challenge to vulgar antistudy pragmatism.

i also think about this in terms of a biographical reflection that's inseparable from forms of collective political and cultural work. i was targeted by my employing university in two simultaneous incidents. One was a deeply reactionary white male student who harassed me and filed multiple grievances against me between 2001-2002, including one of "racial profiling." I later found out that he was connected to the right wing organization founded by David Horowitz, the Center for the Study of Popular Culture in Los Angeles. The UCR administration and the university disciplinary process fully entertained his grievance. It was ultimately thrown out by the [faculty] senate committee because they saw how absurd the whole thing was. That made my life hell for about two years because i didn't know if they were gonna fire me.

The other aspect of my confrontation with the campus as a site of policing and state violence had its origins in my participation in an on-campus demonstration that student activists—almost entirely Latinx and Black women—organized. Students asked me to come as an observer and as a documentarian, so i brought a video camera and recorded the rally. A white male student was there to take photos for the campus newspaper, which had earned a reputation for its anti-Black, sexist, and racist content. This particular student was, perhaps uncoincidentally, also part of a fraternity that had regularly harassed women of color students.

At one point during the demonstration, he became aggressive with one of the student activists and tried to physically intimidate her by raising his fist as if to threaten striking her. i have this on videotape. i physically stood in front of him so he would not be able to advance toward the student any further. He bumped my head with his camera lens, i told him not to touch me, and, predictably, he filed criminal assault charges against me with the UC Riverside Police Department that went to the Riverside District Attorney. Ultimately, they didn't prosecute because there was nothing there and i had ample video evidence. But the threat of prosecution lingered for months. i had to hire a lawyer to get the university to back off of me.

QUESTION *The university administration, along with campus police and municipal police, seem to have played a prominent role in these experiences, is that correct?*

DYLAN RODRÍGUEZ The university administration and police are always inseparable. We should never think about them as separate. The university police and administration, in their symbiosis, were really directing an ensemble of repression against these student activists by way of condoning some of the harassment that was coming, for example, from fraternities. i understood, just by previous experience, how administrators and police at university campuses and surrounding areas are also inseparable: the administration is part of the police and the police are already part of the administration.

What i appreciate about Cops Off Campus is that its commitment to building an analytical framework has been a central part of its organizing practice and internal politics from the beginning. i feel like folks understood that we had to intervene on this notion that the university police are somehow a separate entity from university administration. This analysis informs how we teach, organize, mobilize, and develop different pedagogies.

QUESTION *To elaborate more upon the symbiotic relationship between policing and the university, what issues concern you the most about campus policing?*

DYLAN RODRÍGUEZ   i think that we are in a moment of profound counterinsurgency, which in many ways is centered on college and university campuses. What i mean by that is the following: i think university administrators understand that the primary way for them to re-legitimate police presence at their campuses is to appropriate, expropriate and then rearticulate the rhetoric, concepts, and even the demands of abolitionist movements, of antipolice movements, in ways that are conducive to the administrative reform and restructuring of police power.

This is the moment we are in. i think universities and colleges as institutions are prototype sites for this form of counterinsurgent work. They have been largely successful so far because universities are sites in which there are many people, including my colleagues, who are all too eager to accept administrative invitations onto committees, panels, webinars, town halls, and other ceremonial bullshit, which at best are all about lamenting the casualties that have been created by police violence, terror, and harassment.

After acknowledging and lamenting the anti-Blackness of police violence, they resort to old and thoroughly demystified and rebutted police reform scripts. They are reformist in the sense that they require the continued presence of police as a central part of the university institution. While i put the emphasis initially on administrators and police, i will say that rank-and-file faculty, as well as many liberal-to-reactionary students, are also part of this leading edge of repression and surveillance. That is the counterinsurgency on university campuses.

Cops Off Campus over the last couple of years has generated plenty of imagination and practical solutions that have marinated through collective study to actually build infrastructures of collective security. By security, i'm not just talking about security from interpersonal violence, but security in the deep sense of security. Food security, recreational security, emotional security, health security, all the things for which conditions of institutionalized insecurity generate the conditions for interpersonal exploitation, violence, and harm. That's been central to how Cops Off Campus has thought about police abolition. It's been thinking about security at the center of a robust conceptualization of how campuses are sites in which you can create security for the people in a relatively defined geography, as well as for people in the surrounding community in ways that are immediate and effective.

To the extent that these institutions could become sites of abolitionist practice, restructuring, and redistribution of infrastructure and resources, as well as skill sets, universities could exemplify the possibilities and practical immediacies of police abolition to communities, institutions, and systems elsewhere. It can work as a kind of prototype to be translated elsewhere.

So given that, i think the biggest problem to be confronted in relation to policing and police departments at universities and colleges, is the way that the [schools'] administrations, in collaboration with police departments, have been successful in soliciting consent and participation from students, faculty, staff, and self-appointed community leaders through ceremonies of police reform that are premised on reinvigorating the legitimacy of [campus] police presence. If you want to really cut through to the heart of it, their purpose is to relegitimate police presence at university campuses in the face of massive evidence that the police presence at universities and colleges is not only unnecessary, but counterproductive to their own declared mission statements of what the university and college should be.

QUESTION *What compels faculty to become complicit with policing at the university?*

DYLAN RODRÍGUEZ   There is an inherently individualizing approach that many colleagues internalize when they embrace the idea that their job is to be an "academic." i put academic in scare quotes because most people who embrace this identity think about themselves as individuals and as individual experts. The people who are easily solicited into the university's reformist rituals are almost entirely disconnected if not alienated from communities, organizations, movements, and collectives of people that are involved in the work of challenging police power. Some faculty members have built academic careers that intersect in some way with criminology or related fields that administrators find to be credible enough to include in these reform ceremonies. These faculty members provide cover and credibility for administrative efforts to defend and reinvigorate the police.

The other part of this is that most of the colleagues who participate in these task forces, workgroups, and town halls fundamentally believe and trust in the legitimacy of police power. They believe that the institution can and should be reformed in some kind of way that will more equitably violate and criminalize people. In many ways, there's a disavowed liberalism that's at the core of this type of faculty acquiescence to administrative processes. But again, it only is possible because these colleagues tend to be disconnected from communities of responsibility and accountability that would hold them in serious scrutiny for their participation in administrative reformism.

One of the things that needs to be done is that our movements should do whatever they can to identify and hold faculty accountable for their participation in the reformist rituals that fuel this counterinsurgency. What we can and should do is call that shit out, which some of us are in a good position to do, especially people who are tenured and have relative job security. i think it's incumbent on us to call that shit out. It needs to be named in no uncertain terms as a version of counterinsurgency and participation in political repression. Most of the colleagues i'm thinking about don't like to be held responsible for their participation in repression. They don't want to be on the wrong side of history. They see themselves as being on the right side of history because they see themselves as trying to push towards some version of institutional change. But to help legitimate police power in this moment is to be on the wrong side of history.

QUESTION *How else can faculty leverage their position within the university to organize for abolition on campus, both with respect to campus police specifically, but also beyond?*

DYLAN RODRÍGUEZ First, faculty need to understand that they have expertise, access to resources, and skill sets that they ought to creatively share. Tenured people have an added layer of responsibility to take certain kinds of political and institutional risks that students, people on parole, undocumented people, and untenured junior faculty probably can't or shouldn't take. Putting ourselves in positions of targeting and vulnerability is one way we can lead.

A second action faculty can take up immediately, in a practical way, which doesn't require acute political and personal risks, is resource redistribution. You can redistribute the dirty colonial money of your university into honoraria for local organizers and organizations with whom you may already be collaborating. i think faculty ought to regularly engage with tactical resource redistribution because some of the most important abolitionist collectives are constantly in need of various kinds of resources.

i'm not only talking about honoraria and bits of university money. i'm also talking about how there's something wonderful, ironic, and destructive—in the abolitionist sense of destruction—about actively reinhabiting certain sites and spaces in these institutions with people who are otherwise the generalized targets of the university's institutionalized practices of policing and extermination.

QUESTION *Since so much of what you're saying is grounded in community and doing community work, we're wondering if you might talk about the importance of having people who are not affiliated with the university involved in the Cops Off Campus Movement.*

DYLAN RODRÍGUEZ The university is a fucking beast. Its self-reproduction is premised on border-making and border policing. Its power and its violence exceed its own self-defined borders so much so, that people in surrounding communities, and i'm talking miles and miles away, feel it. And i don't just mean feel it in an existential way, they feel it materially. The context the beastly university presents is one in which people who are not employed or affiliated with the university know that once they come into a certain proximity to the university itself, when they approach the borders of university, or get near university power, meaning university administrators and even faculty members, they need to watch their backs because they will be made vulnerable to the power of that beast. They will be policed, they'll be surveilled, they'll be categorized, and they'll be targeted for displacement and destruction. It's a colonial apparatus in that sense. Black radical colleagues constantly refer to the university as a "plantation." People who are not formally affiliated with universities constantly feel this extended plantation violence.

QUESTION *How have administrators responded to the campus police abolition demands that organizing groups have made, in your experience?*

DYLAN RODRÍGUEZ: They've responded in ways that are entirely predictable and cowardly, that are spineless, which largely means that they don't respond at all. The silence is calculated, intentional, strategic, and tactical. We need to understand the silence in that way, that it's not simple negligence. It's a refusal on the part of the dominant power to acknowledge the existence of an abolitionist position.

Another way that administrators are responding to abolitionist demands and imagination is by actively deforming them. By deforming i mean strategically misappropriating and misunderstanding what abolitionist demands and ideas actually are. i think administrators are generally satisfied that they have quelled the insurgency by engaging in the ceremonies of police reform, by creating multiple ad hoc committees, by doing these modest nominal restructurings of say, campus mental health protocols that they believe are adequate to addressing some of the demands addressing police violence. But it's incumbent on the rest of us to amplify how these reforms actually increase police power by deputizing staff and faculty, including care and health workers, as practical extensions of the police. The administration is deeply dishonest in this way.

QUESTION *What positive efforts or outcomes do you see on the horizon?*

DYLAN RODRíGUEZ: i think there has been evidence of potential to grow abolitionist militancy in the coming time. That's the most optimistic i can be. To do that, we have to come to terms with the complex and sometimes self-implicating forms of counterinsurgency that are happening at colleges and universities. If we are capable and willing to confront those complex forms of counterinsurgency, then i think we can put ourselves in a position to grow that militancy.

i think that there is a necessity and urgency to think about the creatively destructive aspects of abolition as a central part of its historical practice. I'll say that this is an urgent aspiration. What i aspire to be part of in the coming period is a collective critical conversation about what it might mean to center the destructive possibilities of abolition. i honor and participate in the creative and constructive world-making aspects of abolitionist practice. At the same time, those of us engaging in abolitionist practices must not politically disavow the disruptive necessities of our collective praxis. Something beautiful happens when structures of violence are destroyed. i feel like that's something that i want to be part of in the coming time.

AFTERWORD

YALILE SURIEL, GRACE WATKINS,
JUDE PAUL MATIAS DIZON,
AND JOHN J. SLOAN III

Our primary goal for this edited volume was to bring together a group of contributors whose writings and experiences represent a new direction in what might otherwise be considered divergent areas of research and scholarship: the study of policing and higher education administration. What their contributions reveal is that there is an important intersection between these fields: the policing *of* American higher education. Collectively, the chapters in this work provide new narratives, approaches, and frameworks for understanding campus police forces. By combining original research at the cutting edge of multiple disciplines alongside activist interviews, we hope to generate productive discussion on the role of campus policing.

While there are many linkages between the topics covered in the volume's chapters, a few in particular stand out. For example, Andrew Pedro Guerrero's work on the UCLA PD sting operations, Yalile Suriel's chapter on the campus War on Drugs, and Lucien Baskin, Erica R. Meiners, and Grace Watkins's work on campus police unions all explore the relationship between municipal and campus policing. Not only have campus police emulated the practices of city departments, but they have also become close working partners on a range of policing campaigns. Similarly, Jude Paul Matias Dizon's work demonstrates how issues of systemic racism in municipal policing are just as present in the policing of college campuses. Kamaria Porter's chapter on the reporting experiences of Black women and nonbinary students and Matt Johnson's chapter on anti-rape student activism discuss interconnected aspects of the racialization of campus sexual assault—both victims and offenders—and the resulting effects on the growth of campus police and their investigative protocols. Davarian L.

Baldwin, Jacob Anbinder, and Stephen Averill Sherman's chapters each examine different manifestations of the interplay between urban spaces, college grounds, and the borders between them. Finally, John Sloan's chapter on *in loco parentis* and Vineeta Singh's chapter on ed-tech tease out surprising continuities and connections between the evolution of student discipline and the ever-expanding role of campus police.

The future of campus policing takes center stage in the last section of this volume. The activists interviewed in part 4 issue a call to think creatively, strategically, and—most importantly—expansively about the meaning of campus safety. The interviewees highlight different modes of resistance and ask all members of university communities to reflect on our own participation in the legitimization of policing practices within and beyond university spaces.

It is our hope that in addition to capturing a snapshot of this unprecedented moment of reckoning in higher education, these interviews can serve as a resource for the classroom and researchers in the years to come. We also hope that by recording a range of different perspectives and reflections, we can foster discussions that will inform the direction of future activism.

The emerging field of critical campus police studies encompasses a range of issues that have yet to be explored. There are important topics that this volume did not consider that also warrant scholarly inquiry. Below, we identify areas in need of exploration in future research and pose a set of questions that might guide such endeavors.

DIRECTIONS FOR FUTURE WORK

As mentioned, there are identifiable gaps in what is known about the policing of higher education that warrant further attention. For example, many studies of campus police thus far have focused on elite private institutions such as the University of Chicago and those of the Ivy League. The police departments at these institutions are important because they have some of the largest budgets and manpower and were also heavily involved in shaping the field of campus law enforcement and serving as a model for other departments. They also have some of the most detailed university archive materials available. However, the majority of students in higher education are at large public institutions (nine out of ten of which have campus police, at double the rate of private institutions). The history of campus police and student resistance at these institutions are in need of further investigation.[1] Particularly deserving of this attention are community colleges, which constitute over 35 percent of all degree-granting postsecondary institutions and enroll more than five million students.² The study of campus policing is also in need of more comparative work evaluating campus forces across different regions and types of institutions. For example, research into campus policing at HBCUs (Historically Black Colleges and Universities) or HSIs (Hispanic-Serving Institutions) will yield new observations on the role of class, racial and ethnic identities, and the legacy of Jim Crow in higher education. Another promising area of comparative analysis is examining the rise of university policing alongside the development of School Resource Officers (SROs) in K-12 education.

A second area of interest concerns the relationship between postsecondary "police science" programs and campus police departments, as well as the police academies, field training of new campus officers, and in-service training required of active-duty campus police officers. Historically, police science training programs developed during the 1960s as part of the US government's War on Crime initiative and first evolved into associate's degree programs, followed by baccalaureate and finally graduate degree programs in criminal justice. How the establishment of campus police departments coincided with police training programs evolving into postsecondary degree-granting programs is understudied. Also unexplored is (1) how campus police officers are recruited from the ranks of college students and (2) the training received by campus police officers, beginning with their basic law enforcement training at police academies around the nation, extending to their field training, and continuing via annual in-service training once recruits become full-time police officers. Recent quantitative studies of police academies' basic training regiments by John Sloan and Eugene Paoline offer glimpses into specific areas of training that are stressed by academies, but additional work, using mixed-methods approaches or purely qualitative studies, is needed to identify the dynamics of campus officer training.

A third area in need of study is the impact of high-profile campus attacks such as the 1966 tower shooting at The University of Texas, Austin, and the 2007 Virginia Tech shooting. The threat of future mass shootings has frequently been invoked to legitimize the existence of campus police and the militarization of their forces through the acquisition of equipment from the U.S. Department of Defense. Finally, also needed are works that focus on narratives of resistance to the growth of campus police by students, staff, faculty, and local residents.³ Centering these voices is a necessary corrective to the absence of, and limits on, campus police records.

QUESTIONS THAT CAN GUIDE FURTHER RESEARCH

Some of the questions that can guide future research on the policing of American higher education are:

- What does the adoption and overall trajectory of campus policing reveal about the substance and orientation of American higher education?
- How has the presence of internal police forces shaped the daily life of college and university campuses and the many members of those communities, both historically and today? How do the legacies of the presence of campus police continue to play out today?
- How does reconceptualizing universities and colleges through the lens of carceral studies shift how we understand the function and limits of higher education?
- As researchers of campus policing, teachers, and members of the university community, how do we assess and reflect on our everyday roles working in the same sites that we study?

CONCLUSION

This volume responded to calls from critical scholars to depart from a paradigm that assumes the necessity of having sworn police officers present on American college campuses. The chapters questioned how and why campus policing has the "same familiarity and easy intelligibility as other elements of our everyday world."[4] Whereas universities have been hyperfocused on securing their campuses by expanding the powers of campus police, a goal of this work is to question the very meaning of "safety," the tools with which it can be obtained, and the inherent purpose of campus policing.

This collaborative and multidisciplinary approach traverses critical perspectives in fields such as history, sociology, and higher education administration. The contributors to this book mirror the intergenerational, diverse coalitions on college campuses and communities nationwide that are mobilizing to confront the US policing apparatus. Our collective effort signals the need to incorporate different viewpoints in the movement to address campus policing.

Attempts to translate these principles into practice are underway at several institutions of higher education across the country. For example, Portland State

University disarmed its campus police officers in 2021 following a seven-year student-led campaign.[5] It remains to be seen whether these initiatives will grow and continue to be adopted by other institutions as student activists warn of the threat of cooptation and superficial reforms that ultimately do more harm than good. Resistance by students, staff, faculty, and local residents will continue as models of safety are debated, contested, and reimagined.

NOTES

1. Bob Violino, "A Safer Campus?" *Community College Journal* 80, no. 6 (June/July 2010): 26–31.

2. National Center for Education Statistics, *The Condition of Education—2020–2021* (Washington, DC: United States Department of Education, 2022), tables 303.30 and 303.70, https://nces.ed.gov/programs/coe/current_tables.

3. American Association of University Professors, *On Campus Policing* (Washington, DC: AAUP, 2021), www.aaup.org/report/campus-police-forces.

4. David Garland, *The Culture of Control: Crime and Social Order in Contemporary Society* (Chicago: University of Chicago Press, 2001).

5. Kate Hidalgo Bellows, "Portland State U. Is Disarming Its Campus Police. Activists Say It's a 'Media Stunt,'" *Chronicle of Higher Education*, June 17, 2021, www.chronicle.com/.

CONTRIBUTORS

JACOB ANBINDER is a PhD candidate in American history at Harvard University, where he studies the politics of American cities and suburbs in the twentieth century. His dissertation is a history of the metropolitan "growth revolt," its role in the ideological realignment of the late twentieth-century Democratic Party, and the origins of the modern urban housing crisis. His research interests include the political economy of major infrastructure projects, social movements for and against change to the built environment, and the ways in which sprawl and spatial segregation create social inequities. Anbinder is a recipient of the Raymond J. Cunningham Prize and the Albert J. Beveridge Grant from the American Historical Association. His writing has been published in the *Atlantic*, the *Wall Street Journal*, *Business History Review*, *U.S. News & World Report*, *Newsweek*, and *Democracy: A Journal of Ideas*. He holds a master of arts in history from Harvard and a bachelor of arts in history from Yale University. In 2023 he will begin a Klarman Postdoctoral Fellowship at Cornell University.

DAVARIAN L. BALDWIN is an internationally recognized scholar, author, and public advocate. He is the Raether Distinguished Professor of American Studies and founding director of the Smart Cities Research Lab at Trinity College in Hartford, Connecticut. His academic and political commitments have focused on global cities and particularly the diverse and marginalized communities that struggle to maintain sustainable lives in urban locales. Baldwin is the award-winning author of several books, most recently, In the Shadow of the Ivory Tower: How Universities Are Plundering Our Cities. He is currently finishing the book Land of Darkness: Chicago and the Making of Race in Modern America (forthcoming from Oxford University Press). He also sits on the national council of the American Association of University Professors and the coordinating committee of Scholars for Social Justice. His commentaries and opinions have been featured in numerous outlets from NBC News, BBC, and Hulu to *USA Today*, the *Washington*

Post, and *Time* magazine. Baldwin was named a 2022 Freedom Scholar by the Marguerite Casey Foundation for his work.

LUCIEN BASKIN is a doctoral student in urban education at the City University of New York (CUNY) Graduate Center and an instructor of sociology at John Jay College, where they teach courses on the carceral state, social movements, political imprisonment, urban geography, and abolition. Their work focuses on social movements, the Black Radical Tradition, abolition, and education and is rooted in the CUNY, including a dissertation project on radical organizing at CUNY in the era following open admissions. They are also at work on a project about Stuart Hall's educational and pedagogical work and the institutional contexts of his radical intellectualism. They organize with Free CUNY and the Cops Off Campus Coalition and have written about campus policing and abolitionist organizing in the university including "Looking to Get Cops Off Your Campus? Start Here" with Erica Meiners in *Truthout*, and "Abolitionist Study and Struggle in and beyond the University" in the *Abusable Past*.

KACIE LUCCHINI BUTCHER is a public historian who has curated several award-winning exhibits, and currently serves as director of the University of Wisconsin–Madison Public History Project, a multiyear effort to uncover and give voice to histories of racism and discrimination on the UWM campus and resistance to them. She earned a master's degree in heritage studies and public history from the University of Minnesota.

JUDE PAUL MATIAS DIZON is an assistant professor of higher education leadership at California State University, Stanislaus. His research aims to uncover and disrupt the relationship between higher education and the carceral state. He is developing a series of papers from a three-year study, "Broken Windows on Campus: An Examination of Policing and Racism in Higher Education." Dizon's scholarship on campus policing and carcerality has been published in the *Peabody Journal of Education* and the *Journal of Diversity in Higher Education*.

ANDREW PEDRO GUERRERO is a doctoral student in American studies at Harvard University. His research explores the expansion of police power in the twentieth century. A community college graduate from Los Angeles County, he holds a bachelor's degree from UCLA and a master's degree in history from Harvard University.

BRENDAN HORNBOSTEL (they/them) is a PhD student in history at George Washington University. Their research examines the history of policing in Washington, DC, as a key site of colonial-imperial statecraft in relation to DC's simultaneous status as a racial-domestic colony and the world's imperial capital. They are involved in various community organizing efforts around abolition and antifascism, both on and off campus.

MATTHEW JOHNSON is an associate professor of history at Washington & Jefferson College. Much of his work focuses on how universities and colleges help maintain inequality. His first book, *Undermining Racial Justice: How One University Embraced Inclusion and Inequality* (Cornell University Press, 2020), showed how campus officials at the University of Michigan developed techniques to co-opt student movements for racial justice since the 1960s. He is now working on a book about southern universities that adopted the SAT and ACT in the 1950s and early 1960s to resist desegregation. His research has been funded by the American Council of Learned Societies and the Spencer Foundation, and his writing has been featured in the *Washington Post* and *Slate*.

JAEL KERANDI is a financial analyst for Microsoft and lives in Seattle. A recent graduate from the University of Minnesota's Carlson School of Management, she earned a BS in finance and marketing with minors in leadership and business law. During her tenure at Minnesota, Kerandi served as the first Black undergraduate student body vice president and then president. She was also a two-term student representative to the Board of Regents and served as the Chair in her second term. She was a member of the Undergraduate Advisory Board and sat on Carlson's Diversity, Equity, and Inclusion Committee. She is an extremely proud member of Delta Sigma Theta Sorority. At the University of Minnesota, she twice received the President's Student Leadership & Service Award; she was also honored with the Donald R. Zander Alumni Award for Outstanding Student Leadership; the Scholarly Excellence in Equity and Diversity (SEED) Award; and the James A. Johnson Award. Kerandi is passionate about creating a better world; racial justice and working toward a more equitable society is important to her. For her efforts she has been featured on CNN, MSNBC, MTV, and NowThis, and in *Teen Vogue*, *Elle*, *Cosmopolitan*, and more. She has spoken at Notre Dame, Columbia, Princeton, and other postsecondary institutions. She also serves on the UMN Black Alumni Board and tutors third- and fourth-grade students.

ERICA R. MEINERS, a writer, educator, and organizer, has recently coedited the anthology *The Long Term: Resisting Life Sentences, Working towards Freedom* (Haymarket, 2018); coauthored *Feminist and the Sex Offender: Confronting Sexual Harm, Ending State Violence* (Verso, 2020); and coauthored *Abolition. Feminism. Now* (Haymarket, 2022). At Northeastern Illinois University, Erica is an active member of her labor union and teaches classes in education, gender and sexuality studies, and justice studies. Most importantly, Erica has collaboratively started and works alongside others in a range of ongoing mobilizations for liberation, particularly movements that involve access to free public education for all, including people during and after incarceration, and other queer abolitionist struggles.

ELI MEYERHOFF (he/him) is a staff member in the John Hope Franklin Humanities Institute at Duke University He is the author of *Beyond Education: Radical Studying for Another World* (University of Minnesota Press, 2019) and is currently collaborating on projects of abolitionist university studies.

VANESSA MILLER, JD, PHD, is an assistant professor of education law in the Department of Educational Leadership and Policy Studies at Indiana University. Prior to joining the faculty at Indiana University, she was the inaugural postdoctoral associate for the Race and Crime Center for Justice at the University of Florida Levin College of Law. Her research broadly focuses on race, education, and the criminal legal system. Her scholarship has been published in the Missouri Law Review, Washington and Lee Journal of Civil Rights and Social Justice, and the Rutgers Race & the Law Review. She is originally from Miami, Florida, and is the proud daughter of Cuban immigrants.

NICK MITCHELL (she/her) is a faculty member in the departments of Critical Race and Ethnic Studies and Feminist Studies at the University of California, Santa Cruz. Prior to USCS, Mitchell was on the faculty at the University of California, Riverside. Her research is generally on the theory and history of higher education. Mitchell is currently finishing a book on the ways that the histories of Black studies and women's studies interface, intersect, and in some ways prefigure some of the terms that we associate with university neoliberalism (discipline and surplus), Black studies, women's studies, and the birth of neoliberalism. Mitchell also has a long history of abolitionist organizing and organizing around HIV/AIDS.

KAMARIA B. PORTER, PHD, is an assistant professor of education policy studies at the Pennsylvania State University. Porter received her doctorate in higher education from the University of Michigan. Porter's research examines gender and racial inequities in higher education, particularly university response to sexual assault, graduate education, and faculty experiences. Her dissertation, "Speaking into Silence: Intersections of Identity, Legality, and Black Women's Decision to Report Sexual Assault on Campus," examined Black women's perspectives on the legal system in weighing whether to report sexual violence to their university. At Michigan, Porter was the lab manager for the University Responses to Sexual Assault (URSA) Project, which is based on an in-depth policy analysis of 381 university sexual misconduct policies. Before graduate school, she worked as a community organizer in Chicago, focusing on expanding healthcare access and affordable housing. While earning her master's in higher education at Loyola University Chicago, she trained to be a rape survivor crisis counselor, assisting survivors and their families in hospital ERs as they navigated complex medical and legal decisions.

RYAN FLACO RISING is the retention coordinator for the UCI Underground Scholars Program, as well as a PhD candidate in Criminology, Law, and Society at the University of California, Irvine. Rising's lived experience as a formerly incarcerated youth and adult deeply informs the work he does around assisting formerly incarcerated students in their transition into UCI, bringing to the table a unique firsthand perspective. Rising's research interests center on creating pathways for formerly incarcerated individuals into higher education, and analyzing the evolution of programs that serve formerly incarcerated students within the university system. Rising uses his lived experience as a formerly incarcerated student to guide his research, developing tangible findings and methods to best serve this demographic's needs within university and reentry services across California. Rising has been a part of the Underground Scholars program since his release from New Folsom State Prison in 2015. Rising founded the Gaucho Underground Scholars Program at the University of California, Santa Barbara, while completing his bachelor's degree in sociology with a minor in education. There, he played a critical role in the leadership and statewide expansion of the Underground Scholars Programs, now active on almost every University of California campus. Rising has won many prestigious awards, including the Circle of Excellence Scholarship from the University of San Diego. One of the highest honors during his time at UCSB was the distinguished Michael D. Young Engaged Scholars Award, highlighting how Rising built an entire program from the ground floor up to serve the needs of formerly incarcerated students. This is now a fully institutionalized program funded by the State of California. Rising's writing has been published in a variety of newspapers, as well as in the book *Reclaiming Our Stories*. His work is a testament to the power of formerly incarcerated students, and his theory of "organic leadership" demonstrates how formerly incarcerated people continue to produce new solutions, assist in healing, and create sustainable pathways that uplift entire communities.

DYLAN RODRÍGUEZ is a teacher, scholar, and collaborator who is committed to building and supporting abolitionist, liberationist, anticolonial and other forms of radical community and movement. Since 2001, he has maintained a day job as a professor at the University of California, Riverside, where he works in the Department of Black Study and the Department of Media and Cultural Studies. He was elected to serve as president of the American Studies Association in 2020–21, and in 2020 was named to the inaugural class of Freedom Scholars. Rodríguez was Chair of the Department of Ethnic Studies between 2009 and 2016, after which he was elected to two consecutive terms as Chair of the UC Riverside Division of the Academic Senate (2016–20). In 2021, he was appointed codirector of the Center for Ideas and Society. Since the late 1990s, he has participated as a founding member of organizations like Critical Resistance, the Abolition Collective, Critical Ethnic Studies Association, Cops Off Campus, Scholars for Social Justice, and Blackness Unbound, among others. Rodríguez is the author of three books, most recently *White Reconstruction: Domestic Warfare and the Logic of Racial Genocide* (Fordham University Press, 2021), which won the 2022 Frantz Fanon Book Award from the Caribbean Philosophical Association. He was a coeditor of the field-shaping text *Critical Ethnic Studies: A Reader* (Duke University Press, 2016). Rodríguez appreciates participating in all forms of collective study, thought, and planning that build capacities to survive and revolt against oppressive conditions.

ZACH SCHWARTZ-WEINSTEIN (he/him) has a PhD in American studies from New York University and writes about the history of university service workers, mostly food service, custodial, groundskeepers, and clerical workers. Schwartz-Weinstein has also been involved with the abolitionist university studies project since 2018.

STEPHEN AVERILL SHERMAN is a research scientist at Rice University's Kinder Institute for Urban Research in Houston, where he investigates the city-making role of police. An urban planner by training, his research addresses diverse topics—including affordable housing, community economic development, and urban planning methods—while focusing on the role of law and police in each of these research topics. At the Kinder Institute, he primarily investigates housing policy in Houston and Harris County, Texas. Stephen has a PhD and a master's in urban planning from the University of Illinois at Urbana-Champaign and a bachelor's in English and American studies from the University of Iowa. Prior to his research career, he was an urban planner for the City of Tulsa and a manager at an independent grocery store in Iowa.

VINEETA SINGH is an assistant teaching professor in the Interdisciplinary Studies Program at Virginia Commonwealth University. Her research and teaching bring together the history and sociology of higher education through the lenses of Black studies and critical university studies.

JOHN J. SLOAN III is professor emeritus of criminal justice and sociology and Senior Scientist in the Institute for Human Rights at the University of Alabama at Birmingham (UAB). For nearly thirty years he has studied crime and security issues—including campus police—on college and university campuses. Various federal agencies including the National Science Foundation, the Bureau of Justice Assistance, the COPS Office, and the National Institute of Justice have funded his research. He is the author, coauthor, or coeditor of nine books with publishers such as Oxford University Press, Cambridge University Press, and Carolina University Press. His work has appeared in multiple scholarly outlets including *Social Forces, Criminology, Justice Quarterly, Criminology & Public Policy*, and the *Journal of Criminal Justice*. A former automobile mechanic and ex-member of the United Auto Workers (UAW), he earned a PhD in sociology from Purdue University, where he was awarded a National Institute of Justice Dissertation Fellowship to support his work on discretionary justice during felony case processing in Detroit, where he was born, raised, and attended school.

YALILE SURIEL is an assistant professor of universities and power at the University of Minnesota. Her research examines the intersections between higher education and the carceral state. She has published in the *Abusable Past* and *Black Perspectives*. She has been a Turner Fellow, an AERA Fellow, and the recipient of the

Eggertsen Dissertation Prize from the History of Education Society. She is working on a manuscript about campus police and broader university surveillance of Black and Latinx student activism in the latter half of the twentieth century.

GRACE WATKINS is a student at Yale Law School and a doctoral candidate in history at the University of Oxford. She has written on the history of campus police for the *Washington Post,* the *Chronicle of Higher Education,* and the *Comparative American Studies Journal.*

INDEX

abolitionist praxis, faculty, 239–42
abolition of campus police, calls for, x, 37, 147, 203–8. *See also* Cops Off Campus Movement
academic surveillance, 178–86
accountability, lack of, for campus police, 10–12, 25, 88, 197, 200, 241. *See also* qualified immunity
activism: anti-sexual assault, at Penn, 77–78, 83–91; feminist, and the rise of the carceral state, 78, 83–91; suppression of, by campus police, xviii, 20–22, 111. *See also* student protests
"Adamson University" study, 148–56
adultification of Black girls, 169
AFL-CIO, relationship of, with IUPA, 45–46, 48
American Association of Universities (AAU) survey, 160
anticarceral feminism, development of, 78, 84–85, 162–63
anticarceral union power, building of, 48–49
anti-sexual assault activism at Penn, 77–78, 83–91
archives on campus policing: accessibility of, 219–20; collaborative approach to, 220–21; navigation of, 218–19; public availability of, 216–18

Ares, Joe, 114–17
austerity, engineered, within universities, 47, 48
authority, statutory, 17–22, 28–29
automated license plate readers, use of, 186

Barber, John, 112, 114, 115–16, 118
Black campus police officers, racial hostility toward, in the workplace, 26–28
Black feminist thought, 162–63
Black girls, adultification of, 169
Black Lives Matter Movement, x, 90
Black neighborhoods: displacement in, for campus expansion, 38, 80–82, 112; jurisdictional expansion of campus police into, 33–38; stigmatization of, by universities, 151
Black people, overpolicing of, by campus police, 22, 36, 83, 113, 146, 149, 170–71
Black Student Alliance at Yale (BSAY), 66–67
Black women, racialized barrier to reporting sexual assault for, 160, 162–64; study regarding, 164–67
body cameras, use of, 134, 186
broken windows policing as community engagement, 152–54

Brown, Al, 114
"bubble," college campus as a, 127–29, 151
Bureau of Justice Statistics research on campus police, 133

cameras: body, 134, 186; security, 80, 186–87
campus police: authority of, 17–22, 28–29; creation and evolution of, xi, xii–xvi, 5–9, 42, 211; direction for future work on, 246–48; ed tech as an extension of reach for, 178–79; jurisdictional expansion of, 9, 11–13, 33–38, 118–20; legitimacy of, 10–13, 22, 90–91, 96, 102–4, 110; racial conflict within the culture of, 25–29; as a racialized system of social control, 21–22, 145–47, 154–55; unions for, 41–49; and the War on Drugs, 96, 99, 103–4
Campus Security Enhancement Act, 147
carceral responses to campus sexual assault, 172
carceral state, rise of the, and feminist activism, 78, 84–85
carceral unions, 45–49
Caucus of Rank and File Educators (CORE), 49
Chicago Teachers Union (CTU), 49
Citizens Police Data Project, 25
Civil Rights Act of 1964, Title VI of, 83
Clery Act, 145, 156n5
Clery Alerts, 200
Coalition of Graduate Employee Unions, 48
coeducation at Yale, 64, 67
Colgate University, 98, 99, 105
collaboration between campus and local police, 96, 100, 102–3, 115–19
Collick v. William Patterson University, 24

Columbia University protests, 19–20
community-oriented policing (COP), 12–13; broken windows policing as, 152–54
confidential informant (CI) programs, 95–96, 105–6n3
Connecticut National Guard, 68
"controlling images" of Black women and girls, 160, 169
Cops Off Campus Movement, 49, 145, 199, 237, 238–40, 242
crime data, suppression of, 81, 89–90

Dartmouth University ExamSoft incident, 184–86
Davie, Alfred E., 110
defunding of campus police, calls for, x, 48, 109, 144–45
demilitarization of campus police, calls for, x, 28, 48
deputizing of teaching faculty through academic surveillance, 183–86
disarmament of campus police, calls for, x, 48, 248–49
Disarm UC movement, 48
displacement of Black people for campus expansion, 38, 80–82, 112
drones, use of, 186
drugs on college campuses, use of, 97–99, 137

Early, Gerald, 87–88
ed tech as a violation of privacy, 178–79, 180–81
Electronic Frontier Foundation (EFF) database, 186–87
Electronic Privacy Information Center (EPIC), 185

enrollment in postsecondary institutions, growth of, 6
eras of campus security, xii–xvi
ExamSoft, 184–85
excessive force, qualified immunity for, 23
expansion, jurisdictional, 9, 11–13, 33–38, 118–20

facial recognition technology (FRT), use of, 185, 187
facilitator university, 14–15n18
faculty: complicity of, with campus policing, 240–42; deputizing of, through academic surveillance, 183–86
Federated University Police Officers' Association (FUPOA), 41–42, 43, 46, 47
feminist activism and the rise of the carceral state, 78, 83–91
Floyd, George, protests after the murder of, x, 37, 144, 205, 209–10
Fraternal Order of Police (FOP), 43
Freedom of Information Act, xvii, 11
friendliness of campus police relative to municipal police, presumed, 133–34, 145
FTP, acronym, 226

gang activity as a pretense for racial profiling, 113
Geisel School of Medicine at Dartmouth University ExamSoft incident, 184–86
gender-based mistreatment by campus police, 170
gendered racism, legal cynicism surrounding, for Black women & nonbinary students, 164, 173
gentrification, campus police as a means of, 37–38
Georgia State University (GSU), 127–28, 129, 130–31, 132–34

GI Bill, 5
Giles v. Davis, 24
Ginsburg, Ruth Bader, 23
graduate student labor unions, efforts of, 48–49, 226–27
Graham v. Connor, 23
gunshot detection software, use of, 187

harassment of unhoused people by campus police, 44, 112–13, 197
Harlow v. Fitzgerald, 23
Harnwell, Gaylord, 79, 80, 81
Harvard Police Department, 63, 78
House of the Black Family, 83

Immigration and Customs Enforcement (ICE), 48, 49
immunity, qualified, 17, 22–25, 29, 46
impact of policing on the student experience, 206
incarceration rates, post–War on Drugs, 101
in loco parentis: end of, 5–8; history of, 3–5
Inside-Outside Alliance, 224
International Association of College and University Security Directors (IACUSD), xiv, 103
international students, experience of, 127–28, 132, 135–37
International Union of Police Associations (IUPA), relationship of, with AFL-CIO, 45–46
intimate partner violence incident rates, 160
Invisible Institute, 35, 36

Jackson State University, xv, 7, 20, 30n22
Jeanne Clery Disclosure of Campus Security Policy and Campus Crime Statistics Act, 145, 156n5

job protection policies for campus police, 17, 22–25, 29, 46
Johns Hopkins University police force, 36–37, 40n10
jurisdictional expansion of campus police, 9, 11–13, 33–38, 118–20

Kent State massacre, xv, 7, 20
Kerandi, Jael, 144; interview with, 203–8
King of Sting, 117. *See also* Ares, Joe
Kisela v. Hughes, 23
K-9 units, campus: UCLA, 118; University of Minneapolis, 203

labor organizing efforts: by campus police, 42–44; by graduate students, 48–49, 226–27; suppression of, by campus police, 41, 43, 45, 48, 223
Law Enforcement Assistance Administration (LEAA), 113–15
law enforcement training, basic (BLET), x–xi, xvi, 10, 12–13
legal authority of campus police, xv, 19–21, 28
legal cynicism: confirmation of, by campus police, 170–72; cultural frame of, 163–64; personal experiences of, 165–68
legitimization of campus police, 10–13, 22, 110; at Penn, 90–91; resulting from the War on Drugs, 96, 102–4
leniency of campus police relative to municipal police, presumed, 133–34
Los Angeles Police Department (LAPD), 111–12, 113, 115–17, 144, 158n24
Louisiana University Police Association (LUPA), 43

mandatory reporting, 162, 174n13
mass shootings, 147, 247

McClendon v. Lewis, 24
Memoranda of Understanding (MOUs), 12
Michigan State University Department of Police and Public Safety (MSUDPPS), 102–3
migrants, campus police and, 135–37
militarization of campus police, xvi, 10–11, 14–15n18, 101, 118, 247
Minneapolis Police Department (MPD), 102, 144, 203, 205–6
mission creep, 11–12
Morgan, Robin, 84
mortality risk during police encounters, 146
Mutual Aid Agreements (MAAs), 12

narcotics squads, creation of, 102–4
National Guard: Connecticut, 68; Ohio, xv, 7, 20
neoliberal urban university, policing the, 132–34
New York Police Department (NYPD), 20, 25, 167, 172

Office of Justice Assistance Research and Statistics (OJARS), 115
Ohio National Guard, xv, 7, 20
opacity of campus police departments, xvii, 11–12, 18
Operation Hornet's Nest, 116
Operation Sting, 113
Orangeburg massacre, 7
organized abandonment, 47
outreach programs, departmental, 153
overpolicing of racially marginalized people by campus police, 22, 36, 83, 113, 146, 149, 170–71
oversight, lack of, for campus police, 17–18, 25–29, 88

parens patriae, 4, 9
patriarchal power of postsecondary institutions, 8, 9
Peace Officers Research Association of California (PORAC), 42
performative aspects of university policing, 130
Phelps Gate barricade, 57, 58, 68, 71
Pierson v. Ray, 22
police disarmament and demilitarization proposals, x, 28, 48, 248–49
policing: history of, 45, 146, 211; relationship of, with organized labor, 45–46
political censorship, *in loco parentis* as a tool of, 5–6
Powell, John W., 61–65, 70
President's Commission on Campus Unrest, 70
privacy of student data, 185–86
professionalization of campus police, xiv, 10, 60–61, 96, 112, 215–16
Project Rebound, 199
property recovery investigation, UCLA, 114–16
protected status: of campus policing jobs, 17, 22–25, 29, 46; of university students, 129, 132–37
protection of university property, 19, 34–35, 81
protests. *See* student protests
psychological impact of police, 130, 147
Public History Project (University of Wisconsin–Madison), 209, 211–12, 216–17
public vs. private universities, number of campus police at, 133

qualified immunity, 17, 22–25, 29, 46

race-evasive policing, 154–56
racial conflict within campus police culture, 25–29
racialized: barriers to reporting sexual assault for Black women, 160, 162–64; social control, campus police as a means of, 21–22, 145–48, 154–55
racializing of sexual assault at Penn, 87
racial profiling, 33–38, 113, 146, 170–71
racist beginnings: of campus police statutes, 18–22; of policing in America, 45, 146, 211
Ram Attend pilot program, 178, 179–80
records, access to, xvii, 11–12, 18, 42
removal of police from campuses, students organizing for the, 48–49, 144–45
Rename & Reclaim initiative, 204
reporting of sexual assault: barriers to, for Black women, 160, 162–64; options for, 160–62
Reynolds School of Journalism at the University of Nevada, Reno: surveillance database, 186–87
Rhodes, James, 20
Rising-Murrillo Freedom Act, 201
Rising Scholars Network, 199
Ruth, Henry S., 79–80

safe spaces, perception of universities as, 151–52
scholarship on campus policing, xvi–xix, 152
school-to-prison pipeline, 195–96
Schultz, Scout, killing of, 127, 137–39
security for women at Yale, 68–70
security guard era of campus policing, xii, xiv–xv

Index 263

sexual assault: addressing of, at Penn, 83–86; options for reporting of, on campus, 161–62; racialized barriers to reporting, for Black women, 160, 162–73; racializing of, at Penn, 87
sexual harassment by UCPD, 197, 200
shootings by campus police, ix–x, 22, 137–38
sit-in at Penn, feminist activist, 84, 85–86, 88, 89–90
slave patrols as origin of policing in the US, 10–11, 21, 45, 146, 206, 211
social control, campus police as, 21–22, 145–47, 154–55
social justice unionism: contradiction of, with carceral unionism, 45–46; need for, in police unions, 47–49
Sotomayor, Sonia, 23
Southside Together Organizing for Power (STOP), 36
Spelman College, 171
standardization of training, 111–12, 121n21
statutes, creation of, for campus police, 17–22
stigmatization of local neighborhoods by institutions of higher education, 150–51
Stony Brook University drug raid, 99–100
stop-and-frisk tactics, racism of, 146, 153
strike busting by campus police, 41, 43, 223
strikes: campus police, 43–44; graduate student, 41, 48–49, 226–27
student data, privacy of, 185–86
student protests: digital surveillance of, 183; Georgia Tech, 138–39; after the murder of George Floyd, x, 37, 144, 205, 209–10;of the 1960s and 1970s, 6–7, 19–20, 111; Yale, 68–69
students, unlikeliness of sexual assault reporting by, 160–61

Students for a Democratic Society, 6
studies on campus policing: "Adamson University," 148–49; gendered racism, 164–67; Georgia Tech/GSU, 129–31
suppression: of crime data, xvii, 81, 89–90; of labor organizing efforts by campus police, 41, 43, 45, 48, 223; policing as a means of, 45
surveillance: of African Americans in New Haven, 68; of international students and faculty, 136; of labor organizers by campus police, x, 223
surveillance, academic: deputization of faculty and, 183–86; in physical and digital campuses, 178–83

technology, use of, by campus police, 41, 134, 186–88
1033 Program, 11
Title VI of the Civil Rights Act of 1964, 83
Title IX procedure for reporting sexual assault, 161–62, 172, 173
tools, surveillance, used by campus police, 186–87
training: basic, x–xi, xvi, 10, 12–13; standardization of, 111–12, 121n21; warrior aspects of, emphasis on, 12–13
transparency within campus police departments, xvii, 11–12, 18
trauma-informed narrative inquiry, 164–65
Twenty-Sixth Amendment, 6, 8

UCFTP, 226–27
Underground Scholars Initiative (USI), 195, 198–99, 201–2
unhoused people, harassment of, 44, 112–13, 197

unions: campus police, 41–44; carceral, 45–49; graduate student labor, efforts of, 48–49, 226–27
UniverCities, rise of, 34–37
university archives, utilization and preservation of, 216–19
University of California, Berkeley, 48, 99, 105
University of California, Davis, xviii, 9, 48
University of California, Santa Cruz, 41–42, 226
University of California Los Angeles Police Department (UCLA PD): calls for abolition of, 144–45; creation and reformation of, 110–13; interagency task force sting operation, 113–19
University of California Police Department (UCPD), 41–42, 48, 109–10, 115, 144–45, 197, 199–200
University of Chicago Police Department (UCPD), 10, 33–36
University of Florida shooting, 136–37
University of Minnesota, 97–98, 102, 144, 203
University of Pennsylvania (Penn), 44, 77–90
University of Puerto Rico at Río Piedras, 20
University of Southern California (USC), 158n24
University of Wisconsin–Madison (UW-Madison): Public History Project, 209, 211–12, 216–17

University Police Association, 43
uprisings, student. *See* student protests

victim blaming: anti–sexual assault activism as a challenge to, 86–87; as a resistance to the expansion of campus police, 81–82; sexual assault reporting and, 169
video analytics, use of, 187
Virginia Commonwealth University (VCU), Ram Attend program at, 178, 179–80

War on Crime initiatives, xviii, 113
War on Drugs and campus police, 96, 99, 103–4
watchman era, campus, xii, xiii, 3, 110
Westside Major Crime Violators Task Force, 115–18
Westside Narcotics Enforcement Team (WESTNET), 118–19
whiteness as property, 152
wildcat strike, graduate student, 41, 48–49, 226–27
wiretapping at Yale, 68
women, security for: at Penn, 83–90; at Yale, 67–70
Wynne, Charles, 115

Yale Police Department, 9, 43; beginnings of, 58–60; Black students and the, 65–67, 68, 69–70; coeducation and the, 67; transformation of, under John Powell, 61–65

www.ingramcontent.com/pod-product-compliance
Ingram Content Group UK Ltd.
Pitfield, Milton Keynes, MK11 3LW, UK
UKHW030820191224
452479UK00002B/15